The

SALE
of a Lifetime

How the Great Bubble Burst
of 2017 Can Make You Rich

Harry S. Dent, Jr.

Delray Publishing
55 NE 5th Avenue 2nd Floor
Delray Beach FL, 33483
Phone: 1-888-211-2215
www.dentresearch.com

ISBN: 978-0-692-72134-6

Printed in the United States of America

Dedication

To my recently deceased mother, Betty F. Dent (1932-2015)

And to my 310,000 *Economy & Markets* subscribers…
who have the courage to listen to a realistic view
at a time when it is more critical than ever.

To Teresa Van Den Barselaar for an outstanding job
of organizing, crystallizing and editing the material
for this book in such a short time! My readers should
thank her as well, as I'm sure you will instantly notice
the difference between this book and my past ones.

To David Okenquist for his relentless efforts to dig
for the best and most accurate research. His charts
alone are more than worth the price of this book.

"Deciphering demographics and cycles is the key to economic prediction. There is no one on this planet that has a greater knowledge of this subject than Harry S. Dent, Jr. His lifetime's dedication to this work, combined with his incisive ability to identify these patterns, has led to an incredible number of successful predictions. There are more to come! With his unique understanding of economic bubbles together with their consequences, only a fool would ignore what Harry has to say!"

—Andrew Pancholi, www.markettimingreport.com

"Harry Dent's demographic and cycles research helps to create a quantifiable platform and level of confidence from which any investor can plan their financial future years in advance. This latest work ramps that up. A must read!"

—James O. Lunney, CFP®, CEP
CERTIFIED FINANCIAL PLANNER Professional
Certified Estate Planner
Author of *Surviving the Storm* (McGraw Hill)

"I cannot believe how fortunate I am to be watching what I truly believe is history in the making! Harry Dent will one day be looked at by historians of the future as the guy that made sense of economics. To watch it happening before my eyes in really a surreal experience."

—Mel Johnson

"Harry's predictions are spot on because he uses history and cycles of life/economy. History may not repeat itself but it sure does rhyme."

—Todd Black

"Harry does excellent work and highlights what should be elephants in the room, like demographics, that other analysts ignore. He has a great track record."

—Ed Hurlock, ehurlo@gmail.com

"The amazing info Harry brings forward is so encouraging. I want to keep learning and following."

—Katharine Banman

"[Harry Dent] benefits me by giving me thoughtful insights that allow me to capitalize on what the market is doing, instead of being left for dead on the sidelines, like 'a deer in the headlights'."

—Rick

"With [Harry], I look forward to the light at the end of the very dark and circuitous tunnel that I see persisting from a date that is imminent through the end of the decade and perhaps beyond..."

—Ellis Traub

"I have been reading and hearing Harry Dent for 30-plus years. I began in the 1980s as a Rookie Account Executive at Dean Witter. During that career, later Morgan Stanley (1982-2003), I heard him speak and I read about the 2010 Cliff. Harry is a fine thinker."

—Thom

"Harry Dent, carry on the excellent work! I am not an economist, yet I understand the false basis on which many economists practice. You SEE THEIR failed predictions and their rational."

—Aaron Crespi

"I am a big fan of [Harry's] work and I thank you for being one of the few to provide honest insights on the U.S. and global economies."

—Pino Carnovale

"We are loyal followers — amazed by your wonderful work!!"

—Susan Petrick

"I am very impressed with [Harry's] work, especially his work on cycles!"

—Eric Paradis

"I have been following Harry since college, 20 years ago, where I majored in business ... and I have read every one of his books over the years. I also love the newsletters and various information that he sends out."

—Tim Tusa

"Thank you [Harry] for all you do and the incredible research you bring forth for the benefit of us all."

—Steven L. Schatz

"I follow [Harry Dent] with great loyalty, as I believe that he is better than most economists in reading the economy and forecasting its direction. So much loyalty I have placed in him that I have recently cashed in all my investments with the exception of real estate."

—Osvaldo Koch

"I believe in [Harry Dent] and trust his accuracy for market movements based on the demographic studies he does. While past performance is no guarantee of future performance, I believe he will continue to predict with success."

—Mathew Barnett

"Harry Dent has nailed it again. At a time when the markets seem more complacent than ever, he sounds a loud and clear warning bell. The politicians and central bankers are simply rearranging the deck chairs on the Titanic that is our global economy. With each of his key indicators pointing down for the next five years, smart investors must take action now so they are ready to pounce after the crash. There'll be bargains waiting at fire sale prices for those who've read this book and acted on its recommendations."

—Graham Rowan, Chairman, Elite Investor Club
www.eliteinvestorclub.com

"Incredible Insight… and a Rebellious View"

It is with great pleasure that I endorse world-renowned economist and researcher Harry S. Dent, Jr.

From the moment I picked up Harry at Sydney airport for his first tour to Australia with Secure the Future in 2011, the media was in a frenzy. His incredible insight (and often rebellious views) on the future of the world economy is intoxicating.

Harry Dent showed me that he is a straight shooter — he will not accept any incentive to change his view. His only interest is to tell the truth, based on his in-depth economic and demographic research.

I have found Harry to be correct so often, which is why we continue to have large numbers of people turn up to hear him speak every time he comes to Australia. The man is a riveting speaker, who people can sit and listen to for hours and hours. Nobody leaves the room when this man commands the floor.

In 2015, we ran a webinar to launch the forth-coming Secure the Future event, and a staggering 4,000 people tuned in. There were so many people that the webinar system had a melt-down and people complained afterwards that they couldn't tune in. I made the mistake of asking people to email through any questions — we ended up running out of time for Harry to answer them all! This is so telling. It proves that Harry is striking a nerve.

What I am also impressed about with Harry is that some people come to hear him because they think he is totally wrong! They buy a ticket and so often end up staying right to the finish. Maybe Harry and Muhammad Ali have something in common! People came from everywhere to see Muhammad Ali fight because he was so outspoken and there was never an empty seat in the house when he was boxing!

The reality is… Harry S. Dent, Jr. is not your typical economist.

I have built a great friendship with Harry; I find the man the real-deal.

—Greg Owen
CEO of GOKO Management
Sydney, Australia
Founder and Promoter of Secure the Future

About the Author

Harry S. Dent, Jr. studied economics in college in the '70s, but found it vague and inconclusive. He became so disillusioned by the state of his chosen profession that he turned his back on it. Instead, he threw himself into the burgeoning New Science of Finance, where identifying and studying demographic, technological, consumer and many, many other trends empowered him to forecast economic changes.

Since then, he's spoken to executives, financial advisors and investors around the world. He's appeared on "Good Morning America," PBS, CNBC and CNN/FN. He's been featured in *Barron's*, *Investor's Business Daily*, *Entrepreneur*, *Fortune*, *Success*, *U.S. News and World Report*, *Business Week*, *The Wall Street Journal*, *American Demographics* and *Omni*. He is a regular guest on Fox Business.

Harry has written numerous books over the years. In his book, *The Great Boom Ahead*, published in 1992, he stood virtually alone in accurately forecasting the unanticipated boom of the 1990s.

In 1998 and 1999, he authored two consecutive best sellers: *The Roaring 2000s* and *The Roaring 2000s Investor* (Simon & Schuster).

In *The Next Great Bubble Boom*, he offered a comprehensive forecast for the following two decades. In 2008, he wrote *The Great Depression Ahead*, which he forecast to occur from 2008 to 2013.

Then, in *The Great Crash Ahead*, he outlined how there is nothing the government can ultimately do to prevent the inevitable deflationary period ahead.

Harry's book, *The Demographic Cliff: How to Survive and Prosper During the Great Deflation Ahead*, shows why we're facing a "great deflation" after so many years of stimulus.

With Dent Research, he has also published *Spending Waves: The Scientific Key To Predicting Market Behavior for the Next 20 Years* (2015), which is an information-packed guide for any serious marketer, business owner or investor. And in 2016, he published the e-Book, *How to Survive and Thrive During the Great Gold Bust Ahead*, in which he finally puts to rest the argument that gold is the savior to all investors. (It's NOT... avoid gold!)

Today, he uses the research he developed from decades of hands-on business experience, and the cycles he analyses and hones continuously to offer readers an easy-to-understand view of the economic future through Dent Research publications, including *Boom & Bust, The Leading Edge, Ahead of the Curve Webinars, Quarterly Economic Outlook Reports*, and the free daily e-letter, *Economy & Markets*, available at dentresources.com.

Harry received his MBA from Harvard Business School, where he was a Baker Scholar, and was elected to the Century Club for leadership excellence. He was a consultant to Fortune 100 companies at Bain & Company.

TABLE OF CONTENTS

INTRODUCTION

Bubbles: Why We Never See Them

SOME CALL ME the Demographics Guy. Others call me "that crazy guy." But at the heart of it, I'm a cycles guy and we're in a time of extreme cycles. It's the times that are crazy, not me!

I've lived and breathed cycles for as long as I can remember. When I first visited the Louvre in Paris in 1976, I walked through the whole thing in a day. Most people would note the differences in artists and painting styles over thousands of years (the art is presented in historical sequence). I saw something totally different: the cycles of dark and light, human indulgence and repentance, boom and bust through these paintings.

When I look back, *that's* when I realized I was a cycles guy. For me, the most thrilling, enriching and productive days of my life are those spent elbow deep in cycles analyses.

After more in-depth research into cycles in the 1980s, including intense research into the emerging baby boom generation, I stumbled upon the greatest cycle in modern history: the Generational Spending Wave. That's what landed me with the "Demographics Guy" label.

New generations enter the workforce and earn and spend more until their kids leave the nest, creating predictable long-term booms and busts in our economy. That means we can predict economic cycles almost 50 years in advance!

As it turned out, it was the best leading indicator for market and economic movement until 2009, when the Federal Reserve and central banks across the globe began their desperate — yet ultimately

1

futile — efforts to manipulate their way out of this very cycle. It turned down in 2008, as I predicted it would all the way back in the late 1980s.

In so doing, they goosed the markets along, but have done nothing to change the demographic impact on the economy. There is a huge demographic headwind that will only get much stronger in the years ahead. Now we've reached a point where the stock market no longer has any logical connection to reality, making it an extremely dangerous beast (which I'll talk about in the pages of this book).

My Generational Spending Wave takes the population's birth wave (adjusted for immigration) and pushes it forward 46 years for the baby boom so that we can see when people will peak in their spending. The magic number was age 44 for the Bob Hope generation and is likely to be more like 48 for the millennial generation ahead.

We're incredibly predictable. We don't like it, and we are all a bit different, but at the end of the day, as a large group we follow the average, predictable spending pattern as we age.

Generally speaking, we start school at the age of five and graduate by age 18. After that many go on to some level of higher education and enter the workforce at an average age of 20. We get married around age 27 and have children shortly after. Starter home purchases peak around the age of 32 and trade-up home purchases peak around age 42. The kids leave the nest when we're between 47 and 54 years old. Our spending currently peaks at age 47, although, for the most affluent, that peak is at age 54. From age 54 to 64, we start spending dramatically less and saving more. At 63 we retire, again on average, and spend the rest of our lives consuming less and less by living off those savings.

This isn't guess work. This is science! Science based on data we get from the Bureau of Labor Statistics every year. Data that is so detailed it allows us to know exactly when potato chip consumption will peak (age 42)!

While I'll share some more of my demographic research with you later, that's not why I've written this book. Instead, I've written this book because there is something else we predictably do as humans: we create bubbles that we are then utterly blind to.

In fact, we have just seen the greatest bubble in centuries, which I'll prove in the pages to follow, yet most economists and authority figures deny its existence. Denial doesn't make it go away!

There's no debt bubble, they say.

Real estate isn't in a bubble, they say.

The stock market isn't in a bubble, they say.

Gold was not a bubble, they said.

I say they're all in denial and you should question everything they say because no one in power wants a bubble to burst on their watch, including your stock broker!

As I'm going to show you in the following pages, we are drowning in bubbles... and we're witnessing the final moments of the biggest bubble since the U.S. Midwest expansion into 1835.

If you listen to those idiots who assure you "there are no bubbles to be found here," then not only will you be crushed as it all unwinds, but you'll miss out on the sale of a lifetime to follow.

You see, while the crash happens over a short period of time — two, maybe three years — the aftermath lingers, sometimes for a decade or more. This gives us the opportunity to grab stocks at fire-sale prices, real estate dirt cheap, and businesses for cents on the dollar. You'll find details in Chapters 21, 22, 23 and 24.

There's a Time for Every Season

As I've come to appreciate over my three and a half decades spent studying cycles, they all have the same characteristics.

They all have hierarchies.

They all have seasons.

And they all bubble up and end in a terrible burst.

As of 2008, we're in the economic winter season of another cycle I use: the 80-Year Four Season Economic Cycle. It's during this season that we clear the decks with a devastating crash and debilitating deflation. The economy and markets shed the excesses created during the preceding economic fall bubble boom season and prepare the soil for new blossoming in innovation and a spring boom.

After the Roaring '20s came the Great Depression.

After the Roaring 2000s came the Great Recession.

After the blustering bull market of 2009-2015, we are now preparing for a shakeout more painful than anything we've seen before. We have seven years of unprecedented government stimulus and money creation to thank for stretching this bubble beyond imagination and making the burst more painful than anything we've ever experienced.

Winter follows fall without fail (and in the pages to follow, I'll prove it). And while blasting the heat but leaving the doors open has kept the cold at bay, it's done nothing to stop its inevitable arrival... and everything to drain all the resources we had.

Equally, as history shows us clearly, every debt bubble leads to financial asset bubbles that burst. And the bigger the bubble, the greater the burst. No exceptions.

The only near-term exception is central banks around the world printing $10 trillion-plus to offset the crisis and keep the banks from failing like they did in the early 1930s. And it's not an exception, it's a delay.

Over the last 16 years, we have witnessed the creation of the greatest and most global bubble in modern history. Hundreds of trillions of dollars of debt are clogging up the world's veins. Sooner rather than later, it will lead to a massive, global heart attack.

As this book was being edited, the frequency of articles announcing that the debt bubble has begun to unwind spiked. And analysts at Société Générale warned that corporate America is near the point of choking on all the debt it has consumed!

The situation is so dire, and we are so far down this road, that everything central banks and governments try to do now to avoid what's coming will only exacerbate the inevitable outcome.

My Generational Spending Wave was the best leading indicator until 2009, when central banks attempted to come to the rescue after the 2008 crash. There is nothing more frightening and damaging than the person who says: "We're from the government and we're here to help." Or the drug addict that says: "I just need another fix to keep from coming down, then I will be OK and quit."

It's thanks solely to central banker and government efforts to avoid the inevitable seasonal shift from fall to winter... and the inevitable generational shift from spending to saving... that we have a debt bubble so big and out of control that it threatens to blot out the sun.

It's thanks to those people who thought it was their duty to interfere that stock markets have spent the last seven years inflating into a bubble completely detached from reality.

But history shows us one clear fact: every debt bubble leads to financial asset bubbles (in things like stocks, real estate and commodities)... and every financial asset bubble bursts. Dramatically! The greater the bubble, the greater the burst.

Typically, as this chart from Robert Prechter shows, these kinds of bubbles occur every 80 to 90 years or so.

Figure I-1: Stock Prices Since 1700

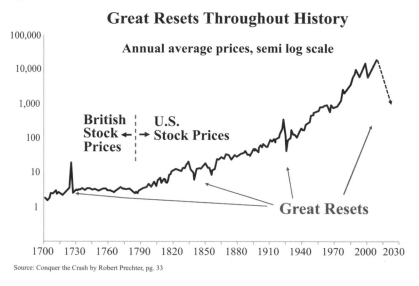

Source: Conquer the Crash by Robert Prechter, pg. 33

Yet, economists never see such major resets ahead of time. Most *people* don't because no one was alive when the last major bubble burst. And people and businesses suffer the most dramatically when these bubbles unravel.

So, the purpose of this book is to protect you from the carnage ahead and allow you to both survive and prosper instead.

When such rare and major debt bubbles burst, there is nowhere to hide except cash and the safest long-term bonds as the entire financial system goes through a massive reboot. That means that the proven asset allocation and diversification systems most financial advisors are preaching will fail, just like they did in 2008 and early 2009. There are no exceptions to this!

That's not to say investing is completely out of the question. Times like these can be very lucrative, but you must follow a time-tested and proven strategy, like the team of experienced and talented investments experts I've assembled at Dent Research (you can learn more about them when you visit dentresources.com).

When people argue with me, trying to convince me that we or China can see a soft landing, I simply ask: "When last did you see a bubble burst slowly?" China's recent bubble burst started with a 45% crash in 2.5 months, as did the Nasdaq in 2000 and the Dow in late 1929. And that was just the start.

They never have a good answer for me!

We have witnessed the greatest and widest-reaching bubble in modern history, and it will burst — painfully — like every bubble that has come before it. And since this bubble has now mutated as a result of artificial stimulus into something beyond imagining, its bursting will be like nothing we've ever endured before.

Yet so few see it coming because, according to the experts, there is no bubble!

I say: if it looks, walks and quacks like a bubble... it's a bubble, damn it!

Don't be fooled!

Instead, be ready!

My goal with this book is to prepare you NOW to recognize the obvious and pervasive global bubble you've witnessed since 1995, and how central bank interference has turned it into an even more dangerous monster since 2009...

To help you gain enough insight so you never have to simply accept what mass market economists and authorities try to shove down your throat...

And to guide you towards the once-in-a-lifetime opportunities these events will hand you if you have cash and cash flow available to take advantage.

I'm going to explain the seven guiding principles of bubbles and then show you the bubbles and resets we've seen before... you'll very quickly see they are all very similar!

And I'll dissect why it seems so hard for people to see bubbles when they're right in front of them, despite it being so obvious from an historical view. This will empower you to step out of the crowd of no-bubble blindness and see what's *really* happening… This next and final bubble crash will impact your life and business more than any financial crisis in your lifetime! It's vital you see what's going on and take action.

But, most important, I'm going to show you what makes the years after a massive bubble reset so valuable to investors and businesses ready to make the most of the opportunities that fall from the sky. Bursting bubbles have made many investors breathtakingly rich. Taking advantage of the fire sales after a major crash is how you can create "extreme wealth" in a short period of time! I'll show you how they did it, and then how you can do it too.

I'm also going to teach you how to predict when bubbles will crash, although that is never an easy skill to acquire. Bubbles always have a new twist to them. But I have four key indicators that I've developed over the years that can help. When they converge downward — which they have only done four times since the early 1800s — you'd better run for cover. They're currently in complete convergence for the fifth time. I'll explain exactly what that means to markets, the economy and you.

And finally, there are short-term signs that a great crash already began in mid-2015 and is likely to accelerate into the second half of 2016 forward. I'll share those with you, too.

I'm going to break down the greatest debt bubble in history for you and show you why there is no stopping the bursting.

The potential that lies ahead will be like what investors saw back in July 1932 and what real estate investors saw in 1933! You could have bought sea salt or roach droppings back then and made money for decades! Basically, I'm giving you the keys to the candy store. All you need to do is walk in and pick out whatever you want.

But an early warning: the best investments will be in sectors and countries you may not be considering today… that's the ultimate secret to the sale of a lifetime ahead.

So let's get to it. There's a lot to cover and limited time for you to take action…

PART I

How to Identify a Bubble

CHAPTER 1

How to Identify a Bubble:
Guiding Principle #1

IT'S ACTUALLY QUITE SIMPLE. You start the bubble identification process by looking at cycles. That's because a few key cycles give you the power to see what will impact your life, your business, your family, and your investments over the course of your entire life!

So I'm surprised when I hear someone say: *"I don't really believe in cycles."*

What!?

You mean you don't believe that the sun will rise tomorrow morning, like it did this morning?

You don't believe that the tide will peak twice a day and that we can know, down to the minute, when this will happen on every beach around the world?

You don't believe winter comes once a year?

That you are born and will die?

That your teenager will hate you when they turn 13?

Have you looked at an EKG… *ever*?

Did you know our stock market, adjusted for inflation, has peaked every 39 years in the last century, that commodity prices peak every 30 years, and boom/bust cycles peak around every 10 years?

Did you know that the average household peaks in spending at age 46 and that causes predictable booms and busts that we can see decades in advance? (For Japanese households, that peak in spending is at age 47… it differs from country to country, but only by a year or two on either side of 46.)

What about the 500-Year Mega Innovation Cycle, which Henry Phelps-Brown and Sheila Hopkins discovered? It shows that inflation rises and peaks every 500 years. It did so in 1154 and again in 1648. It's due to peak next around 2150.

What about the 250-Year Revolution Cycle? The Protestant Reformation… the American and French Revolutions… the Industrial Revolution. The next one is coming in the next decade or so!

What about the 165-Year East/West Cycle? Power shifts from the East to the West like clockwork! You can guess it's heading back East for the next century.

There's a 5,000-Year Civilization Cycle shifting from towns to cities to megacities… oh, and have we seen megacities emerge in the last century… the 10 million-plus club.

A 100,000-Year Glaciation Cycle, with cooling longer-term, except CO_2 cycles are causing man-made warming first…

A Billion-Year Climate Cycle…

Sunspot Cycles…

Population Cycles…

Ovulation Cycles…

Sleep/Wake Cycles…

I think you get my point. Everything… EVERYTHING… follows some (if not dozens) of cycles. I won't get into the details of many of the cycles — it's not in the scope of this book — but I have written about them before in my *The Leading Edge: Harry Dent Unplugged* bi-monthly newsletter. Visit dentresources.com if you're interested in learning more.

So do yourself a favor: don't trust anyone who doesn't "believe in," or denies the existence of, cycles. I certainly don't. They're either ignorant or short-sighted… and both conditions are extremely dangerous to you.

But while I believe Cycle Blasphemers and Cycle Atheists are asleep at the wheel, I understand their deep-seated unwillingness to accept the obvious. The truth is that many people don't want to believe in cycles because they don't like change and they especially don't like the challenging part of each cycle.

They don't want to die (who does, really?). Although, I would propose that birth is actually more challenging and shocking.

Few parents welcome the puberty of their children.

We don't want to endure economic downturns, even though that's where all the great innovations happen and future prosperity is born.

Humans generally abhor change and cycles are all about change and progress. Constant change. So many people just deny the existence of such forces because that gives them the feeling of power where they have none.

It doesn't stop the inevitable… but it can mutate it when the ones holding the national and global purse strings refuse to see what's right in front of them. In Chapter 7, I'll go into the details of how they did this, and the resultant damage they have done. I'll also show you the only outcome that's possible… but let's first truly come to grips with the nature of cycles and the bubbles they bring about.

Of course, this is a book about bubbles and how this latest one is opening up the sale of a lifetime for you as an investor and for the best businesses, including yours. But as I'm about to show you, cycles and bubbles are inextricably linked.

The Ultimate Economic Model

Like it or not, everything in life is cyclical. And all cycles have four seasons. Our annual weather cycle is the most obvious example: spring, summer, fall, and winter. Not so different are the four stages of our life: youth (spring), adulthood (summer), midlife (fall), and retirement (winter). There are four stages of the business cycle, too: innovation, growth, shakeout, and maturity.

Just as there are four weeks in a month and four phases of the moon, I've found that the economic cycle evolves through four seasons as well, only over the approximate duration of a human lifetime, currently about 80 years.

The first credible economic cycle I studied in the early 1980s was the Kondratieff Wave, revealed by the Russian economist Nikolai Kondratieff in 1925. Back then this was a 50- to 60-year cycle (we didn't live as long) that saw peaks in inflation rates in 1814, 1864, 1920, and more recently 1980.

This cycle of inflation and deflation was characterized as having four seasons:

- A spring boom with mildly rising inflation.

- A summer recession with inflation rising to a long-term peak and major wars.

- A fall boom with declining inflation, powerful new technologies moving into the mainstream, and a credit bubble that leads to high speculation and financial bubbles.

- And a winter deflation, during which time bubbles burst, debt deleverages, prices deflate, and depression takes hold (and wars can follow such upheaval as well, like it did with World War II).

Note that the great resets I showed you in Figure I-1 on page 6 in the Introduction all tend to come during this economic winter season, which indeed resets the economy from all of its excesses and imbalances so it can grow again. And it happens once in a lifetime!

But, Kondratieff's original cycle seemed to lose its power to predict a couple of decades ago when the winter deflationary season was expected in the 1990s. I believe there are two reasons the cycle failed: we saw the first middle class generation to emerge after WWII and the massive baby boom generation followed!

When the Bob Hope generation, born between 1897 and 1924, entered the workforce after winning WWII, they were the first middle class generation that could afford to broadly buy homes using longer-term mortgages. They made the everyday person more important to the economy than ever before. They put demographic cycles to the forefront and such cycles have dominated ever since.

The Bob Hope generation's family cycle and spending boom dominated and stretched beyond the 30-Year Boom/Bust cycles, which were based on commodities and innovation, to nearly 40 years! The generation's boom stretched from 1942 to 1968, followed by its bust from 1969 through 1982.

Then the largest generation in 250 years hit. The massive baby boom took place from 1934 to 1961.

When they entered the workforce en masse during the economic summer season of the '70s, the economy saw massively higher inflation trends. The cost of incorporating young people into the workforce is high. Until they become productive, they drive up inflation.

And their impact on the economic fall season was also outsized, extending that greatest and inevitable boom to grander heights, and, again, for longer than Kondratieff's original cycle allowed for. So when his cycle showed it was time for the economic winter season to set in, we got the greatest boom in history instead.

That's why there was a rash of books in the late 1980s and early 1990s calling for a great depression: Ravi Batra, Robert Prechter, James Dale Davidson, and Harry Figgie wrote them, and they all sold boatloads of books. I respect most of these authors and read their books because they have a much greater perspective of history and cycles than most clueless economists who aspired to be accountants but didn't have the personality. Of course, their forecasts were wrong because Kondratieff's cycle no longer "seemed" to work.

They lacked the insight into the demographic impact of the new generation cycle of middle class spending and the massive baby boom… and how it altered the economic cycle.

From the research I was working on at the time, I understood that there was no way we could have a great depression when the largest generation by far was in its sweet spot for spending, house buying and borrowing in the 1990s.

So I wrote my second book in late 1992 called *The Great Boom Ahead* (my first book, self-published in 1989, was *Our Power to Predict.*) I presented my thoughts on a new four-season economic cycle that spanned roughly 80 years with two 40-year boom and bust cycles.

I saw that the baby boom had exaggerated the Kondratieff cycle in terms of the magnitude of inflation and booms.

Besides, our life expectancies took a big leap between the 1930s and 1960s, extending all human-related cycles, including the length of the booms and busts.

The Kondratieff four-season cycle is still valid, but it has been stretched and magnified. Just by projecting cycles in spending and inflation through demographics, we can more accurately time this powerful and overarching, four-season economic cycle into the future.

That's why it's important to be able to accurately project the fundamental trends rather than just following historical, clockwork-like cycles (although many are still very clockwork-like and I will look at those later).

The deeper explanation for the shift from a 60-year to an 80-year cycle is that our economy changed dramatically in the last century.

Up until the late 1800s, the United States (and even most of Europe) was still an agrarian nation with 80% of its population involved in agriculture, mining, and trapping. Even in the early 1900s, it was still 60% rural. Of course, agrarian consumers don't have nearly the effect on the economy that the urban, affluent, middle-class consumers have today.

Even today in China and India, rural consumers have lower economic impact because they're mostly self-sufficient farmers (I'm not talking about commercial farmers here).

But after the Roaring '20s, we saw the first mass affluent middle-class society in history. Their spending cycles started dominating the economy instead of the 30-Year Commodity Cycle. This stretched the boom and bust cycle to 40 years each, so a full four-season cycle is now 80 years long.

All of this explains why most Kondratieff proponents were wrong about a depression in the 1990s. On the extended, 80-year cycle, that depression was only due 20 years later… and that's what we're seeing now.

Figure 1-1 below shows you what this new 80-Year Economic Cycle looks like:

Figure 1-1: 80-Year Four-Season Economic Cycle

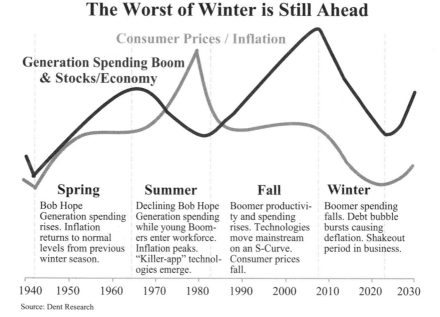

The Worst of Winter is Still Ahead

Consumer Prices / Inflation

Generation Spending Boom & Stocks/Economy

Spring	Summer	Fall	Winter
Bob Hope Generation spending rises. Inflation returns to normal levels from previous winter season.	Declining Bob Hope Generation spending while young Boomers enter workforce. Inflation peaks. "Killer-app" technologies emerge.	Boomer productivity and spending rises. Technologies move mainstream on an S-Curve. Consumer prices fall.	Boomer spending falls. Debt bubble bursts causing deflation. Shakeout period in business.

1940   1950   1960   1970   1980   1990   2000   2010   2020   2030

Source: Dent Research

This 80-Year Economic Cycle perfectly summarizes what started in 1942, after the Great Depression that marked the end of the last winter season with deflation in prices and massive bank and business failures that generated 25%-plus unemployment.

The inflation index (the gray line) in Figure 1-1 follows the traditional pattern of the Kondratieff Wave: moderate and rising inflation in spring, high and peaking inflation in summer, falling inflation in fall, and deflation (falling prices) in winter.

Think of inflation like temperatures in our annual weather cycle. High temperatures are like high inflation and low temperatures are like deflation. Both are uncomfortable and present challenges for the economy and stock markets, which paradoxically is the greatest driver of breakthrough innovations that make us wealthier and live longer over time.

The black line in Figure 1-1 is the Generational Spending Wave. The Bob Hope generation's Spending Wave rose from 1942 into 1968, which is also when we saw a great bull market in stocks. When adjusted for inflation, the S&P 500 peaked in 1968. This was the economic spring.

Then there was an on-and-off recession from 1969 through 1982, as the Bob Hope generation slowed in its spending — the economy kept going into recession after recession. But that time period saw the emergence of the massive baby boom into the workforce that paradoxically created high inflation along with a series of wars (as is typical in the summer season).

Then the baby boom started up on its Spending Wave from 1983 to 2007, and again we saw the greatest stock market boom in history, from August 1982 to October 2007.

This was the economic fall and bubble boom season, paradoxically with falling inflation and interest rates as that generation and its new computer technologies created much higher productivity.

In 2008, the baby boomers' spending began its slowdown, and so started the great recession. That spending slowdown accelerates into around 2020, then flattens out and doesn't turn up with the echo boom or millennial generations until around 2023 forward. That is the winter economic season.

This economic winter will see deflation in prices from massive debt and financial bubbles deleveraging, just like what happened in the 1930s. And we'll see a depression, not a recession.

But governments around the world have pulled out all the stops to prevent this... good luck fighting Mother Nature on this one!

Everything I just described to you is how I was able to forecast, back in the late 1980s, that we'd see trouble after 2007! I understood how the Kondratieff economic cycle had changed and when I lagged the baby boom birth index by 46 years to see their predictable peak in spending, I had a very clear view of the future.

And this is **Guiding Principle #1** of bubbles: they occur in the fall economic season, which consumer spending now predictably drives. The combination of a strong boom and falling inflation will always create bubbles. They're cyclical... which means they're unavoidable and more easily predictable!

Incidentally, this is how I also successfully forecasted, in 1989, that Japan would collapse.

My claims didn't make me very popular because, back then, everyone was saying that Japan would become a super power. Today, the country is the poster child for how demographics drive the economy and market... and what NOT to do when these inevitable busts roll in.

Why every economist, central banker and government official isn't studying Japan is a mystery to me. They absolutely should be because we're seeing one country after the next go over the demographic cliff... and one bubble after the next reaching their limits. But, they seem to live in a world of their own, untethered from reality, where bubbles don't happen and they think they can control consumer spending like puppets on a string.

Japan was the first to see its great economic, stock and real estate bubbles inflated by the unprecedented demographic cycles. Its baby boom peaked 12 to 19 years earlier than the one we saw in the U.S. (it saw a double peak between 1942 and 1949 in births on either side of World War II). It was also the first to see its stock market and real estate bubbles burst as its Generational Spending Wave first turned down from 1990 forward, and then much more so after 1996.

And it was the first to embrace quantitative easing (QE) in 1997, to fight that devastating collapse.

Twenty-six years later, Japan is an aging retirement home in hock! It's a coma economy that faces a bleak future, with an ever-depleting workforce, a shrinking population, and rising government debt. The reality is, Japan is dying, as all things do in cycles.

Just look at the country's real GDP growth since 1997 in Figure 1-2, when its baby boom generation finally peaked in spending and its QE program started:

Figure 1-2: GDP in Japan

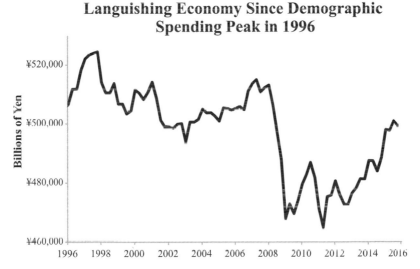

Languishing Economy Since Demographic Spending Peak in 1996

Source: St. Louis Federal Reserve

Again, these are predictable trends!

Predictable *decades* in advance.

I predicted the demise of Japan when it looked invincible (as China does today) in my first book, *Our Power to Predict*, in 1989.

They were simply nearing the top of their baby boom spending cycle with massive real estate and stock bubbles that were crying to burst… and they did!

Yet people simply can't see the bubbles. Couldn't see them then, can't see them now. Besides our natural blindness to them, they mostly happen only once in a lifetime, so by the time the next bubble inflates, very few people remember the giddy highs and devastating lows of the last one. Anyone who lived through the Great Depression was likely too young back then to grasp the significance and learn any lessons from it, or they have Alzheimer's or are dead by now!

This brings me to the **Guiding Principle #2** of bubbles…

CHAPTER 2

How to Identify a Bubble: Guiding Principle #2

QUITE SIMPLY, INFLATING BUBBLES is in our nature. We can't help ourselves. We work hard to improve our lives and once we've reached a good place, we don't want it to end. We want to stay in that place forever. If we do move, it's only towards something bigger and better.

It's also this very nature that prevents us from seeing the bubbles we create.

When they occur, the overriding response is denial. This isn't a good thing, because it sets up millions of hard-working people (perhaps even more so high-net-worth investors), for a devastating financial collapse precisely when they need all the money they can get. It prevents people from taking the necessary steps to protect their wealth. And it stops them from having the resources or courage to grab the opportunities when the sale of a lifetime opens up in front of them.

But why is there such a blind spot to bubbles in human nature?

It's because we don't understand or project reality as it *really* is. And we don't like change (as I explained in Chapter 1), especially exponential change. We prefer the world to grow incrementally and in a straight line… without cycles. We reject the reality that is historically clear: that growth is both cyclical and exponential (more on this soon).

The biggest cause of this massive "blind spot" in human nature is best shown in The Human Model of Forecasting, which you can see in Figure 2-1:

Figure 2-1: The Human Model of Forecasting

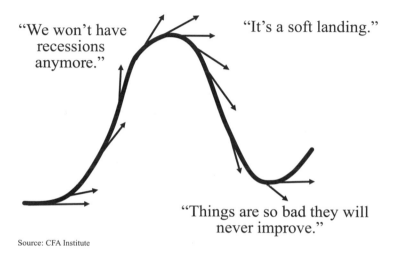

Why We Can't See Bubbles

"We won't have recessions anymore."

"It's a soft landing."

"Things are so bad they will never improve."

Source: CFA Institute

We project the future in a linear way when the reality is instead both exponential and cyclical. That's why so few people can see ahead of the curve.

Most people were slow to see the great boom of 1983-2007, and no one saw how high it could go even halfway through the 1990s.

The good news is that once you're aware of it, you can break yourself of the habit and change your future for the better — by better seeing the future!

Unfortunately, people generally don't like the play of opposites of life. We don't like the bursts that inevitably follow booms, so we just pretend that life doesn't work that way. We don't like good and bad, hot and cold, inflation and deflation. Even men and women, while we're attracted to each other, can't understand and deal with our obvious, almost incompatible, differences. But the economy, like a battery, can't have energy and growth without this play of opposites... our creator was not stupid!

When the economy is booming, we project the rising trend in a straight line, and so over-project bull markets and overvalue stocks. Eventually, we begin to use this view as evidence that no bubble exists. We are in "a new plateau of prosperity" — a famous quote from the Roaring '20s bubble. That's a euphemism for "going to heaven."

Real estate is probably the best example of this.

As the property market was peaking in 2005/06, anyone with an opinion said "real estate prices can only go up!" Everywhere I spoke, from San Francisco to Australia to Dubai, the comments were the same.

"Our property market is unique because..." (said everywhere).

"There's limited land..." (said in Florida, California or Australia).

"It's in the heart of the entertainment/technology/financial industry..." (said in Los Angeles, Silicon Valley and New York).

"We have strong demographic growth from baby boomers and immigration..."

"We have an endless source of foreign buyers, especially from the Chinese and Asians..."

I've heard every excuse there is... and every single one is wrong!

As history has proved, time and again, property prices are fallible. And when they fall, they bring the house down on hard-working people! The greater the bubble (because such areas were so "special"), the harder they burst.

If I had a nickel for every time someone said their city wasn't in a bubble, I would be a billionaire.

The real estate bubble in the U.S. burst just a few months after I forecast it would in early 2006. It took six years to bottom out, but most of the damage came in 2008 and 2009, in the Great Recession.

Massive quantitative easing brought interest rates and mortgages down, helped the economy recover and brought home prices back up, but not back to their highs in most places.

Now home prices are bubbly again just as the worst demographic trends will hit between 2016 and 2022. Any sign of economic weakness, which is inevitable ahead, will send buyers running because they're much more aware of the downside after experiencing the first real estate crash in their lifetimes.

In the most extreme areas, like Manhattan, San Francisco, Vancouver, and South Beach, home prices have become way more bubbly than the last time around. We're about to see another six-year slide that will be greater than the last one and take home prices back, at least, to their early 2000 levels, where the bubble began.

If you have the courage, look up the value of your home or real estate in January 2000! You will be shocked at your downside potential.

Of course, when the trend turns, as it inevitably does, we hope — to the point of delusion — for a soft landing. We project an indefinite flattening. But no such thing has ever happened. Not once throughout history!

And then, as the floor drops out from under our feet, we settle into the belief that things will never be good again… because now we're paying for our sins.

That's something we've done throughout history. It's something I noticed while walking the halls of the Louvre in 1976. I could see the times of brightness and self-indulgence followed by the times of darkness and repentance… it was crystal clear from the paintings of history — long-term booms and busts happen all the time.

It's my goal, with this book, to break you of this natural straight-line forecasting tendency once and for all!

Ultimately, human beings are all about finding Nirvana and then digging in their claws to stay, no matter the consequences.

Almost everyone has that dream of retiring early, of never needing to work again, of simply living a life of ease and pleasure. Personally, I don't believe humans are designed to retire and do nothing — and we don't grow or evolve much in such times of ease. Regardless, that's the goal most people strive for and you might achieve it if you take high risks, bust your ass for years or decades, are highly skilled and determined... and lucky.

You could strike oil in your back yard like Jed Clampett did, become famous like Lindsay Lohan... or you could win the lottery. I wouldn't hold my breath, if I was you. Your odds are extremely low.

That doesn't stop *anyone* though. The Powerball Bubble of January 2016 is actually the ultimate example of our human tendency to inflate bubbles to insane extremes in our desire to find the easy life.

When we get caught up in the excitement and hope of a bubble, it's simply irresistible, no matter how irrational it is. The more and the longer something goes up, the more appealing and less risky it seems. So more people pile in and build on the bubble.

Never mind that the odds of winning the $1.5 billion Powerball jackpot on January 13, 2016 were only one in 292 million! You'd have had more chance of being bitten by a shark (11.5 million to one), being in a plane crash (11 million to one) or being dealt a royal flush with the first five cards (655,750 to one) than of winning that billion-dollar lottery.

But that didn't stop anybody. In fact, for $2, most people thought they'd be insane NOT to get a ticket just to be in the running.

Look at this perfect illustration of a bubble in Figure 2-2:

Figure 2-2: The January 13, 2016 Powerball Bubble

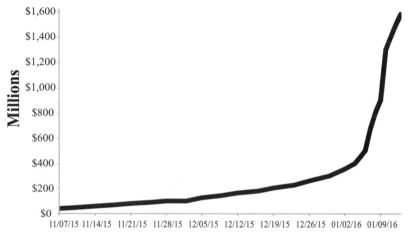

Everyone Piled In As the Jackpot Rose

Source: http://www.arkansasmatters.com/news/local-news/15-billion-powerball-jackpot-timeline

In the first eight weeks, the jackpot grew to $350 million. Then, after a few no-wins, things went exponential! In less than two weeks it went up 4.6 times.

I get it. Bubbles will always exist because life is hard, despite its rewards. Life is cyclical and challenging. It's natural to want to follow the path of least resistance, but it's not realistic. And I hope this book proves this to you (and then helps you avoid becoming victims of bubbles again).

I always remember something my father said to me: "People are unrealistic, and therefore irresponsible." He was trying to tell me that most people don't intend to be irresponsible or to harm themselves or others, but if you make unrealistic assumptions about life to defend against your fears, you're likely to do just that. He was a wise man.

An average, everyday Chinese father returned from a long business trip in August 2015 to discover that he'd lost his family's entire net worth when the Chinese stock bubble burst. The market had gone up an astounding 160% in one year and then crashed 45% in just two-and-a-half months.

Figure 2-3: Shanghai Composite

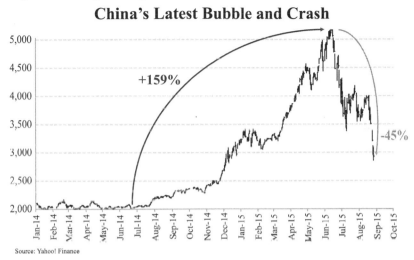

China's Latest Bubble and Crash

Source: Yahoo! Finance

Did he intend to be irresponsible? Of course not. He was swept up in the bubble mania… and he — and his family — paid the price!

He sobbed while telling his story to a news crew. He was terribly embarrassed to tell his family.

Students (and their parents) aren't trying to be irresponsible when they sign on the dotted line for that $30,000-plus student loan for a college education. They're faced with little option thanks to the student-loan bubble and the education-costs bubble.

Yet those young adults suffer the consequences for decades after they leave college.

But that's the thing: as humans, we just can't help ourselves. That desire for an easy life for us, and even more so for our children, is deeply entrenched, as is our blindness to bubbles and our ability to send them soaring to the moon… which brings me to **Guiding Principle #3** of bubbles… It's ALWAYS a moon shot.

CHAPTER 3

How to Identify a Bubble: Guiding Principle #3

BUBBLES ALWAYS GO exponential at some point.

Look back at the China stock bubble last year in Figure 2-3. Look back at the Powerball bubble in Figure 2-2. Both turn up steeply and then shoot for the moon.

The seven-year bull market from 2009 to 2016…

Figure 3-1: Dow, Early 2009 to Mid-2015

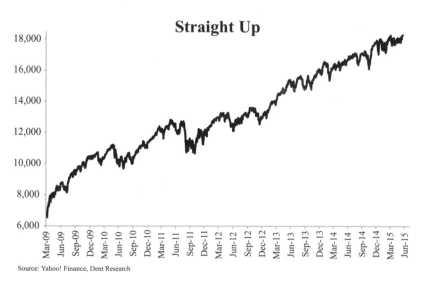

Source: Yahoo! Finance, Dent Research

Exponential.

Mom and pop investors just can't resist the notion that they can get rich quick in the stock market, even after the 2007 crash.

The student loan bubble I mentioned earlier...

Figure 3-2: The Student Loan Bubble

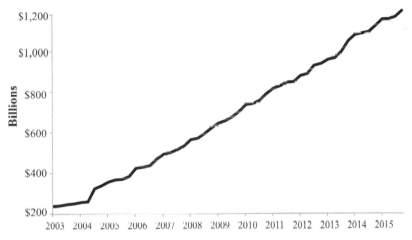

Student Loan Debt Surged Nearly
$1 Trillion Since 2003

Source: New York Federal Reserve

Exponential.

Most Americans want their kids to go to college. They believe that without a college education, job prospects and earnings capacity would be limited. This is no longer the case today, yet we have a student loan bubble of epic proportions.

The tuition and health care cost bubbles...

Figure 3-3: The Health Care & College Bubbles

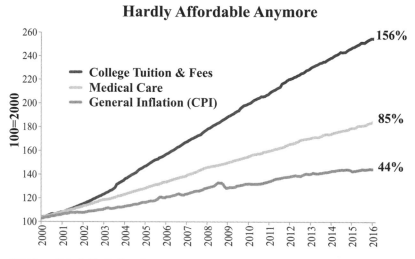

Hardly Affordable Anymore

Source: Bureau of Labor Statistics, Dent Research

Exponential.

Colleges are riding the coattails of the student loan bubble, so costs go up every year. It can now cost hundreds of thousands to send your kid to one of the best colleges.

For the average household, who has not felt much (if any) of the "recovery" since 2007, the only option is a student loan.

The car-stocks bubble before the Great Depression...

Figure 3-4: The S&P Auto Stock Index Bubble Before the 1929 Crash

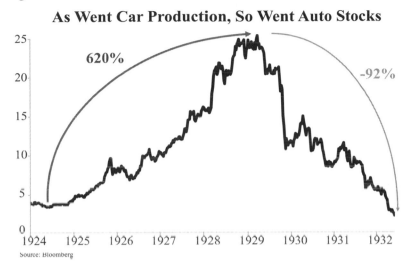

As Went Car Production, So Went Auto Stocks

Source: Bloomberg

Exponential.

The Japanese real estate bubble in the '80s…

Figure 3-5: Japan Real Estate Bubble

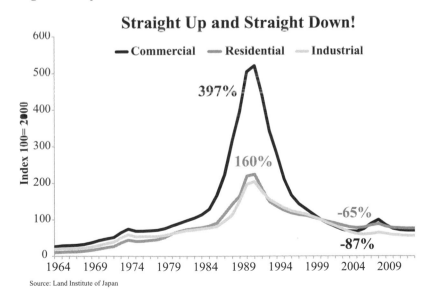

Source: Land Institute of Japan

Exponential.

And Japan's stock market went up 5.6 times between 1983 and 1989 and then crashed 80%!

The first modern-era bubble: the Tulip bubble…

Figure 3-6: Dutch Tulip Bubble

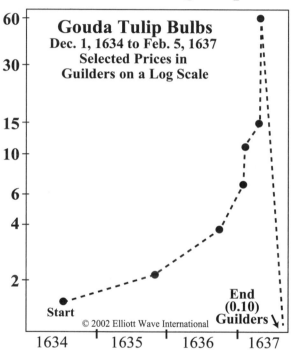

Almost Straight Up!

Source: "Conquer the Crash" by Robert Prechter, pg. 80

Exponential.

Bubble after bubble… it's all the same.

Figure 3-7: Stocks, Real Estate, Biotech & Gold

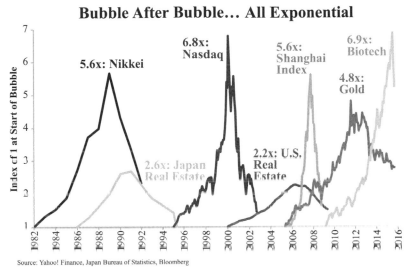

Source: Yahoo! Finance, Japan Bureau of Statistics, Bloomberg

This is probably a good point at which to give you two warnings.

Firstly, to help demystify bubbles once and for all, and empower you to take advantage of the sale of a lifetime ahead of you, it's important that you SEE as many bubbles as possible. This means there will be many   many   charts throughout this book.

Secondly, I'll be repeating some charts in following chapters, where I go into more detail about what was going on as each bubble was inflated and deflated.

I think for now though, you can see for yourself that bubbles always go exponential, which, when you consider the other guiding principles of bubbles as well, is why they are so dangerous!

Stock and commodity bubbles tend to be much steeper than real estate, but most real estate is leveraged by mortgage loans, which make it riskier than it seems and the worst bubble bursts have been the ones where real estate was at the core.

Here's the thing: growth is exponential, not linear.

Two great visionaries — George Gilder (co-founder of Discovery Institute) and Ray Kurzweil (the futurologist who was involved in inventions such as optical character recognition and text-to-speech synthesis) — see this as well, as do most evolutionary scientists.

It means that bubbles are inevitable, especially in the late stages of any long-term growth trend.

But, like I've said, humans naturally tend to think in linear terms **(Guiding Principle #2)**. We do this because we don't look very far back at history. We tend to look just behind us and just ahead. But the farther you go back in history, the clearer the pattern of exponential growth and progress is.

Think about it. How do rabbits multiply? Exponentially.

How has the human population grown? For our entire existence, it's been exponential and even more so since 1800.

How have technology and our standard of living grown? Again, exponentially. We've made more progress in our standard of living in the last century than in all of history. In fact, our standard of living adjusted for inflation has experienced eight times growth just since 1900.

The learning curve of progress and evolution has its own momentum. Cells get together and evolve into greater organisms… towns grow into greater cities and countries, faster and faster.

And a mere 3% annual economic growth rate compounds into an exponential growth curve over time. This, after all, is the proven principle of compound growth… the "magic" that financial planners show you.

If you save regularly from an early age, even in small amounts, you will grow rich. But most people don't do that because they're overly optimistic and driven by instant gratification.

I love David Bach's book, *The Automatic Millionaire* (updated in April 2016), because he perfectly captures this logic of compound interest in the simplest and most human way: just save that $3 a day instead of buying a latte and then invest it systematically over the rest of your life.

His other concept — pay yourself first — is also brilliant. Before anyone else gets a piece of your paycheck, put money into a 401(k) or other savings vehicle. Treat savings like you would your rent. It's not something you do if you have money left over.

It's these small actions that compound into great wealth.

I used to speak for David and his father's clients in San Francisco. He's become one of the best-selling authors in personal finance ever. If you haven't read his book, get yourself a copy when you're done with this one!

Now, let's move on to **Guiding Principle #4** of bubbles.

CHAPTER 4

How to Identify a Bubble:
Guiding Principle #4

QUITE SIMPLY: financial bubbles are orgasms!

Think about it: what is more bubble- and burst-oriented than an orgasm?

Here's the original Masters and Johnson Human Sexual Response Cycle, first scientifically documented in the late 1950s and early 1960s.

Figure 4-1: Masters and Johnson Male Orgasm Chart

The Ultimate Bubble and Burst

Source: Masters and Johnson

This cycle starts with desire and arousal, then expands into a growing excitement, then into a final blow-off phase, or orgasm.

The most important thing to note here is that the drop-off after that is **sudden and steep**. As I always say, bubbles don't correct, they burst.

It's also important to note that this graph is actually of the male orgasm, which is more extreme and with only one peak. Female orgasms are different. I'll explain this shortly. First, let's look at the key stock bubbles over the last century so you can see the correlation here. This, again, is my view: if it looks like a bubble and walks like a bubble… it's a bubble, damn it!

Figure 4-2 shows the Nikkei stock bubble that peaked in late 1989:

Figure 4-2: Nikkei Bubble, 1985 – 1992

The Nikkei Orgasm

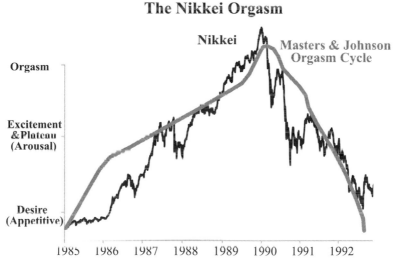

Source: Japan Statistics Bureau, Masters and Johnson

Is that a close correlation or what?

Here's another one for you.

Figure 4-3 shows the infamous Roaring '20s bubble in the Dow:

Figure 4-3: Dow Bubble, 1924 – 1932

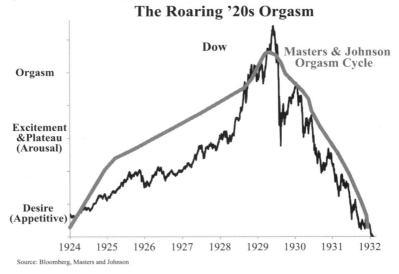

Source: Bloomberg, Masters and Johnson

Look at that. A perfect financial orgasm!

Figure 4-4 shows the Nasdaq bubble that peaked in early 2000:

Figure 4-4: Nasdaq Bubble, 1995 – 2003

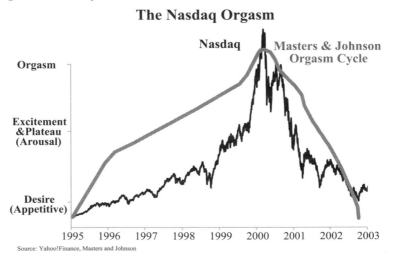

Source: Yahoo!Finance, Masters and Johnson

I did warn you that there would be many charts. In fact, in this book, you're going to see more bubbles than anywhere else I know of.

As you can see from this latest batch of charts, while no two bubbles are the same, they act in the same way. They build up, increasing in intensity until they suddenly go exponential, then climax, and crash!

And the whole process has a prolonged effect, in men AND the financial world. Men are DONE after sex. That's why they don't want to talk!

In fact, countless studies have been done in an attempt to prove the old wife's tale that warns professional athletes and sportsmen not to have sex 12 hours before competition.

The jury is still out on this, but a study by the University Hospital in Geneva sums up the general scientific consensus nicely. It says that while sex doesn't weaken an athlete, it does slow down his ability to recover during competitions. Anyone who takes their sporting or athletic activities seriously knows that recovery is a vital part of their overall performance! Economies don't recover quickly after bubbles either.

Clearly, financial bubbles are orgasms (**Guiding Principle #4**)!

They're part of our natural process of progress through the play of opposites: success and failure, inflation and deflation, innovation and creative destruction, conservative and liberal, women and men, dark and light, waking and sleeping, good and evil, pleasure and pain... and of course, boom and bust.

Before moving on to discuss the next guiding principle of bubbles, I just want to briefly return to something I said earlier: female orgasms are a bit different.

See for yourself:

Figure 4-5: Female Orgasm Chart

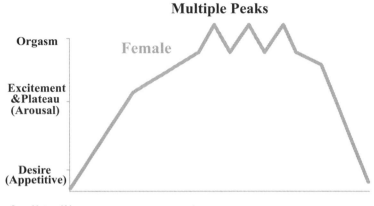

Source: Masters and Johnson

When women orgasm, they tend to have three intense peaks and the crash is a bit slower. That's why they want to talk after sex, but men don't. They have some energy left!

Look at this chart of the Dow in Figure 4-6, which shows the index all the way back to its last major bottom in late 1974:

Figure 4-6: Dow vs. Female Orgasm

Source: Bloomberg, Masters and Johnson

As you can see, there have been three peaks before, what I believe is, the last and greatest bubble burst.

The whole boom in stocks, from the last major low in late 1974 through mid-2015, has been a financial female orgasm: desire and arousal into 1987, growing excitement into a first orgasm peak in early 2000, a second peak in 2008, and just one more and most dramatic one in 2015… and we're done!

I've been warning this crash would come.

Yes, I was early with my forecast at first, but I have refined my analyses and our subscribers have had opportunities to profit during this bubble.

But in markets like this, you're playing Russian roulette with the Devil if you try to time the top in the hopes of squeezing out that extra, tiny bit of profit. Markets can drop faster than you can react, which is typical in most bubble bursts in the early stages.

By my broader projections, it will take us until around 2022 (maybe a little later) before we come down from this broader boom and bubble bust, wrapping up the current 39-Year Generation Spending Cycle. But most of the damage in stocks will likely come by late 2017. I will explain in more detail later.

Now let's explore **Guiding Principle #5** of bubbles: they always fall back to near the point where they started (if not a little lower).

CHAPTER 5

How to Identify a Bubble:
Guiding Principle #5, #6 and #7

TURN BACK A FEW PAGES and look at a couple of the bubble charts I've shared with you so far. Hell, look back at every single one and you'll notice something remarkable: every bubble goes back to at least the point where it began (meaning where it started to turn exponential), if not lower! Flip forward and look at all the rest of the bubbles I'm going to show you. You'll see the same thing.

I didn't cherry pick bubbles to show you in this book. I didn't study only bubbles that did what I thought they should. I've spent the last three decades studying every bubble I could get my hands on, mostly in the financial and economic world, but also in other areas, like climate, sunspots, life. Of course I can't share every one with you. There are simply too many and we'd need to publish an encyclopedia-sized series of books to be able to. But I assure you, nine times out of 10, when a bubble bursts, it resets at least to very near its starting point.

This next chart of the U.S. housing market, long-term (adjusted for inflation), is a great example to add to all the others in this book. It shows this **Guiding Principle #5** repeating itself time and time again: bubbles always reset close to where they began to go exponential (if not lower).

Figure 5-1: U.S. Home Prices Adjusted for Inflation

Back to Where We Started Every Time

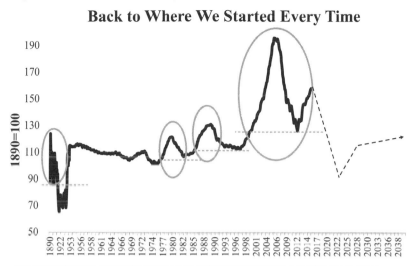

Source: Figure 2.1 in Robert J. Shiller, Irrational Exuberance, 2nd. Edition, Princeton University Press, 2005, 2009, Broadway Books 2006, also Subprime Solution, 2008, as updated by author

The simple truth is that real estate is not an appreciating asset, like stocks. It only reflects inflation and higher building costs.

This is true of gold and most commodities as well. Unlike gold, real estate can be rented out for income, and/or bought to save on rent.

But since this bubble, starting in early 2000, is so extreme, it won't just burst back to normal levels (adjusted for inflation). It's likely to go even lower! After that, it will resume its natural trend of little or no appreciation outside of inflation.

In short, real estate will never be the same again. It can't be. Not with slowing demographic trends. More people are dying and thus selling than younger people are buying in more and more wealthy, developed countries.

Prevention is Impossible

Guiding Principle #6 is that preventing a bubble burst is impossible, although you can go to great lengths at first to try… which is what we've seen governments do over the last several years. What we haven't ever seen before is them go to lengths of this magnitude!

Trying to stop a bubble from bursting only damages the system... and, in fact, makes the burst all the more painful. That hasn't stopped the Federal Reserve and other central banks around the globe from jumping to the rescue.

As I said in the Introduction, possibly the most dangerous thing in the world is someone who comes knocking and says: "We're from the government and we're here to help," or a drug addict who says: "Just let me get high one more time, and then I will finally quit. I promise."

Worst Idea EVER: Give Addicts an Unlimited Supply of Drugs

Quantitative easing is the crack cocaine of the financial world.

It's also the stupidest thing ever done!

The first, really strong burst of QE came in response to the U.S. financial meltdown in late 2008. Since then, every time the economy slowed down (as it inevitably would because QE only delays, it doesn't cure), the Fed and central banks around the world would up the ante with even more stimulus.

When it looked like the drug addict was coming down from his high, they'd pump ever larger doses of crack into the veins.

Of course, anyone with any sense knows this can't go on indefinitely. They also know how destructive this approach is. It's a one-way ticket to a dead drug addict.

Unfortunately, very few mainstream economists and central bankers seem to have much common sense!

This has led to two things: a delay in the inevitable and a third stock market bubble with nothing substantial behind it!

In fact, the stock bubble from early 2009 into mid-2015 is a rare and perfect example of an artificial bubble created solely by pouring money created out of thin air into the financial system.

Without massive government intervention to save the banks and some major companies — and to pump up the spending of the asset-rich upper class that control over 50% of spending — we'd have seen a 1930s-style depression. 2008 was looking exactly like 1930.

The $4 trillion in QE ($10 trillion-plus globally), along with $7 trillion (and rising) in fiscal deficits, have created a mere 2% average GDP growth. That's about $320 billion growth a year.

That's a bad deal and a high price to pay!

I mean, seriously!?

An average stimulus of $1.6 trillion per year, or about 10% of GDP, for barely 2% growth?

Ouch!

However, there would have been no recovery at all without such unprecedented stimulus. And I assure you, I use the term "recovery" loosely here because barely getting 2% growth is just about the weakest-ass recovery you could imagine and the worst in modern history!

There are many reasons why the Fed's quantitative easing efforts haven't had the desired effect, but that's worthy of a book on its own. For now, suffice it to say that a big stumbling block has been that the "printed" money didn't largely go into bank lending as hoped and as has happened in past recoveries.

Consumers and businesses are already too indebted thanks to the debt bubble that mushroomed from 2000 to 2008. Private debt more than doubled from $20 trillion to $42 trillion in those eight years while government debt doubled from $5 trillion to $10 trillion (and is now at $19 trillion and rising).

Instead, the money injected went into speculation, and often at high leverage, and BOOM! We have a stock bubble.

David Stockman, in his book, *The Great Deformation*, chronicles this better than anyone.

As he tells it, 40% of the earnings-per-share gains since 2009 have come from stock buybacks, made easy by the Fed's ultra-low, short-term interest rates and lower long-term rates. Lower borrowing costs from artificially low rates likely account for another 20% or more of the earnings gains. Companies also borrowed cheaply to finance mergers and acquisitions.

So the earnings surge into 2015 wasn't so much driven by sales or business growth, but more by financial engineering, or magic!

And *this* is a bubble, let me assure you… despite all of the classic public denials by politicians, central bankers, economists and analysts.

Here is a clear representation of this fact:

Figure 5-2: Dow, Late 1994 — Early 2000 vs. Early 2009 — Mid-2015

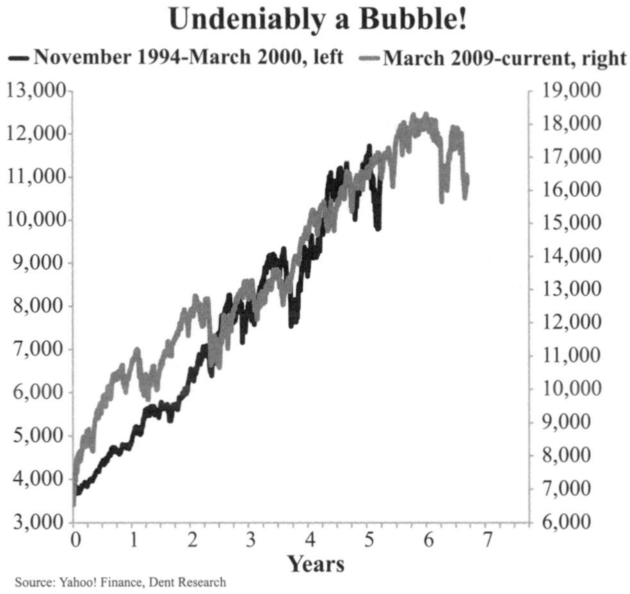

Undeniably a Bubble!
—November 1994-March 2000, left   —March 2009-current, right

Source: Yahoo! Finance, Dent Research

Figure 5-2 compares the Dow Jones from 1994 into early 2000 — the largest and clearest bubble in modern history — to the Dow Jones from 2009 into 2015.

There's not a single person or economist (that I'm aware of, at least) that denies 1995-2000 was a bubble. It was the most extreme in U.S. history and driven by technology and the Internet mania.

Look at how similar 2009-2015 looks to that uncontested bubble. The only significant difference is that the newer bubble has lasted a year longer due to artificial stimulus.

How can anyone possibly argue we've not witnessed a bubble these past six-plus years? They can't, unless they're in denial… and clearly that's exactly what they are. In denial!

I'll say it again: if it looks like a bubble and quacks like a bubble, it's a bubble!

I'll examine this 2009-2015 bubble in more detail in Chapter 20. For now, I'll quickly note that I believe we're looking at a Dow 3,800 or a bit lower by 2020-2022 — to go back to where it started in early 1995 — once this bubble has fully unwound. Most of that crash is likely to come by late 2017, so you need to prepare NOW! More on that later though…

Right now, it's important that you understand that debt and financial asset bubbles ALWAYS burst. No matter what desperate measures the Fed or other central banks around the world attempt, they will fail. Country after country is trying on negative interest rates for size, and at the time of writing, they too have failed to achieve the desired results. If zero interest rates and pouring $4 trillion into the U.S. economy is not enough… then what is?

You can't fight declining and predictable demographic trends forever, nor keep debt from deleveraging once it has gone to extreme levels… just like no one can keep an orgasm going forever.

And this takes me to the final guiding principle of bubbles…

At the Bottom of Every Hill
Is Unprecedented Opportunity

Guiding Principle #7 of bubbles is that, once they've burst, it takes years for the excesses to be worked out of the system. It's during that time that you find an abundance of opportunities.

In short, at the end of every bubble is "the sale of a lifetime" on financial assets and businesses.

Look at the money investors were able to make after the great depression!

Jesse Livermore shorted the stock market and became a billionaire in modern terms in a few years...

Joseph Kennedy sold stocks at the top and rebought at the bottom and established a family dynasty...

The mafia turned its bootleg cash flow of the 1920s into a massive loan shark, high cash-flow business in the 1930s...

General Motors used the downturn to catapult from #2 (behind Ford) to #1 in market share and clear dominance all the way through the 1960s.

Those fortunes all came from seeing the opportunities right in front of them just before and after the 1929 bubble burst.

It's during times like that when businesses are at rock bottom and available for pennies on the dollar. The strongest businesses see their competition fall like flies and gain massive market share. Real estate is in the dumps and just waiting to be snatched up. Stocks are cheap and looking for some love. Commodities reach lows never to be seen again. And everyone is too terrified to see it and take advantage because they've just had their legs cut out from under them.

Remember that human model of forecasting I shared with you earlier (on page 22)? Well, when things are at their worst, people naturally believe that they'll never get better again (it really is a flawed way to view the world!). They're gun shy and hiding away, licking their wounds... so they miss the buying opportunities. And most lose most or all of their assets in the bust anyway, so they have nothing to take advantage of it, even if they did have the courage.

But none in your lifetime will compare to the one we're about to see. It could even be bigger than the 1930s, given the potential for growth in the emerging world for decades ahead. You could have bought anything between 1932 and 1933 and made a fortune for decades to follow! That opportunity will come around again, but more selectively, where demographics will point us.

Quite literally, the world will be littered with pearl-filled oysters from which you can take your pick of treasure. I'll give you all the details you need in PART V.

So let's recap...

The Seven Guiding Principles of Bubbles

Here's a summary of those seven guiding principles of bubbles...

Guiding Principle #1:

Bubbles are cyclical and since the 1930s, generational. They occur in the fall boom season every other generation. That makes them easy to forecast *decades in advance*. It also makes them inevitable and far enough apart so that they only happen once in a lifetime like the late 1920s... and now.

Guiding Principle #2:

Bubbles are human nature. We love stocks and real estate and anything else that goes up exponentially and gives us "something for nothing" (like the lottery). We are suckers for this. This not only makes bubbles inevitable, it also makes us blind to them.

Guiding Principle #3:

Bubbles are exponential, not linear. This makes them unsustainable. They have to burst. But they are also representative of long-term trends, which are also exponential. This also makes them inevitable.

Guiding Principle #4:

Bubbles are financial orgasms. They build up, go exponential, climax and peak, then deflate rapidly, not slowly. From time to time, they'll follow the female orgasm of a triple peak before bursting, like now. That is even more ominous, as history shows.

Guiding Principle #5:

Bubbles always return to where they began their exponential move, if not lower. There are few exceptions here. This makes it easy to see how much downside there is, and how big the buying opportunities will be before the next boom.

Guiding Principle #6:

There is no stopping the bubble burst cycle. The Bank of Japan has tried for 20 years and has seen no success. The European Central Bank has tried, with no long-term luck. The story's the same with the Fed. Despite their persistent efforts, the bubble will unwind; painfully. In fact, thanks to their efforts, the bubble is far worse than it was when they got involved and we can now expect a devastating crash. While we'll be ready to grab the opportunities this will present us, those unprepared will suffer!

And finally...

Guiding Principle #7:

Bubbles, once they've experienced their initial, sharp burst, continue to unwind for years, presenting us with a sale of a lifetime, where we can pick up businesses, real estate, stocks and everything else for a fraction of their value. Despite the crisis, this presents the once-in-a-lifetime opportunity to create extreme wealth in a short period of time... if you see it coming. With this book, you'll be ready to back up the truck and position yourself for wealth beyond your imagining!

Before we move on to Chapter 6, I'd like to clarify a point for my long-time readers. In my previous books, I've explained bubbles in terms of 10 to 12 principles, not seven. Over the years, I've tightened up this list, condensing it without losing any of the points. All the salient points remain, just worded differently.

For new readers, here's the full list (for the sake of continuity across my books) to illuminate a few minor points...

1) All growth and evolution is exponential, not linear. We don't like that.

2) All growth is cyclical, not merely incremental. We like that even less.

3) Bubbles, when they go exponential in the short-term, always burst. There are no exceptions.

4) The greater the bubble, the greater the burst. Most people assume the greatest assets will hold up the best but they never do. They burst harder, even if they start to burst a bit later!

5) Bubbles tend to burst at least twice as fast as they build, so getting out a bit early is better than a bit late. They don't correct, or go down in stages. They crash and burn!

6) Bubbles tend to go back to where they started to grow exponentially, or a bit lower. Sometimes, like in 1932, they go much lower.

7) Financial bubbles tend to get more extreme over time as credit availability from higher incomes and wealth expand the capacity to both borrow and speculate.

8) Governments have become larger and more powerful in more complex urban societies and they always find ways to develop new tools for expanding credit and economic stimulus — like endless QE today.

9) Bubbles are like a drug and they make most people feel better (or high). We don't want this to end so we go into denial as the bubble evolves, especially in the late stages. Governments and major financial institutions go even more overboard.

10) Bubbles become so persistent and attractive that they ultimately suck in even most of the skeptics. Sir Isaac Newton — the smartest man of his era — was sucked into the great 1720 stock bubble after initially warning against it.

11) Major bubbles only occur once in a human lifetime, so it is easy to forget the crash and lessons from the last one.

12) Bubbles may seem fruitless and cruelly destructive when they finally burst, but they actually serve a very essential function in the dynamic play of opposites and progress. They help launch many potential innovations mainstream so that a few can become long-term game-changers. But many more fail in the process. You can't get evolution and success without failures!

Seven principles or 12, the golden threads remain the same... bubbles are inevitable (they're human and universal in nature)... they aren't easy to see because we don't want things to change or such bubbles to violently burst — as they do... they're cyclical and generational... but, they're predictable... and they're unstoppable when they do burst.

Most importantly, they present smart investors and business people, like you, with opportunities to really make money!

While everyone else is hurting from the crash, convincing themselves things will never be better again, you'll be taking the next bull by the horns (so to speak) and getting ready for the next wild ride!

Before we move on to the next chapter, I must give credit when it's due...

Which Country Has the Biggest Stock Market Bubble?

In April 2016, www.feddashboard.com published an article asking the question: which country has the biggest stock market bubble. I'm not the kind of guy who ignores when someone or some agency does the unexpected. The Fed Dashboard, and a handful of others, are slowly starting to admit to the bubble I've been warning of for years now.

I'll give them credit for that.

They shared a very interesting chart, which I'll now share with you:

Figure 5-3: Stock Market Indices Divided by Business Gross Value Added

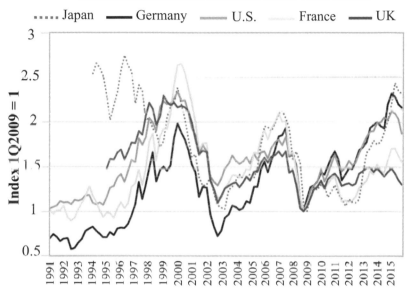

Which Country Has the Biggest Bubble
Stock Market Indices / Business Gross Value Added
..... Japan ——— Germany —— U.S.   France ——— UK

Data Sources: Nikkei, FTSE Russell, Deutsche Börse, Euronext, Eurostat, U.S. Bureau of Economic Analysis, Japan Cabinet Office/ESRI

Source: www.feddashboard.com
(http://feddashboard.com/which-country-has-the-biggest-stock-market-bubble#prettyPhoto)

Stock indices were selected for broadest coverage in companies and history, and readily available.

Japan is shown dashed because Japan rarely publishes Business GVA (GDP). Thus, Private Consumption was used to eliminate an aspect of government from the denominator. Private Consumption and GDP tracked fairly closely until 1Q 2014 when the combination of consumption tax and QE cut the relationship from nearly 62% down to just above 58% in 4Q 2015.

Variations in exports and foreign investment matter. Gross National Product to GDP ratio for these countries varies from 100% to 102%, Japan tends to be higher and the UK lower.

Most recent government data releases are for 4Q 2015.

This is a beautiful chart, making the bubbles around the globe easy to see, not only in their current form, but in comparison to previous bubbles. Nicely done!

They did leave out the greatest bubble: China, especially its real estate boom, but I'll cover that in Chapter 17!

That said, the majority of economists and people remain blinded to the stock market and global debt bubble, and it's to their and everyone else's detriment.

Now, on to Chapter 6…

PART II

A Brief (But Thorough) History of Bubbles

CHAPTER 6

Lessons From History

AS I MENTIONED EARLIER, bubbles have occurred back as far as humans can remember, and have recorded. They've happened all throughout natural growth and evolution. The sudden explosion of new species, like trilobites or humans, is an example. So is the massive growth and then sudden extinction of the dinosaurs.

It's clear that we, as humans, have a psychology that is prone to bubbles. Life is challenging and even though such trials are key to our personal and collective growth, no one likes the hard stuff — including me! So we have a natural propensity to hope that things will only get better and then stay that way.

Having studied the history of everything (I literally read a set of encyclopedias on "The History of Western Civilization" — 10,000 pages plus — over a period of three months when I was 29), I can tell you that no matter how much we hope and wish, life has never been easy or simple!

Every time things get good and the economy grows faster than usual, we see a crash with a recession or depression that follows.

Prices go up, then they go down.

Booms always turn to busts. In most booms, life gets better and easier in many ways… we want that trend to go on forever. So we go into denial and find every plausible explanation for why "this time it will be different."

Mainstream economists proclaim that recessions are only a thing of the past and that any undeniable bubbles will enjoy soft landings. That has never happened. We really are masters at self-delusion!

The thing is, as I explained in previous chapters, bubbles are unavoidable… particularly towards the end of any long-term boom. And they inevitably burst ferociously, whether we admit their existence or not.

This makes my job of warning people about bubbles almost impossible! I nailed it when I identified the real estate bubble peak in the United States in late 2005, but no one would listen, except for my newsletter subscribers (and my ex-wife), whom we had been preparing with evidence for a long time before the collapse.

Bubbles are irresistible. They keep building beyond logic as more people are drawn in. "Come into my parlor, said the spider to the fly."

As 2014 and 2015 unfolded, I found myself pulled into debate after debate over the stock market bubble. For the most part, I was speaking to deaf ears. People who warn about bubbles almost always look like idiots as the black hole continues to suck people in. Ultimately they always burst, and as I'm about to show you — there are no exceptions in history! But it's tough to stand your ground when everyone around you is throwing rocks.

The story now is that governments have been able to keep the economy going after the Great Recession and the crisis is over… No! They have only created a greater bubble that now must burst more violently. There is no other way this can end.

By the end of this chapter, you'll have all the evidence to see the inevitability for yourself!

Blooming into a Great Bubble

There are so many bubbles throughout history that it's a difficult task limiting myself to just a few. Let's start by looking at the first bubble in modern history that preceded the stock markets: the Great Tulip Bubble.

While Holland is famous for its tulips, they're actually native to Central Asia and Turkey. In the 16th century, they were brought over to Holland, where they became an instant hit! Such a big hit, in fact, that around 1634 the first modern "commodity futures" market was formed so people could buy tulips before they were harvested and lock in a price. Before that, tulip bulbs weren't really worth much. Then suddenly anyone could put a little money down and speculate on the value of the harvest ahead. And so people lost their minds!

As they developed, futures markets allow agricultural producers to lock in their profits at a certain price as well. But given the low price of doing so early on, futures markets also led to speculation among the rich.

In the case of 17th century Holland, as tulip prices went up, more people bought such futures. The more they went up, the more people speculated. We all know how that ended.

The reality is we're greedy bastards who want to get rich quick, with no effort. So when everyone starts doing something, it looks less risky. Just like during the Powerball of January 2016: you begin to believe that you can't win if you don't play. Of course, even if you do play, you're not likely to win, either.

With futures, there is always risk, no matter how many people pile in. In the case of the Dutch, the wealthy speculators were caught off guard and they were crushed under the weight of the tulip bulbs they didn't own.

Just look at that collapse. It's almost vertical!

Figure 6-1: Dutch Tulip Bubble

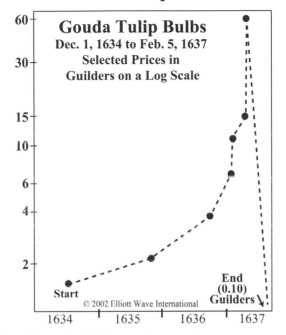

Source: "Conquer the Crash" by Robert Prechter, pg. 80

Bulb prices went exponential from 1634 into 1635, advancing 120 times in less than two years.

Then they collapsed 99.8%, just below where the bubble started.

This was the most extreme bubble in history as investors were even more oblivious to bubbles back then, but it was restricted to a very minor portion of society.

One factor in its occurrence was that it came at the top of a 500-year cycle of rising inflation into the mid-1600s, with everyone expecting commodity prices to go up forever (the trap, again, of straight-line forecasting).

The Tulip Bubble had little reality to back it up — it was pure speculation, based not on rising productivity or value, but just on higher prices. Sound familiar?

The next great bubble occurred in the early 1700s as the first trading companies developed around long-term sailing expeditions for trade in the East Indies (India and beyond), led by the East India Trading Company that was founded in 1706.

Spreading Bubbles Across the Ocean

Investors could buy shares in such trading companies and share in the profits. Functionally, this was the very genesis of stock markets, which inevitably led to a speculative surge. But that financial orgasm only occurred after the British government sold off its shares in its state-owned South Seas company to finance its war debts with low interest rates and easy financing for investors.

By mid 1720, the South Seas bubble was ready to pop.

South Seas shares had gone from 110 to 960, or 8.7 times, in less than two years. Then they collapsed 94% within a year, as you can see in Figure 6-2:

Figure 6-2: The South Seas Bubble

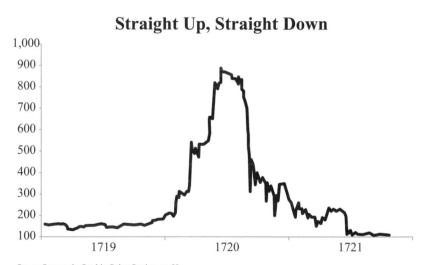

Straight Up, Straight Down

Source: *Conquer the Crash* by Robert Prechter, pg. 80

This is also another example of bubbles collapsing back to where they started or a bit lower.

The story of the Mississippi land bubble in France in Figure 6-3 was even more telling, since it saw the first bubble fully induced by a central bank and its government.

John Law had ascended to the top levels of finance in France after Louis XIV's long wars that had nearly bankrupted the country. He conceived the idea of having the Bank of France raise money by selling shares in French-owned lands in Mississippi and Louisiana to pay off its debt.

To do this, Law created the first central bank that could create money by loaning artificially created funds against such speculative purchases in what turned out to be largely swamp land in America. The interest rates were low and government guaranteed (is there an echo?).

The result was like the South Seas… an intoxicating bubble and a devastating burst.

Figure 6-3: The Mississippi Bubbles

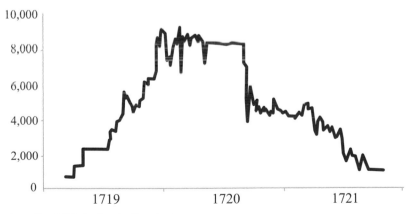

Central Banks Start Their Shenanigans

Source: François Velde, http://www.heraldica.org/econ/

The Mississippi land bubble was much worse than the one Fannie Mae and Freddie Mac produced into 2007/08 because the land being sold in North America was nearly worthless at the time, and so far away no one knew otherwise. To the investors, it all sounded like the bright new future of things… and the government was recommending it and providing low cost financing!

Of course, the Mississippi bubble collapsed just as the South Seas bubble had (and all bubbles do). And a long-term economic slowdown followed, with lower stock prices into the late 1700s.

These twin bubbles exploded into 1720 from low-cost interest rates, encouraging speculation, courtesy of governments. They then burst, losing more than 90% into 1722. A depression followed and stocks went essentially nowhere into 1787 — that's 67 years!

Only when the Industrial Revolution (along with free-market capitalism) and the American Revolution (democracy) took center stage did the momentum change — the bigger the burst, the greater the innovations it spawns. In the greatest "Big Bang" in economic history since the Agricultural Revolution 10,000 years before, stocks and the economy blasted to the moon… until the next great bubble peaked and burst, which showed up first and most in the rapidly growing American Midwest…

CHAPTER 7

Bubbling America

CANALS TURNED CHICAGO into the new "Oz," with access to the Atlantic Ocean through Canada and the Great Lakes. The U.S. government financed this massive migration using — you guessed it — cheap and guaranteed financing and cheap land to induce people to move westward.

When land is cheap and easy to finance, you always get a speculation-fueled bubble!

Andrew Jackson was credited as the only U.S. president to balance the federal budget, but he didn't so much slash spending. In fact, he funded it with those massive land sales to the public, like John Law back in France... some things never seem to change.

Thanks to cheap land and financing, land in the Midwest skyrocketed and Chicago suddenly bubbled up close to New York-level prices in a matter of years. This formed the most extreme real estate bubble in U.S. history.

Real estate prices in Chicago soared 40,775%! That's not a typo.

They shot up from $800 an acre in 1830 to $327,000 in 1836.

Then they crashed 90%, back to $34,000, by 1841.

Figure 7-1: Chicago Real Estate Bubble, 1820-1843

The Most Extreme in U.S. History

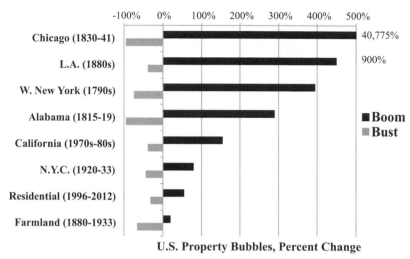

U.S. Property Bubbles, Percent Change

Source: "Betting the house," *The Economist*, 4/6/2013

The equity market topped in 1835 and then there was the panic of 1837. Stocks lost 60% between 1835 and 1843. What followed was a terrible depression the likes only to be exceeded in the 1930s and both with deflation, not inflation — the economic winter season.

Then there was an aftershock into 1857 and another depression before stocks and the economy advanced again. The whole affair resulted in one of the greatest resets in U.S. history lasting 22 years, as you can see in Figure 7-2:

Figure 7-2: Stock Prices Since 1700 on a Logarithmic Scale

Two Massive Shocks Created
a Great Reset: 1835-1857

Source: *Conquer the Crash* by Robert Prechter, pg. 33, Dent Research

The railroad boom before and after the Civil War came next.

The dominant theme of the 1800s, from around 1830 forward, was the great railroad boom. These were the first mega companies in American and European history.

There was a long depression in the U.S. and Europe between 1873 and 1896, with the most devastating crash from 1873 to 1877, then a milder one from 1883 to 1885 and a final one from 1893 to 1896. This depression was not as deep as 1835-1843 or 1930-1942, but it was the longest since the 1700s.

Most people don't appreciate how the invention of railroads in England in the 1820s ultimately exploded growth in the U.S. While their use in the UK and Europe boosted economic growth there, in North America they united a vast continent and so brought about the birth of a mega nation!

Railroads became the new way to become rich in business and in stock speculation. And as usual, a bubble developed and burst just after the first transcontinental railroad was completed in 1869.

Railroads boomed strongly into the Civil War as they were the backbone of logistics. After the war, 33,000 miles of track were laid between 1868 and 1873, with lots of government backing through land grants and subsidies. Every great bubble has had encouragement from governments.

Railroads became the largest employer in America outside of agriculture.

Figure 7-3: Railroad Bubble

The Crash of 1873-1877

Source: Arthur H. Cole and Edwin Frickey. "The Course of Stock Prices, 1825-66". *The Review of Economics and Statistics.*
Vol. 10, No. 3, August 1928. page 117-139.

The first bubble started in 1857 and built into a double top between 1864 and 1869 (there's that female orgasm!). The first serious crash came in late 1873 when the dominant investment bank, Jay Cooke & Company, failed to float a bond offering to continue to fund the highly leveraged second transcontinental railroad, Northern Pacific. Cooke went under and that spawned a series of bank and railroad failures, and layoffs.

That created the panic of 1873. The New York Stock Exchange closed for 10 days. Most major railroads, 60 in total, went under in the first year. 18,000 businesses failed. Unemployment grew to nearly 9%

in 1878. There was a railroad strike in 1877 that required President Hayes to send in the troops to end it.

The longstanding Bubble Bill that was passed after the horrific South Seas Bubble crash was repealed in 1825 and that allowed investors to speculate again and for companies to publicly promote their stocks… and, of course, that led to greater bubbles like 1835 and 1869. This was much like the Glass-Steagall Act being repealed in 1993, just in time to allow the recent series of dramatic bubbles and banking leverage. There just is no stopping human nature when it comes to bubbles. If you allow, they will speculate.

After the depression into 1878, there were aftershocks and some minor depressions and crashes between 1883 and 1885, and again from 1893 into 1896. Consumer prices eventually bottomed in a long-term, 500-year inflation/deflation cycle in 1896.

Railroads continued to boom and become increasingly mainstream from 1897 into 1920, where they finally peaked in passenger miles and revenue in 1920, marking the turn of the Innovation Cycle into its slowing phase (I'll share more details on this cycle in Chapter 12).

The Roaring '20s and The Great Depression of 1929-1942

The greatest depression in U.S. history hit not long after our country became the world's leading growth engine thanks to those canal and railroad innovations, and then the early stages of the explosion of autos, electricity and phones into the economy. (China has been following an even more aggressive and massive expansion track in recent decades, which will end catastrophically as I'll explain in Chapter 18.)

Not only did we surpass Great Britain in basic innovations after the 1870s, bringing to the world things like the telephone, the combustion engine, electricity, the Model T, and the assembly line, but we benefited from massive migration from Europe into World War I. In fact, that war catapulted the U.S. into the limelight.

The war-torn European continent needed our newly found agricultural and industrial capacity. So we expanded rapidly to meet that and became the China of that era (you could see China today as the U.S. of *this* era).

That war caused a natural explosion in inflation and commodity prices, and when that was over, both collapsed into the deep recession of 1920 to 1922. That was actually a minor depression with deflation in prices and a collapse in commodity prices right on my 30-Year Commodity Cycle, much like we saw in 2008-2009 (more details later).

But downturns in that commodity cycle, no matter how big or small, don't result in deep contractions or depressions. Real estate collapses walk away with that honor, hands down!

The Great Depression occurred after the U.S. continued to expand agricultural and industrial capacity, even after Europe came back online to compete globally. That's just not smart business! Unfortunately, that's another human tendency: once we've started growing, we don't know when to stop. We just push growth harder and faster until we overdo it… and everything blows up in our face.

The trouble that played a heavy hand in making the Great Depression so devastating was the creation of the Federal Reserve in late 1913. Ironically, its creation was intended to counter interest-rate and depression cycles from all of the off-and-on depressions between 1835 and 1896… Ha! What a joke!

It's worth noting here that there was no central bank between 1836 and 1914. The first central bank founded by Alexander Hamilton operated from 1791 to 1811. The second central bank was renewed from 1816 – 1836. When its charter expired, it was not renewed. By 1914 the thought was that the series of depressions from 1835 through 1896 were the result of not having a central bank to stabilize interest rate cycles, i.e., like today, there was a mistrust of free markets with the assumption that governments can manage better (think China). No one wants the pain of natural adjustments and rebalancing — just straight-line growth on the way to heaven… when will we ever learn?

As all central banks have always done, the Fed tried to offset downturns by lowering interest rates and protecting banks. In so doing, they lessened the effect of naturally occurring recessions, creating greater imbalances down the road and encouraging even greater speculation in stocks and real estate. In the end, the Fed only created a greater depression and higher volatility by trying to over-manage the economy from the top down. Apparently, very little has changed.

Hence, we saw the Roaring '20s wherein wages didn't grow that much, but speculation did, especially in stocks, farmland and equipment.

The Roaring '20s was not just an auto bubble, but ultimately a farm bubble thanks to the introduction of tractors! That created a bubble in farmland prices and borrowing on farm equipment and when *that* bubble burst it triggered the Great Depression.

The 1930s crash first hit the stock market and industrial firms like Ford and General Motors. Then it took out everyday people and local banks with real estate, particularly in rural areas where 60% of people still lived.

Figure 7-4: Dow Bubble and Crash in the Great Depression

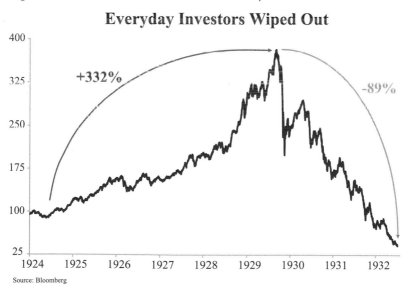

Everyday Investors Wiped Out

Source: Bloomberg

The Great Depression represented the greatest detox in debt and production capacity in U.S. history. And it set the stage for the greatest boom that followed.

World War II and the first middle class generation to emerge from the mass production/assembly line revolution created a massive boom from 1947 into 2007, with only a brief, predictable interruption when the Bob Hope generation began to spend less from 1969 into 1982 and the baby boomers began entering the workforce, creating unprecedented inflation into the late 1970s (the economic summer season).

The United States came roaring out of the Great Depression to become the greatest country and world leader since Great Britain in the 1800s. Why? Because what doesn't kill you makes you stronger! We didn't gloss over our debt and slowing demographic trends like we're doing today. Instead, we eliminated most of our private debt. We allowed banks and companies to go under. It was a massive detox of the system, which made it more efficient and stronger in the end.

And we saw the incredible baby boom bubble…

Figure 7-5: The Baby Boom

A Generational Bubble of Epic Proportions

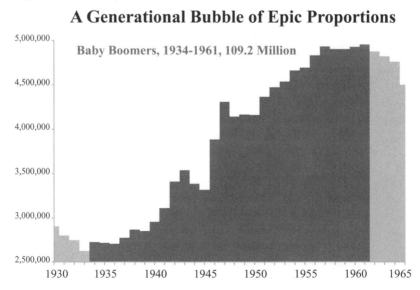

Source: U.S. Census Bureau, National Center for Health Statistics

I will talk about this bubble generation in more detail in Chapter 14, but I mention it here because it plays a critical role in the position we find ourselves in today… and has most certainly earned its place in the halls of bubble history.

109.2 million people were born in just 28 years when you count the large wave of immigrants that are here now and were born in the same cycle! It's unheard of… and as yet, unrepeated.

The baby boom generation became a pig moving through a python, distorting everything around it as it grew up, got jobs, had kids, and is now starting to retire. It has played a significant part in creating the bubbles we've witnessed since 1995… and for the inevitable burst ahead. This generation was destined by its sheer size to be a bubble generation.

That's quite a burden to place on one generation's shoulders. We could rage against them as so many have done, or thank them for the sale of a lifetime (I vote for the latter).

In Chapter 15, when I discuss the greatest debt bubble in history — the one we're all experiencing — I'll explain the role central banks have played in creating this mess we're in. So how could I not blame the baby boomers as well?

Quite simply, it's their sheer numbers that distorted the economy health care, social security, employment — and as they sip their sundowners in greater numbers, they're draining the economy of its spending blood!

More than that, it is members of the baby boom generation who lead the Fed and other central banks… organizations that are only reacting to the trends this generation has created with their predictable patterns. They've been guiding us down this path both to heaven and to hell. So broadly speaking, the generation continues to stamp its mark on the world.

But then, that's what bubbles do!

CHAPTER 8

Bubbling into the '90s
and Beyond

THE JAPANESE NIKKEI peaked near 39,000 in 1989 and then plunged 62% to around 24,000 in late 1992 before enjoying a strong, but brief, rally.

I predicted the long downturn in Japan in 1989 in *Our Power to Predict*. Everyone thought I was nuts for that, until it happened!

The real estate markct in Japan followed the stock market and peaked in 1991. Then it collapsed by more than 60% and has never rallied back… and it's now 25 years later!

Figure 8-1: Japan Real Estate Bubble

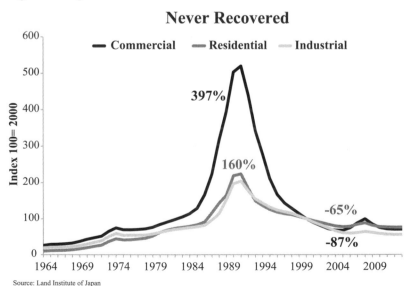

Source: Land Institute of Japan

Japan's property peak in 1991 was right in line with peak spending on trade-up homes, which happen around age 42 there (remember, it varies by a year or two from country to country, and generation to generation).

It's been all downhill since. Japan is the retirement home "in hock" of the developed world. It has no demographic growth or future, only decline. Sadly, Japan is dying.

Then came the high-tech and Internet bubble from 1995 to early 2000. It really made a go of challenging the South Seas bubble for heights attained and losses recorded. Here's a more detailed chart of that:

Figure 8-2: Nasdaq Bubble, 1995 – 2003

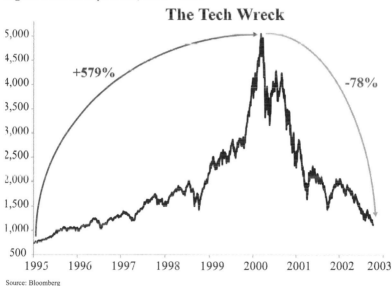

Source: Bloomberg

The Nasdaq advanced from 750 to 5,050, or 6.8 times, from late 1994 into March 2000, and then fell 78% to 1,100 in October 2002.

The Internet index rose nine times and fell 92%.

This bubble was driven by the sweet spot of baby boomer spending in the 1990s (which I predicted in the late 1980s) and the S-curve acceleration of Internet, cell phones, and broadband into the mainstream economy (much like the prior fall season boom from 1914 to 1928 when cars, electricity, phones, and radios moved mainstream rapidly).

The 1990s was totally predictable as the greatest boom in U.S. history if you simply looked at projectable demographic trends and cycles of technology innovation and the S-curve projections of progress. But economists don't dirty their hands with such consumer fundamentals. They don't consider them as important as the intricacies of government policies. That's why they totally missed the greatest boom in history and will now miss the greatest bust just ahead.

After the punishing crash in tech stocks, a bubble formed in U.S. real estate, peaking in early 2006 (again, in late 2005, I predicted this would be the case).

Property prices then fell 36%, adjusted for inflation, into early 2012, more than what we witnessed in the Great Depression (26%).

Figure 8-3: U.S. Home Prices Adjusted for Inflation

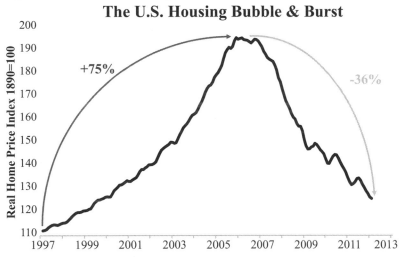

The U.S. Housing Bubble & Burst

Source: Figure 2.1 in Robert J. Shiller, Irrational Exuberance, 2nd. Edition, Princeton University Press, 2005, 2009, Broadway Books 2006, also Subprime Solution, 2008, as updated by author

We've seen booms and busts in real estate and occasional bubbles throughout history. Two, one-time trends caused an unprecedented and seemingly non-stop surge in real estate after World War II.

One was the first middle class generation in modern history returned from the war and bought homes financed with long-term mortgages with support from the GI Bill. This allowed them to buy on a new, larger scale.

The other was that, from the late 1970s forward, the baby boom generation distorted home-buying trends simply because of its unprecedented size.

It's worth noting at this point that since World War II, it has seemed that real estate is a perpetually appreciating asset. This is absolutely not the case historically. Adjust for inflation and you can clearly see that property isn't the ticket to riches it's thought to be.

The Bob Hope generation was the first middle class to emerge after WWII and be able to broadly afford homes and long-term mortgages, with a little help from the GI Bill to boot. Then their boom was quickly followed by the massive baby boom generation.

Hence, from 1947 to 2005 it seemed like real estate only went up and they just weren't making any more land. So, we baby boomers don't have a realistic view of real estate's more typical boom and bust scenarios prior to WWII, and that it's a non-appreciating asset adjusted for inflation.

Today, a second minor bubble has developed in real estate and major new bubbles in places like Manhattan, San Francisco and South Beach. This too will crash... and more importantly, it will never appreciate the way the baby boomers enjoyed up until 2005.

With the generation retiring and eventually dying en masse, more die-rs will drain out of the property market than buyers into 2039.

That's why Japan's real estate market never recovered, even when a smaller millennial generation entered the real estate buying cycle... and that's why real estate will never be the same, as I explained in Chapter 3 of my book *The Demographic Cliff*.

Beyond the bubbles in real estate, first in Japan and then in the U.S. and around the world, nothing compares to the real estate bubble in China where major cities like Shanghai have seen appreciation of

587% since 2000, and still rising sharply recently, signaling a blow-off top. I'll talk more about China's bubble in Chapter 17, including its crazy property prices.

But let's look at the Red Dragon's recent stock market bubble... the one they can't hide with questionable statistics.

China's stock market, in Figure 8-4, epitomizes the emerging market bubble that was even stronger than the tech bubble in the 1990s. Its Shanghai Composite went up nearly six times, to 6,000, in just two years and then collapsed 70% in just one year into late 2008. Bubbles tend to collapse twice as fast as they build!

Figure 8-4: Shanghai Composite

Twin Sharp Bubbles and Crashes

Source: Yahoo! Finance

China's market rallied only modestly into February 2010 and was back near its 2008 lows in mid-2013.

This called into question China's growth rate of 8% to 12%. How could its market perform so badly if its growth was so great? As usual, the answer is that China was (and still is) overbuilding everything. Besides that, it isn't known for being honest about its statistics.

The country's stock market tells the real story, with its feeble rally into February 2010 and its decline to near-2008 lows.

In late 2015, its stock market bubbled again, this time up 159% in just one year as its government encouraged speculation in stocks to offset the slowing real estate markets. Then it crashed 45% in just a few months, much like the first crash in the Dow in late 1929.

Bubble Mania in Commodities and Bonds

According to the Commodity Research Bureau Index, commodity prices were the next bubble to peak first, in March 2008 and then secondarily in late April 2011. There is no more bubble-prone sector than commodities.

Oil went from $18 in late 2001 to $147 in mid-2008. That's an increase of 716%.

Then it came tumbling down, losing 78% in just 4.5 months. I've never seen the late-stage surge and crash occur so fast... ever!

Talking about commodities in general... after the first steep crash in 2008, prices had in Elliott Wave language, a "B-wave" or bear market rally into 2011, and have continued to collapse.

Figure 8-5: CRB Commodity Index

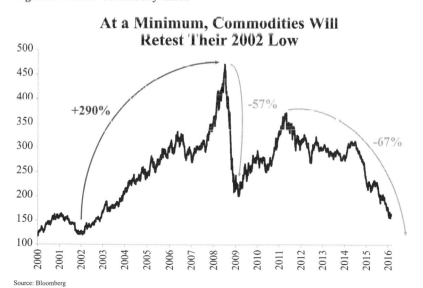

Source: Bloomberg

Falling commodity prices create a vicious cycle of falling exports and profits in emerging countries, and that, in turn, creates lower exports for China.

Silver peaked in that cycle at $48, rivaling its 1980 bubble peak.

At Dent Research, we gave a sell signal on silver and gold on that day in late April 2011 right at the top, at $48.

Gold was the next major bubble to peak (Figure 8-6).

The crisis metal market saw escalating money printing around the world, but it had to start throwing in the towel when inflation fell back toward a modest 1% rate in mid-2013. This reinforced my long-standing argument that money printing would not create substantial inflation in the economic winter season of debt deleveraging and deflation.

Gold staged a rally into mid-2016, as I forecasted a bear market rally was due, but will likely steadily deflate again...

Figure 8-6: The Gold Bubble

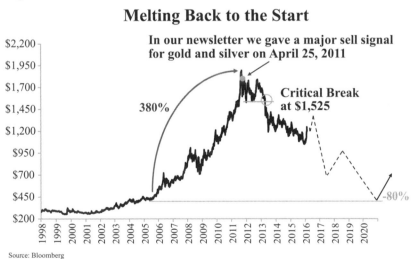

Source: Bloomberg

Gold went up 674% (7.7 times) between 2001 and 2011 and crashed to as low as $1,050 in January 2016.

The bubble didn't kick in until late 2005 when it started to go up exponentially and advanced 4.8 times, or 380%, in six years. So it has much lower to go to erase that bubble. In fact, my next target for the precious metal is around $700 an ounce by mid-2017 or a bit later.

Ultimately, gold is likely to bottom around $400 between 2020 and 2022 when the clockwork-like, 30-Year Commodity Cycle turns back up again. At its worst, it could go back to its 2001 low of $250 before seeing a long-term boom again, led by emerging countries. After all, they are big gold and commodity consumers and they will totally dominate the demographic trends in the next global boom.

Remember in 1980, when gold soared to $840 and was projected to go to $5,000? That's bubble logic for you. And we've heard the same wild projections for gold in recent years. But that is not going to happen anytime soon. Gold could hit $3,000, even $5,000, in the next 30-Year Commodity Cycle peak… but that will only be around 2038-2040… when you're dead!

Let's look at two last bubbles before we move on…

The first is HYG, an ETF index that tracks high-yield bonds.

It peaked in May 2013 at around 96, right where we gave a clear sell signal in our newsletter.

Figure 8-7: Junk Bonds

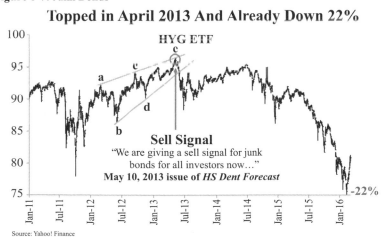

Source: Yahoo! Finance

And the second is the very last bubble to peak: global stocks. They very likely peaked back in mid-2015.

This last chart, Figure 8-8, shows what is called a Megaphone Pattern for the U.S. stock market. As you can see, each step of this bubble has seen higher highs and lower lows.

Figure 8-8: Dow Megaphone Pattern

The Greatest Crash of Our Lifetime Has Begun

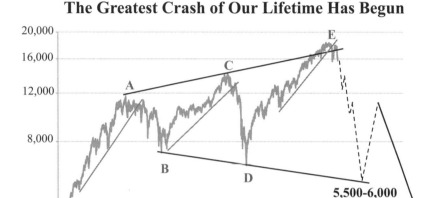

I will discuss this bubble in much greater detail in Chapter 20. After all, it's what's going to present us with the sale of a lifetime ahead.

For now, let me say that I expect the Dow to fall to around 5,500 by late 2017, the lower trend line of this megaphone pattern.

If stocks take out the bubble that started in late 1994, then the Dow would ultimately fall to 3,800 or a bit lower between early 2020 and late 2022. Only after that will the demographic trends turn positive again, as we shift into the economic spring growth season.

What History Shows Us

By now it should be clear to you that once a trend goes exponential, it ultimately peaks and crashes. Once that's happened, it tends to go back to that launch point.

Gold started going exponential in 2005, from $400 upward. So again, $400 is the most likely bottom target. That would mean a 79% fall from its top in late 2011. A fall all the way back to the last low of $250 is also possible. That would mean an ultimate collapse of 87%.

The typical range for a normal, long-term bull-market correction, like the one we saw in 1968-1982, is 50% to 60%. But when a bubble boom peaks — like in 1929 or 2015, or 1989 in Japan, or in gold in 2001 and oil in 2008 — the corrections tend to be between 70% and 90%! That's why I am more cautious now than any time in my forecasting career.

That's why I've been pleading with my readers and newsletter subscribers to get out of any passive investments they may hold. As Barron Rothschild said when asked how he amassed his great wealth: "I always sold a little early."

Sharp crashes, as you can see in all the charts and bubbles I've shared with you so far, happen fast… too fast to give you time to react and get out unscathed.

In this environment, your only hope is to follow a proven strategy, like any of the several the Dent Research team of investment experts have developed through years of research and decades of back testing. You can find details on all of these at dentresources.com.

And for those passive investments you do have — like the ones in your 401(k) — follow someone with a proven track record of solid allocations that keep you in the game but out of the danger zone. This is exactly what our *Dent 401K Advisor* newsletter aims to do.

The bubble burst in Japan's stock market was 80% from late 1989 into early 2009. Most of that drop took place in the first crash into late 1992.

The bubble burst in U.S. stocks from late 1929 into mid-1932 was 89%! The first three-month drop was 42%!

The Nasdaq bubble burst from early 2000 into late 2002, rapidly losing 78%... and it's not likely bottomed yet. Its first three-month drop was 42%.

The overall commodity bubble that peaked in mid-2008 has already been down as much as 70% as of January 2016. It clearly has further to go and will ultimately be down 80% or more by the end of this cycle.

The stock bubble in China, on the Shanghai Composite, went up 570% in just two years — into late 2007 — and then crashed 70% in just one year, into late 2008. That's the second most extreme bubble and crash since oil in 2008. Its second bubble peaked in 2015 and went down 45% in its first three months, just like the Dow's collapse in 1929.

The skies darken fast in the world of investing and business. Keep reading to not only discover how to predict the next crash, but how to make the most of the sale of a lifetime that it will present you.

Before we get to that, though, there are many more bubbles that don't fall under the category of financial assets, like the student loan bubble and the tuition inflation bubble, or the health care cost bubble, now seemingly exaggerated by Obamacare. Childcare cost is another bubble that's affecting the young millennial generation.

The chart below shows the sectors of our economy that are seeing inflation rates far higher than the average CPI. I showed you a similar chart in Figure 3-3, but this time, I've added childcare.

Figure 8-9: Education, Health Care and Childcare Costs vs. Consumer Price Index

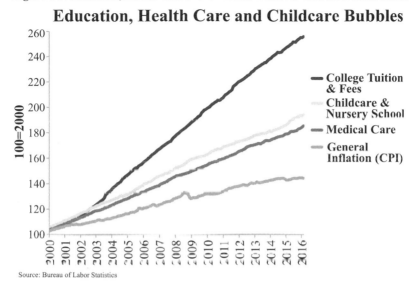

Source: Bureau of Labor Statistics

And here's the student debt bubble that has risen to a whopping $1.23 trillion, with nearly a trillion coming into existence just since early 2003. This has been the only way to keep the education bubble going — with government-backed loans that are crippling more and more young people.

Figure 8-10: The Student Loan Bubble

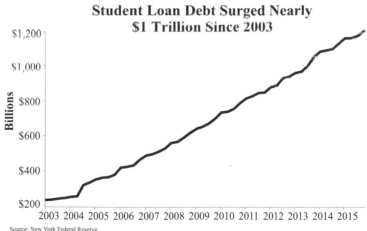

Source: New York Federal Reserve

Before we move on to Chapter 9, one last comment: most economists don't see the tuition, student loan, daycare or health care bubbles as comparable to financial asset bubbles like stocks, real estate and commodities. That's just short-sighted... and stupid.

No sector can inflate much faster than average forever. These are bubbles, and they will burst when the demand pressures and special interests that caused them meet the great depression and deflation of 2016-2022.

Falling health care costs will bring relief to the aging baby boomers.

Declining education and childcare costs will greatly relieve the emerging millennial generation.

Great resets occur once in a lifetime for good reasons — to restore sanity and balance after long-term booms create extreme bubbles and imbalances in their late stages. This is necessary to allow us to grow and innovate again, yet still painful if you don't see it coming.

Depressions are like death: "the pause that refreshes."

PART III

Our Power
to Predict

CHAPTER 9

How to Predict When Bubbles Will Crash

FOR MOST PEOPLE, the essential characteristic of the future is uncertainty. Most economists and investors operate from the basic assumption that the economy, not to mention life itself, is unknowable. The conclusions they reach and decisions they make are done under conditions that remind me of a party of blindfolded children playing pin the tail on the donkey.

Imagine if you were a farmer and couldn't relatively accurately predict the four seasons? Or if you were pregnant and had no idea when the baby would come? Or if you're a fisherman who couldn't forecast the tides, or the weather? You wouldn't be a farmer or fisherman for very long!

Imagine if you could get a glimpse of what lay ahead of you…

Imagine the edge you'd have!

The fact is: you absolutely can see around the corner, and in this chapter, I'm going to show you how.

This is my passion… my reason for getting up early in the morning and going to bed after midnight.

My aim (and that of my team at Dent Research) is to continuously identify reliable indicators that provide signposts to the future, which you can use as the basis for all your investment decisions.

History *does* repeat itself (as I've showed you over and over again since the beginning of this book), albeit always with a few new twists — like the unprecedented money printing by central banks around the world in their attempts to stave off the inevitable and necessary economic winter season, only to create a greater bubble that will burst more dramatically.

The secret of knowing what's coming next — and when — is all contained in the predictive power of cycles and human behavior!

That's why I've painstakingly developed a hierarchy of four key cycles over the last three decades. I have many more cycles that I study and watch — I'm a sucker for cycles — but there is a right and wrong number of cycles to use. I call it the "optimal minimum" number of cycles to explain the key trends that will impact your life, your business and your investments over the rest of your lifetime.

Too many and you're just as blind as if you had none. Too few leave you missing something important.

But I've found the sweet spot. four cycles that collaborate perfectly. Only with *all* four can I see the whole picture for developed countries like the U.S.

Developing this hierarchy has been a process of trial and error over the last 30 years. When something happened that I didn't expect with my best cycles, I dug for an explanation and then a new solution to better forecasting the markets and economy.

I still do this today. My research is perpetual and I'm constantly innovating in an effort to bring readers like you, and subscribers, to my newsletters better, more useful, information.

As the cliché goes: knowledge is power.

If you know what's around the corner, there are always ways to invest profitably. If you know that a sale of a lifetime is coming soon, you can take maximum advantage!

In short, cycles help you identify when bubbles are most likely to occur and when they're most likely to pop in their usual spectacular fashion.

Here's an overview of my four key cycles for developed countries (note that I use a slightly altered hierarchy of cycles for developing countries).

Figure 9-1: Hierarchy of Macroeconomic Cycles

Our Power to Predict

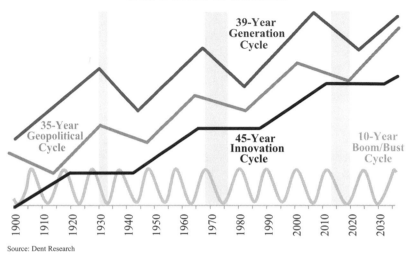

Source: Dent Research

As you can see in that third vertical gray bar on the right of the chart, **all four of my cycles are currently in their downward phase**.

This convergence is rare, having happened only twice in the last century (the other two vertical gray bars). The first time this happened, we suffered the worst ravages of the Great Depression (late 1929-1934). The second time it happened (1969-1975) we endured a major stock market collapse and deep recession that included the OPEC oil crisis and the greatest stock crash since 1929-1932!

And as you can see from the above chart, we have several more years in which to witness major market and/or economic upsets. After that, we have good times to look forward to again. That's because it's not only noteworthy when the cycles all point down together. It's important to see when they're all heading up together as well. It's during such "up" times that we see the markets and economy boom. The period from 1989 into 2000 is a good example of this. And from what the cycles are saying, we can expect another such boom period from 2023-2036, just not as strong in the U.S. because the demographic trends won't be as propelling.

But I'm getting ahead of myself. Let's take a step back so I can show you why I trust these cycles as much as I do (and why you should, too).

The four key cycles that currently make up my hierarchy, in order of my discovery, are:

• The 39-Year Generational Spending Wave;

• The 34-36-Year Geopolitical Cycle;

• The 8-13-Year Boom/Bust Cycle; and

• The 45-Year Innovation Cycle.

Let's look at each one in detail…

The Generational Spending Wave: The Ultimate Leading Indicator

I discovered the Generational Spending Wave in 1988. It's a 39-year cycle in the last century that tracks the movement of a new generation as it increases, plateaus, and then decreases in spending as it ages. The stock market put in major long-term peaks adjusted for inflation in 1929 and 1968, and then 2007 — 39 years on the nose.

To know what a generation's spending wave will look like, you simply move the birth index forward by 46 years (after adjusting for immigration). At 46 years old, most people are peaking in their spending, having bought the largest house they'll own when they were about 41 and helping their kids through high school, maybe college, and then into the big, wide world. These numbers were for the baby boomers.

Figure 9-2: Immigration-Adjusted Births Lagged for Peak Spending

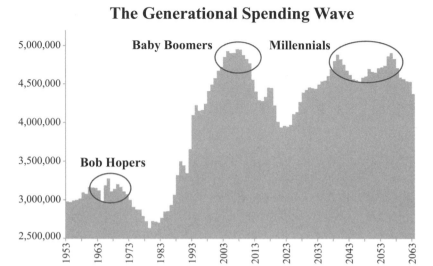

The Generational Spending Wave

Source: Dent Research, U.S. Census Bureau, Bloomberg

For the Bob Hope generation, that peak in spending came at age 44 because they got married earlier and went to school for a shorter time, on average. For the millennial generation, it will likely come at age 48 or so. The peak spending age also differs from country to country. As I've mentioned before, in Japan, it's 47.

This cycle proved powerful enough to predict the unprecedented boom and bubble into late 2007. And when I back-tested it, it "foresaw" the '50s and '60s boom and the '70s extended recession and inflation crisis. That's because demographics allow us to predict inflation trends decades in advance as well.

As my demographic analysis has been my claim to fame — what I'm best known for in economic and investment analyst circles — it would be best to share with you what I've learned over the last three decades…

A Pig Moving Through a Python

Essential to understanding broad economic trends is the recognition that new generations of consumers enter the workforce around age 20 and spend more money as they raise their families, buy houses and cars, etc.

The demographic climaxes in average peak spending led to the rising boom from 1983 to 2007, then the slowdown in 2008 that will continue until 2020, when trends flatten and bottom out into late 2022 before turning up again.

Yet the world's economists simply have not come to terms with what happens when the largest generation in history reaches its spending peak. Nor do they appreciate the impact of a smaller generation following a mammoth one in most developed countries

We need to consider hard questions, such as what happens when Japan, most of the countries in Europe, North America and China face shrinking workforces and reduced population growth.

What happens as more people retire than are entering the workforce? How does that affect economic growth and commercial real estate and inflation rates?

What happens when more homes go onto the market as people die than there are younger buyers to buy them? That's already happening in Japan and most developed countries will follow suit.

Such situations have never happened before, so we have no history to learn from Yet there's no doubt they'll radically affect the global economy and we can project the demographic trends that will predictably result.

The thing is, when you give demographics the significance it is due, you get an invaluable edge. That's because *people do predictable things as they age*. So when the largest generation in 250 years comes along, the baby boomers, those predictable trends are magnified and easy to see decades in advance.

As I showed in Chapter 7 (and I'll go into more detail in Chapter 14), the baby boomers have stretched every trend to extremes, from inflation when they were young and expensive to raise and educate... to spending into their peak... to investing in stocks and real estate until they could no longer sustain the bubbles they'd created... to retiring en masse and morphing health care and retirement services into behemoths that will eventually crumble under their own weight. Their retirement is also destroying the Social Security, Medicare and Medicaid systems... and we ain't seen nothing yet (but that's a topic for later).

And they've done all of this in a predictable way, that we can track and project.

The Consumer Expenditure Survey (CE) from the U.S. Bureau of Labor Statistics measures more than 600 categories of spending by age... which changes according to age.

The average boomer family borrows the most when the parents are about 41 years old. That's typically when they buy the largest house they'll own. They spend the most at age 46, although more affluent households reach that peak between ages 51 (top 10%) and 54 (top 1%). People save the most from age 55 to 63 and have the highest net worth at age 64 (later for more affluent households).

Predictably, as we live longer, these peaks slowly move up in age. The Bob Hope generation, born from around 1897 into 1924, reached its spending peak at age 44 in 1968. Baby boomers peaked in their spending at age 46 in 2008. Millennials will most likely peak in their spending at age 48-49, in 2055-2056.

Here's what that predictable spending cycle looks like for the maturing baby boom generation:

Figure 9-3: Consumer Life Cycle

Predictable from Cradle to Grave

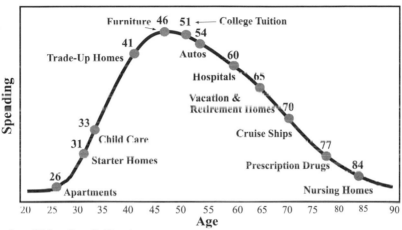

Source: U.S. Census Bureau, Dent Research

Let's look at this more closely...

The average person enters the workforce at age 20, an average of those who complete their education with a high school degree at age 18 and those who graduate from college at age 22.

Typical baby boomer couples got married at age 26 (millennials are getting married a little later, around 27-plus).

Apartment rentals peak shortly after, and the average kid arrives when his or her parents are 28 or 29 years old. That stimulates the first home purchase at about age 31.

As the kids become teenagers, parents buy their largest house. That's between the ages of 37 and 41. They do this because, at that point, both parents and kids need more space between each other. You want the kids to be way over there while you're way over here — and the kids couldn't agree more!

We continue to furnish our homes into our 40s, and thus spending on furniture peaks around age 46. This is also the peak in spending overall for the average household.

In the downward phase of spending, some sectors continue to grow and peak. College tuition peaks around age 51. And cars are the last major durable goods item to peak, at around the age of 54. That's when parents finally trade in the mini-van and splurge on a luxury car. Some get fancy sports cars (I have a cherry red Jaguar). Some get big pickup trucks. So it's no surprise that these sectors did so well throughout 2015. Their future, though, isn't so bright!

Savings start to rise from 46 forward, but surge the most from age 55 to 63 toward a net worth that peaks at age 64 (a year after the average person retires at age 63).

Spending on hospitals and doctors peaks between the ages of 58 and 60… vacation and retirement home spending peaks around age 65… and cruise ship travel peaks into age 70. After the stress of travelling with kids for 20 years, who wouldn't want the luxury of relaxing on a floating hotel and casino where you can stuff yourself with food and booze until you collapse!

Then there are the peak years for prescription drugs and likely vitamins (age 77) and nursing homes (age 84).

I've highlighted only some key areas. The data can tell you much more, such as when consumers spend the most on camping equipment, babysitting, or life insurance. If you want to see more, get a copy of my in-depth research report, *Spending Waves: The Scientific Key to Predicting Market Behavior for the Next 20 Years*. It delves into hundreds of categories of consumer spending, with charts that show you the trend for each. You can find more information on that at dentresources.com.

The Pig, Up Close and Personal

All of this becomes critical to understanding and forecasting the markets and economy because the baby boomers are like a pig moving through a python. As the largest in history, they're the ultimate bubble generation. And that's why my Generational Spending Wave is the core cycle in my hierarchy.

However, members of the mainstream media (and others) — a May 2013 article in *Barron's*, for example, and an on-air piece at CNBC — often challenge me on my argument that the baby boomers are bigger than all other generations that have followed.

"How can I say that," they ask. "There are clearly more millennials."

I cringe when I hear this. Actually I cringe when I hear any broad statements concerning demographics because too often the speaker hasn't done in-depth research *and* has reached the wrong conclusions.

It's quite simple really: when you factor in immigration — which I do for all my Generational Spending Wave analysis — the baby boom generation takes top count. That makes millennials the first generation to be slightly smaller than their predecessors. This pattern is consistent throughout the developed world, with the exception of Australia and the Scandinavian countries. Many southern and central European and East Asian countries have no echo boom generation at all.

More subtly, but no less simple: yes, the millennial generation has bigger numbers than the baby boom.

But, it's not only about the numbers.

It's ALSO about the growth rate and time it took to reach those numbers and the ultimate heights to which they rose.

In the U.S., the birth rate for the echo boom group started at a higher level, and rose to its final peak over a period of 32 years (1976–2007).

The baby boomer births peaked in just *28 years*!

And, it has an advance, from bottom to top, in immigration-adjusted births of 90%, compared to only 27% for the millennials.

Figure 9-4 shows you what this looks like:

Figure 9-4: U.S. Births Adjusted for Immigration

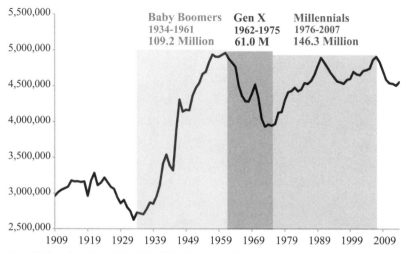

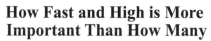

Source: U.S. Census Bureau, National Center for Health Statistics, Dent Research

This time-to-peak makes a significant difference to the economy. It's like five people trying to squeeze through the door standing shoulder-to-shoulder rather than the same number going through two by two.

That's the key to demographic trends and forecasting: reading the wave — namely, the rising wave of births and growth — and distinguishing the relative size of the acceleration of each generation.

The baby boom is the 10-foot-tall wave crashing onto the beach. The echo boom is a five-foot-tall wave sliding up the sand. The Bob Hope generation prior was more like a three-foot wave.

A surfer instantly can tell you the difference — it's like night and day!

Although the echo boom wave is only slightly wider in its scope, the baby boom wave is taller and greater in magnitude and peak numbers.

That's why it's a bubble generation!

And *that's* why I call it the biggest generation in modern history.

In the next boom, from about 2023 forward, the number of households needed to keep the economy going through spending and borrowing money, buying homes, investing, and other economic activity simply won't grow as fast or to the same levels as we witnessed the baby boomers do since the 1980s.

Yes, many (but not all) developed countries will experience another demographic-driven boom about a decade from now, but it won't be as strong as the one precipitated by the rising spending and borrowing of the baby boomers, except in rare smaller countries like Australia or Singapore. Like any true bubble, they were a once-in-a-generation phenomenon!

After the baby boomers, growth is more likely to come as a result of technological advances, especially those that will increase longevity and working years, which could help compensate for the lower number of workers. Such areas as biotechnology, robotics, nanotechnology, and cleaner energy sources will be drivers, but it will be a long time before they affect the economy broadly. After all, it takes decades for new innovations to gain momentum.

Clearly demographics have a pervasive effect on modern economies and the baby boomers have reshaped our world, quite literally.

Take inflation for example...

Most economists view inflation as largely a monetary phenomenon, but it's not (sorry, Milton Friedman). It's driven more by people. And the baby boomers turned it into a bubble in the '70s.

Bubbly Inflation and Deflation

Young people cause inflation. They cost everything and produce nothing. That's because, quite rightly, they're in a learning stage until ages 18 to 22.

It costs, on average, about $250,000 for parents to raise a child, not counting college costs if they go. It costs governments a big portion of their budgets for education. And just as a new generation enters the workforce, businesses have to invest in workspace, equipment and training.

In effect, young people are an investment in the future for all sectors of our economy. They begin to pay off when they enter the workforce and become productive new workers (supply) and higher-spending consumers (demand).

Conversely, older people tend to be more deflationary. They spend less, downsize in major durable goods, borrow less, and save more. They don't require investments in new infrastructures like offices or larger homes, or in major education; they ultimately leave the workforce and downsize to smaller homes or even nursing homes.

I discovered this in 1989, one year after I discovered the Spending Wave, when I noted a surprisingly strong correlation between inflation rates and a 2.5-year lag on workforce growth (it apparently takes that long for their productivity or contribution to exceed their costs). This is an amazing short-term correlation, given how many factors affect inflation: food and gas prices, monetary policy, swings in economic cycles, currency exchange rates, and others. And there are swings against this indicator in real life from such variables. But the long-term trend follows very accurately, just like the Spending Wave, despite such short-term volatility.

And so, as the baby boomers grew into young working adults, they bubbled up inflation into the early '70s.

Now, as they amble into the sunset, they're bubbling up deflationary trends as well.

Figure 9-5: Inflation Indicator and Forecast

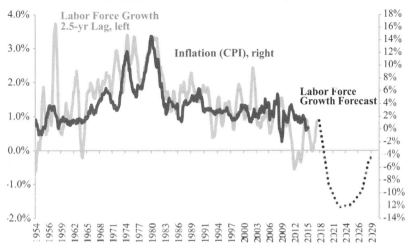

Deflation Ahead Into 2023

Source: Bureau of Labor Statistics, Dent Research

Central bankers didn't cause the greatest inflation in modern history. Politicians didn't create the high workforce growth of the 1970s. Creating 16% inflation and 18% mortgage rates wasn't in their best interest. *That* was mostly the baby boomers' doing.

The most important trend to note from Figure 9-5 is that it points toward deflation in prices into 2023, without any impacts from debt deleveraging we'll see as the greatest debt and financial bubble in history bursts.

My Inflation Indicator can only give us a 2.5-year window on inflation trends, but, since we can predict the number of 20-year-olds who will enter the workforce and the number of 63-year-olds who will exit, we can roughly project workforce growth and inflation two decades in advance. But the 80-Year Four Season Economic Cycle gives us clear insights into such up and down trends many more decades out.

Back in the late 1980s, when I was predicting the greatest boom in history into 2007 or so, I also saw inflation falling to near zero by 2010. And what do you know? That's exactly what happened.

Workforce growth went from a high of 4% in the late 1970s to 3% in the late 1980s to 2% in the late 1990s. It currently stands at around 1% and will be 0% by 2020-2023… despite massive stimulus.

The bottom line is, if you want to see the future, watch demographic trends. They're the ultimate leading indicators.

Even better: most economists, investors, and businesspeople don't understand this, so it creates a unique advantage for you as an investor or business.

To wrap up this chapter, here's a summary chart on the impacts the baby boomers had on these three broad areas as they've aged:

Figure 9-6: Three Generation Waves of Impact

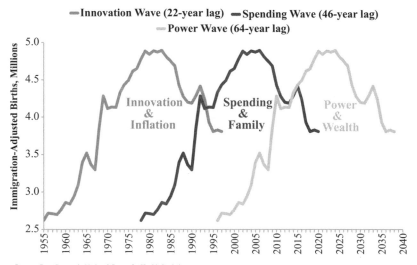

Baby Boomers Leaving Their Mark

Source: Dent Research, National Center for Health Statistics

The first wave of impact is the Inflation and Innovation Wave. As I mentioned earlier, into 1980 we saw an inflation bubble from the baby boom. That peaked in 1980 and the entire information revolution Innovation Cycle peaked around 1983.

Then came the Spending and Family Wave. We saw the greatest boom and bubble in modern history from 1983 into 2007.

Finally, we're witnessing the Power and Wealth Wave right now. A revolution in institutions with massive social and political change is coming in the next decade. But this phase also sees the bubble burst, with revolts against income inequality and the private and public institutions.

As you now better understand, this is all why the Generational Spending Wave is my most fundamental cycle, and the most predictable, so it's at the top of my hierarchy.

CHAPTER 10

The Geopolitical Cycle: When it's Bad... it's Horrid

MY NEXT CYCLE BREAKTHROUGH was in early 2006, when I found the Geopolitical Cycle, which oscillates from favorable to unfavorable every 17 to 18 years... and oh, has it been unfavorable since 2001 (9/11)!

The last positive arm of this cycle was between 1983 and 2000, during which time nothing significant went wrong in the world.

Since the cycle turned negative in 2001, however, we've seen an endless series of destructive geopolitical events: 9/11, two failed wars, endless civil wars from Syria through the Arab Spring, the Russian invasion of Crimea and Ukraine, the rise of ISIS (worse and more brutal than Al Qaida), the twin Paris attacks followed by Brussels, rising racial tensions in the U.S. over police brutality, and now Donald Trump and Bernie Sanders showcasing the extreme political polarity in the U.S. more than at any other time since the Civil War.

Here's what it looks like:

Figure 10-1: The 35-Year Geopolitical Cycle

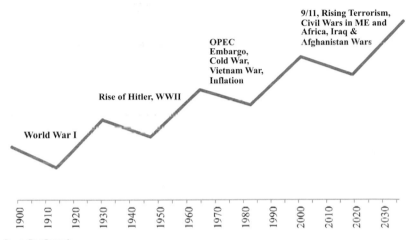

17-18 Years Up... 17-18 Years Down

Source: Dent Research

This cycle has an impact, not as much on GDP growth or corporate earnings, but on the risk perceptions of investors because markets and economies are highly charged during the negative period of this cycle. Volatility is high. Fear simmers just under the surface. As a result, stock valuations during negative turns tend to be half of what they are during the positive swing, as I will show later in this chapter.

In November 2015, I recorded a monthly *Ahead of the Curve* webinar for my *Boom & Bust Elite* members in which I broke down the events that have taken place since this Geopolitical Cycle turned down in 2001.

It was shocking to see the timeline of events, but reinforced the power this cycle has on every aspect of our lives.

I'll share this with you now:

Figure 10-2: Geopolitical Timeline

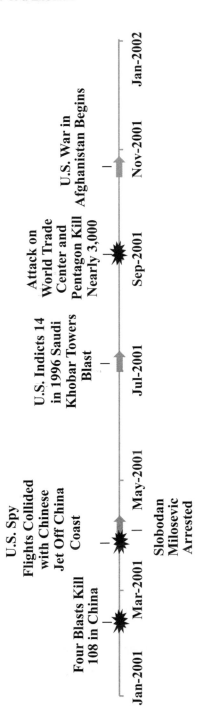

Figure 10-3: Geopolitical Cycle

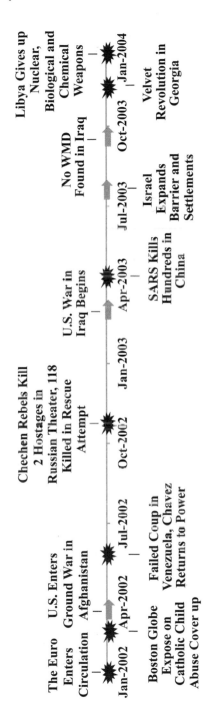

Figure 10-4: Geopolitical Cycle

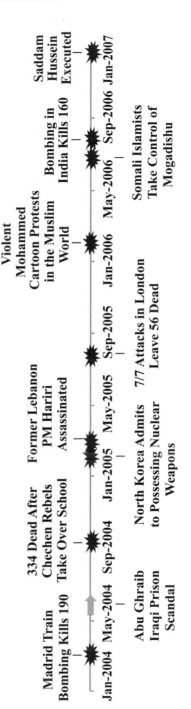

Figure 10-5: Geopolitical Cycle

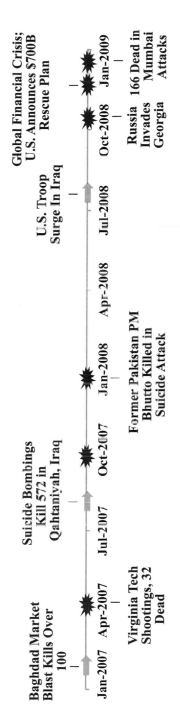

2007 & 2008

✹ Isolated, High-Impact Events ➜ Part of Ongoing Conflict

Figure 10-6: Geopolitical Cycle

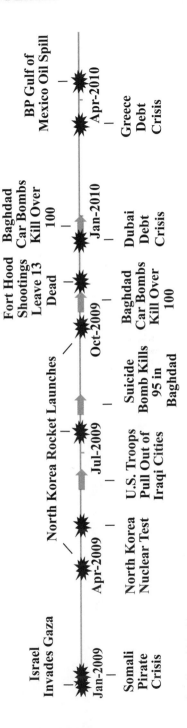

2009 & 2010

✸ Isolated, High-Impact Events ⬆ Part of Ongoing Conflict

Figure 10-7: Geopolitical Cycle

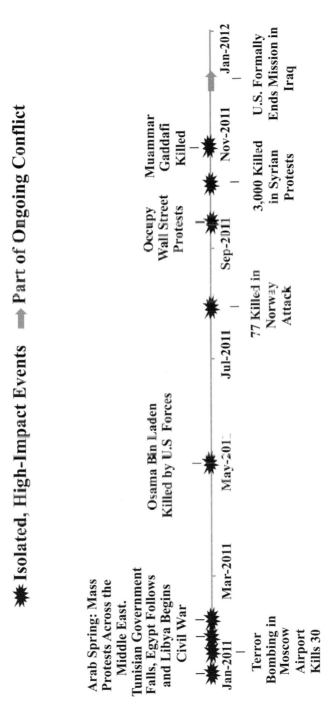

2011

✸ Isolated, High-Impact Events ➡ Part of Ongoing Conflict

Arab Spring: Mass Protests Across the Middle East. Tunisian Government Falls, Egypt Follows and Libya Begins Civil War

Osama Bin Laden Killed by U.S Forces

Occupy Wall Street Protests

Muammar Gaddafi Killed

Jan-2011 Mar-2011 May-2011 Jul-2011 Sep-2011 Nov-2011 Jan-2012

Terror Bombing in Moscow Airport Kills 30

77 Killed in Norway Attack

3,000 Killed in Syrian Protests

U.S. Formally Ends Mission in Iraq

Figure 10-8: Geopolitical Cycle

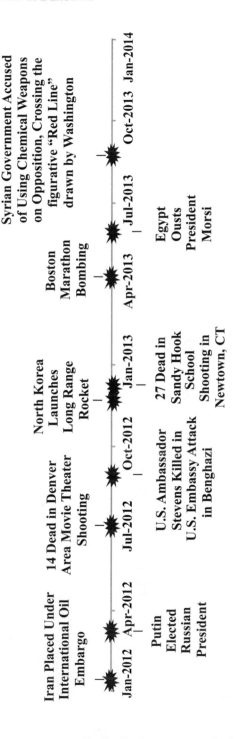

Figure 10-9: Geopolitical Cycle

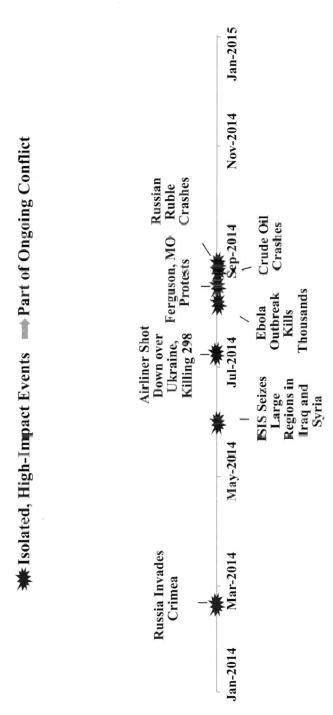

Figure 10-10: Geopolitical Cycle

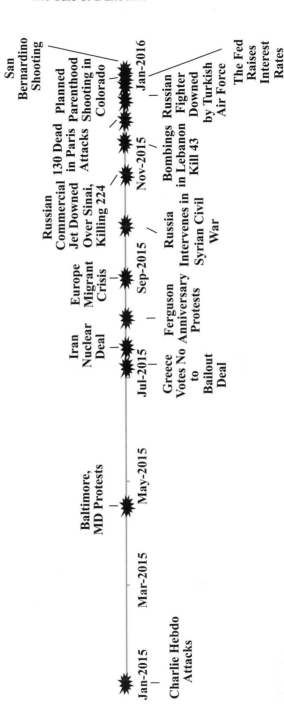

Figure 10-11: Geopolitical Cycle

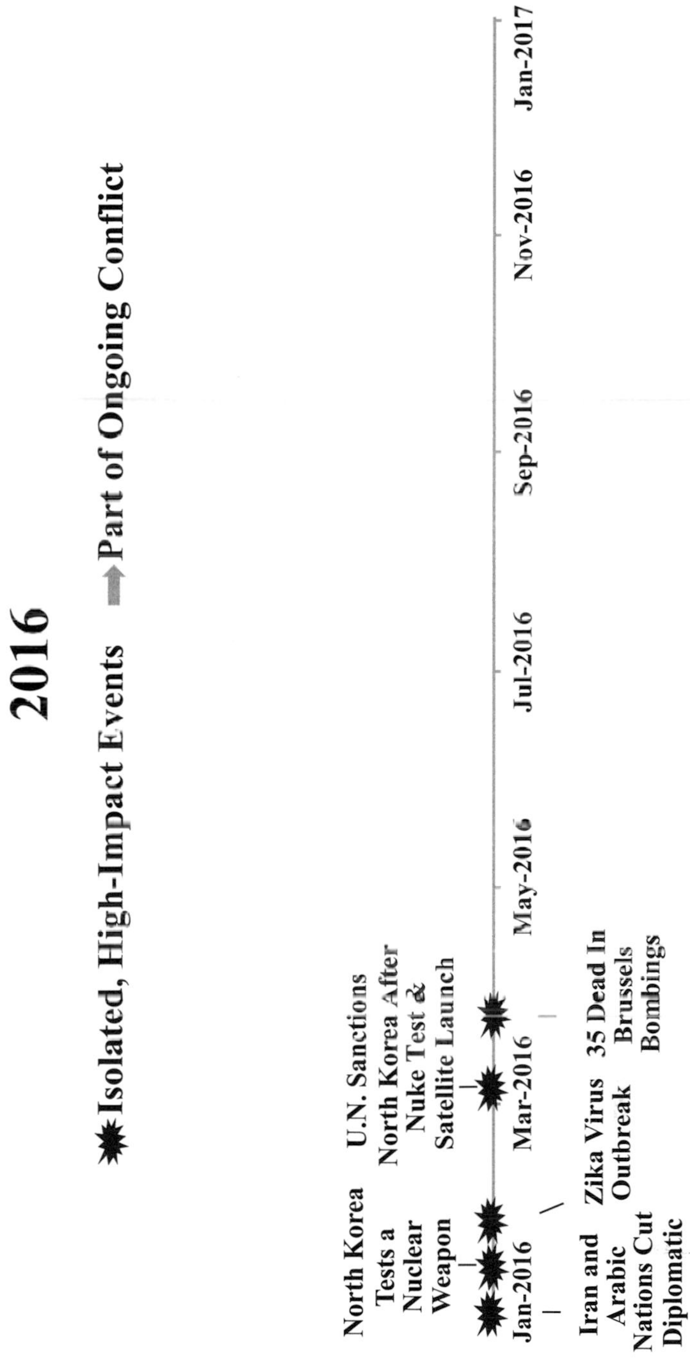

2016

✴ Isolated, High-Impact Events ➡ Part of Ongoing Conflict

Jan-2016	Mar-2016	May-2016	Jul-2016	Sep-2016	Nov-2016	Jan-2017

North Korea Tests a Nuclear Weapon

U.N. Sanctions North Korea After Nuke Test & Satellite Launch

Zika Virus Outbreak

35 Dead In Brussels Bombings

Iran and Arabic Nations Cut Diplomatic Ties

And those timelines don't even cover every single event. Like I said: it's shocking to see.

Now, when we look at my Generational Spending Wave and the Geopolitical Cycle together, we see that they both trended upward between 1983 and 2000… the exact period in which we saw the greatest boom and bubble in U.S. history.

They also both trended down together during the 1930s, when the world suffered one of the deepest and most painful economic depressions in history.

This highlights **the key to harnessing the predictive power of cycles**.

As I've already indicated, individual cycles don't give the full picture. That's why I never rely on just one, and why I don't become emotionally attached to any one particular cycle. Instead, I look for collaboration and correlations between cycles. When you combine a group of powerful cycles a reliable pattern emerges, just like it takes a cluster of key technologies like autos, electricity, phones and radios to create a technology revolution — and *that's* when I pay attention.

Adding the third cycle to my hierarchy made the pattern clearer: the time frame between 2000 and 2009 was fraught with dangers to investors, businesses and the world… as early 2014 to early 2020 will see an even greater set of bubble bursts and financial crises.

CHAPTER 11

Booms and Busts...
And the Power of Innovation

THE THIRD CYCLE I watch closely stems from the Decennial Cycle that Ned Davis originally conceived. He reviewed 100 years of stock data and found that the most significant stock corrections and recessions occurred in the first three years of each decade, like the 2000-2002 tech wreck.

That cycle worked like a charm from the early 1960s forward, but then derailed in 2010 with only a 20% correction in stocks and no recession in 2011. So I locked myself in my office and went digging again. The 2010 to 2012 down cycle should have been the worst after such a great bubble peaked in late 2007 on cue.

After intense research, I concluded that Ned's 10-year cycle is ultimately driven by sunspot cycles that vary between eight and 13 years — not as clockwork like as many cycles I study.

Now, hear me out on this one...

When I first mentioned this cycle to my colleagues, they laughed at me. Then they begged me not to talk about it in public or even to subscribers because it made me look like a crack-pot, and I didn't need to lend any more credence to the popular view that I'm just plain crazy for seeing bubbles that no one else sees. (I'm not on crack, the economy and government policies are.)

But my live-and-die-by-the-sword personality wouldn't let me follow their advice. In fact, their warnings just drove me deeper into the research to prove the value of this cycle. And the more I researched, the more evidence I found that this cycle is very real, very powerful… and has impacted markets and the economy for as long as we have data to review!

I'm also not the only economist or financial researcher who believes in the power of this cycle.

In fact, I first came across it when reading an article in *Barron's*. One of the largest fund managers, formerly at Pimco, said it was the Sunspot Cycle that saved him from the 2000-2002 crash.

As I have since discovered, sunspot activity affects many things, from satellites to electronic infrastructures to weather. Do you know that both sunshine and rainfall are 20% higher at the peak of the sunspot cycle!? Shouldn't all farmers be following this cycle?

In the recent cycle, the best scientists called for a peak in late 2013. They were early by a couple of months. It finally peaked in February 2014. But, in the world of cycles, that's close enough to be spot on.

Now the scientists are calling for the next bottom to occur around late 2019 or early 2020. And from my back testing of this cycle, I warn you not to ignore this.

The good thing about this cycle is that it is more intermediate-term and better focuses on booms and busts within the larger cycles that my other three cycles are good at predicting.

Even better, scientists are very good at predicting it.

As a cycles guy, I read more scientific articles than economic ones because scientists are great at identifying and predicting cycles — so far out it would make your head spin.

Again, this cycle is not as clockwork-like as many other cycles, so scientists are constantly researching and refining their forecast in this area, and that's invaluable.

Richard Mogey, the past director of the Foundation for Cycles, attributes this variation of eight to 13 years to the gravitational pull of the larger outer planets on the sun. That could be why it's not as clockwork-like as the sun coming up every morning.

Figure 11-1: The 10-Year Boom & Bust Cycle

88% of Crashes Happen in
the Downturn of this Cycle

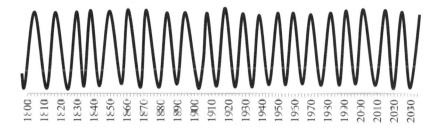

This cycle is best at pinpointing when we'll see major crashes, financial crises or recessions/depressions.

Eighty-eight percent of the recessions and stock crashes since the mid-1800s (where we have good economic data) have come in the downward phase of the Sunspot Cycle, which has been documented in detail back to the 1700s, and which scientists from NASA to Stanford diligently project.

There is almost no chance this is a coincidence, and I consider this the most important cycle I've discovered since I created my Generational Spending Wave in 1988.

Important to note is that when the Sunspot Cycle, the Spending Wave, and the Geopolitical Cycle have all moved through their negative phases simultaneously, markets have almost always tanked.

The last sunspot cycle peaked in March of 2000 and the tech bubble crash followed. It bottomed between 2008 and mid-2009, right when the great recession hit. The current Sunspot Cycle peaked in February 2014, and points down into around late 2019 or early 2020.

If we don't see a major financial crisis hit by early 2020, I will quit my profession and become a limo driver in Australia (my favorite country)!

That gives us *three* cycles in negative territory, indicating the greatest likelihood of a market crash between now and early 2020... and most definitely a global depression according to the extent of this bubble and the economic winter season of the 80-year cycle from 2008 through 2022!

Thus far stocks look to have peaked in May of 2015, with some markets, like the Dow Transports, peaking as early as November 2014. In fact, most major global markets peaked in 2015 and have already entered bear market territory of 20%-plus declines, except for the largest-cap markets in the U.S., like the Dow, the S&P 500 and the Nasdaq.

The U.S. stock markets also saw the worst January in history, which doesn't bode well for the markets historically.

As this was going to print, the markets were still failing to make new highs since the May 2015 top. They look likely to crash again into July (or December at the latest, if they hold up into early July). A break lower than 20% from that May top will finally signal clearly that this bubble is over and done.

If two powerful cycles confirm the trend that my proprietary Generational Spending Wave shows — as predictive demographic trends drive the economy up or down — then a third seals the deal. And that's exactly what this final cycle in my hierarchy does from a broader and less volatile impact.

The 45-Year Innovation Cycle

For many years, the four cycles in my hierarchy contained the three I've discussed, along with the 30-Year Commodity Cycle. But something was off. As we moved deeper into the new century, I found the Commodity Cycle had more relevance for developing nations than for the developed ones, because they are largely commodity exporters. Most developed economies revolved largely around commodities until the early 1900s.

I knew that innovation and productivity had a lot to do with these new clusters of technologies emerging and I tried to correlate that with the simple 22-year lag for the impact of young people. So back into my office I went and began digging… again. Before long, I found what I was looking for…

The peaking of major mainstream technology surges every 45 years, not quite in line with the generational Innovation Cycle.

In 1875, steamships peaked and then dropped off rapidly long term. Into 1920, railroads roared and followed. By 1965 cars had raced into the hearts and homes of middle class citizens. In 2010, the Internet and mobile computing became ubiquitous and had changed how we work and interact with each other. Google and email tripled the productivity of my research business, at a bare minimum!

Figure 11-2: The 45-Year Innovation Cycle

Technology Transforming Life

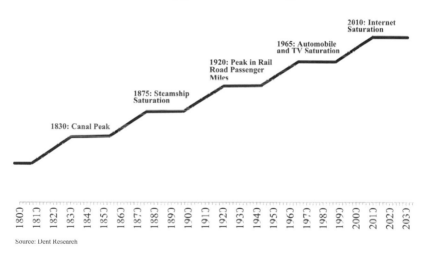

Source: Dent Research

This cycle turns positive when clusters of technology move mainstream for 22.5 years. This is what happened with portable computing and the Internet from 1988 into 2010; with cars from 1942 into 1965; with railroads from 1897 into 1920, and steamships from 1852 into 1875. These tend to be high-growth, high-productivity periods due to the advance of such major driving industries.

Although I am highlighting the most dominant technology in each cycle, they always come in clusters: steamships, canals, and the McCormick reaper; railroads, telegraphs, penicillin and elevators; autos, electricity, phones and radios; personal computers, the Internet, wireless phones and broadband.

For example, the number of railroad passengers and revenue grew strongly into 1920, just as cars and trucks first emerged and began gaining traction with consumers.

Figure 11-3: Railroad Passengers and Passenger Revenue

Peaked in 1920 and Fell Off a Cliff

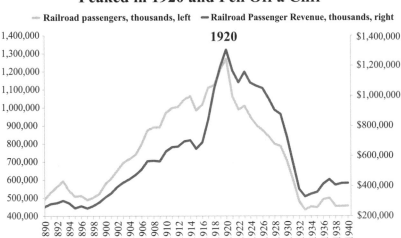

Source: Statistical Abstract of the United States, Colonial Times to 1970

1920 marked a first, clearly documentable peak in the impact of railroads on passenger travel. They were a much better way to travel compared to Conestoga wagons, stage coaches and steamboats. In fact, railroads united the U.S., connecting cities for travel and commerce. Actually, steamships connected the north and south and railroads the east and west. And automobiles and trucks connected it all.

A cluster of key technologies allowed the mass production and assembly line revolution, which was followed by the massive shift from city living to the suburbs from the 1940s into the 1960s.

Suddenly everyday people could have more land and space, enjoy safer living conditions, and commute to and from work with ease. They didn't have to be within walking distance of their job, the nearest bus terminal or train station.

I use the automobile trends and Federal money spent on highways to summarize this revolution because they're the easiest to measure and the most fundamental.

See for yourself how the acceptance of cars accelerated toward market saturation (in 1965), well after the railroad peak... and how the Federal Interstate Highway System flourished from the late 1930s into the mid-1960s.

Figure 11-4: Federal Highway Miles and Money Spent, Peaks in 1966

On the Highway

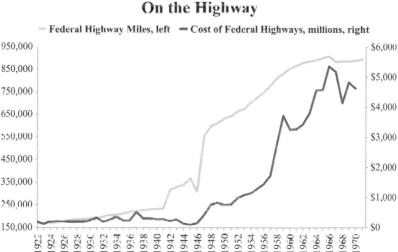

Source: Statistical Abstract of the United States, Colonial Times to 1970

By 1965, 80% of households had cars and most people lived in suburbs, totally unlike the early 1900s and even the Roaring '20s boom. The highway systems that linked all our major cities and allowed commuting to and from suburbs were in place.

The other side of this cycle is more neutral. It's not like the other cycles that turn negative. After all, there is *always* innovation. Only, it's during those neutral periods that the next new technologies are emerging into niche markets while the older wave is maturing and declining.

The perfect example of this is biotechnology. Innovation continues exponentially in this arena, but much of the breakthroughs are not yet accessible to the masses. Watch out for this to burst into the mainstream when this technology cycle turns upwards again, around 2032. Other breakthrough technologies like 3-D printing, robotics, and especially nanotechnologies are nowhere near mainstream. Robots were predicted to have much more impact by now, but they are still dumb and clumsy.

When adding the 45-Year Innovation Cycle — which more broadly impacts productivity and wage gains — to the other three cycles in my hierarchy, the picture of what the rest of this decade will look like is even more crystal clear... and grimmer.

All FOUR cycles — the Generational Spending Wave, the Geopolitical Cycle, the Innovation Cycle and the Boom/Bust (Sunspot) Cycle — have been moving down simultaneously since early 2014... and they all continue with that trend into early 2020!

As I've explained, this convergence has proven devastating the previous times it happened.

Note the progression in this hierarchy of cycles... how the crisis has built since early 2000:

- The Geopolitical Cycle peaked first in late 2000. That's when we had the worst of the tech wreck and devastating 9/11 attacks to follow.

- The Generational Spending Wave peaked in the U.S. in late 2007. The great recession and second major stock crash followed.

- The Innovation Cycle peaked in 2010 and we saw a 20% stock correction in 2011, the largest since the early 2009 bottom.

- The Sunspot Cycle was the last to peak in February 2014 and stocks have gone nowhere since late October 2014 despite greater levels of QE from Europe and Japan and accelerated debt and overbuilding in China... That tells me the next major financial crisis and stock crash should come between now and late 2017, with another lesser crash and aftershocks likely between late 2018 and early 2020. We'll only see the bottom by late 2022 before three of these four cycles turn up again together. The last (the Innovation Cycle) joins in 2032.

And because central banks have had years to inflate the greatest bubble in modern history, the coming crisis should be much greater than we've seen thus far.

Clearly we're in a dangerous investment environment, but one that's filled with extraordinary opportunities.

And as you can see, with the right cycles in your arsenal, seeing ahead of the curve is entirely possible... if not easy!

Of course, all of this looks good in theory, but what does this look like in real life?

Well, let's see...

CHAPTER 12

Evidence of the B.S. Recovery

AS I SAID EARLIER, with my Generational Spending Wave (in-novated in 1988) I lag births and adjust for immigration to identify baby boomers' peak spending in the U.S. That peaks at age 46 (for the middle class) and peaks at around 54 for the affluent.

Now, here's the Spending Wave again, this time overlaid with the Dow Jones Industrial Average adjusted for inflation.

This is what this cycle looks like in real life:

Figure 12-1: The Generational Spending Wave in Action

An Undeniable Correlation and the Impact of QE

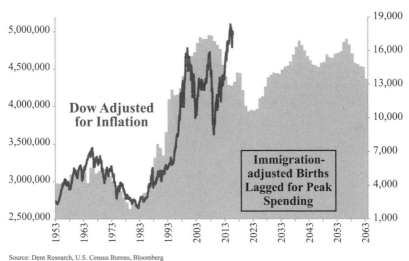

Source: Dent Research, U.S. Census Bureau, Bloomberg

This chart has always been a show stopper!

The correlation with the Dow Jones Industrial Average (adjusted for inflation) is incredible, proving the long-term effectiveness of this indicator.

If you or anyone else can find a long-term leading indicator better than this one, I'll hire you (or them) on the spot!

Note the stark divergence since QE began in late 2008. The market is now way more overvalued, and so is defying this fundamental trend. That will not last... mark my words! With every failed attempt to keep the system alive, from bazooka-sized money printing to negative interest rates, we move closer to the inevitable via desperation.

The Generational Spending Wave has the broadest and most pervasive impact on stocks and the economy... and it's clear to see. However, the rise of a new generation into its peak family and spending cycle affects not just stocks, but spending, productivity and corporate earnings as well.

After all, people are the *real driver* of our economy, not government policies as most economists would have you believe. *That's* the secret to our research... *that's* what sets us apart from those other guys: we look at the most important element — you!

Here's a table to show you a little more detail about the impact of this cycle:

Figure 12-2: Real Growth Rates In Economic Indicators

The Impact of the Generational Spending Wave Cycle

Years	Cycle Direction	Real S&P Total Return, with Dividends	Real Corporate Earnings	Real Retail Sales	Real Personal Consumption Expenditures	Real GDP
1930-41	Down	-1.1%	1.6%		1.98%	3.32%
1942-68	Up	11.2%	3.0%	2.9%	3.96%	4.39%
1969-82	Down	-0.8%	-0.1%	1.3%	2.98%	2.57%
1983-2007	Up	9.2%	4.0%	2.6%	3.65%	3.38%
2008-current	Down	6.5%	17.2%	0.8%	1.29%	1.14%

Source: Dent Research, MeasuringWorth.com, www.econ.yale.edu/~shiller/data/ie_data.xls, Bureau of Labor Statistics, Bureau of Economic Analysis

Note that I measure all of these indicators in real terms, adjusted for inflation.

As you can see, stocks feel the impact of the Generational Spending Wave the most. That's because, historically, they rise faster than earnings. And, of course, earnings rise faster than the economy.

Stocks, including reinvested dividends, were up 11.2% in the longer up cycle from 1942 to 1968. Then they were down 0.8% in the down cycle from 1969 into 1982. That's a swing of 12.0%!

The next boom and bust cycle saw a 9.2% move up and a drop to just 6.5% in the down trend. That's thanks to QE, which has provided unprecedented support for stocks during this down cycle.

Corporate earnings also have very clear shifts through this cycle.

The first up wave saw 3.0%, with the down wave resulting in an average of -0.1% real growth annually.

The recent up cycle, from 1983 into 2007, saw a whopping 3.96% increase. However, the current down cycle is anomalous, with the Fed's monetary policies encouraging unusually high levels of stock buybacks and fruitless mergers.

For retail sales, during the upturn from 1942 into 1968 we again see the trend for numbers to more than double during the cycle's up-ward wave: 2.9% versus 1.3% growth and 2.6% versus 0.8% growth in the current up and down cycle.

Interestingly, and perhaps tellingly, QE has *not* caused a break from the pattern of past cycles on the retail sales front, even while corporate profits and stocks buck the trend. The current wave down has seen slower growth, at a mere 0.8%. That's even lower than what we saw during the last down cycle and we haven't remotely seen the worst of it yet!

There are similar trends in personal consumption, which we can measure back further. The 1942 to 1968 boom cycle saw real growth at 33% higher than the down cycle that followed. The 1983 to 2007 up cycle was 3.65% while the current down cycle is already at a paltry 1.29%.

Here again, the numbers we're seeing in this down cycle are much lower than past ones, which proves to me that the Fed's monetary policies are not benefiting the broad economy or everyday households.

Finally, real GDP also clearly correlates, but it isn't as strongly divergent in up and down cycles. That's because governments tend to counter the private economy and run deficits and stimulus programs to help offset the slowdowns. On average, from 1930 to 2007, real GDP grew 0.94% faster in the up cycles. That's significant when you compound it over 26-year average boom periods.

When all is said and done, my Generational Spending Wave clearly shows that quantitative easing has boosted stocks and corporate earnings, but done little for the broader economy or consumers.

The Role Risk Perceptions Plays

The major impact of the 35-Year Geopolitical Cycle is on risk perception. When everything in the world is hunky-dory, stock valuations and P/E ratios soar. When it feels like the world is one step away from global war, those indicators tend to be suppressed.

See for yourself in Figure 12-3:

Figure 12-3: Geopolitical Cycle vs. P/E Ratios

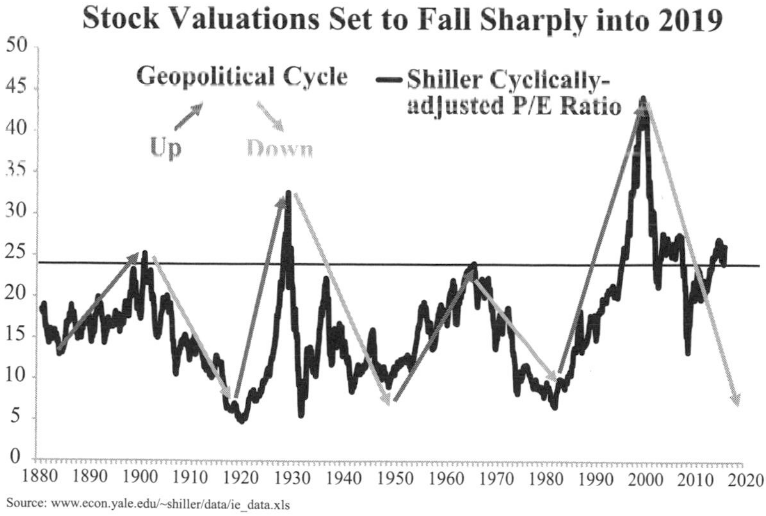

Stock Valuations Set to Fall Sharply into 2019

Source: www.econ.yale.edu/~shiller/data/ie_data.xls

Remember, the Geopolitical Cycle averages 35 years — 17 to 18 years up and 17 to 18 years down (the last positive part of this cycle was 18 years).

Look at the astounding correlation with P/E (price to earnings) ratios, which vary in long-term down cycles as much, if not more, than earnings or sales growth for stocks.

At peaks, investors are willing to pay well over 20 times the long-term earnings. They even went as high as 44 times earnings in early 2000!

During the troughs of this cycle though, they'll only pay five to 10 times earnings. That is a huge difference.

Note that I use the Shiller cyclically-adjusted P/E ratios in this analysis, which use the real average earnings over 10 years. This removes the extreme volatility in the earnings cycles. Regardless, this indicator correlates closely with normal P/E ratios based on current annual earnings as well.

So the Generational Spending Wave largely affects the "E" or earnings while the Geopolitical Cycle largely affects the "P" or price that investors are willing to pay for those earnings based on their perceptions. And that's where these two cycles overlap.

When a boom starts to turn into a bust as a result of a negative shift in demographic trends, investors will perceive greater risk. But they also perceive such risk when the world looks dangerous because of things like wars, civil wars, terrorism, oil embargos, or even droughts and plagues. We've endured most of these nonstop since 2001. Prior to that — from 1983 to 2000 — almost nothing of significance went wrong in the world. And we can see the effects of this on P/E ratios.

In fact, that's what convinced me that this cycle mattered. The ratios changed so dramatically after 2000. We've never come close to the high valuations of the Tech Bubble peak, despite even stronger earnings from the free-money bonanza of QE. The reason for that is that all three of my longer-term cycles were positive at the same time from mid-1988 into 2000. And the demographic cycles were the strongest in history, thanks to the massive baby boom spending acceleration in the 1990s.

I think the Geopolitical Cycle is actually one of the reasons many long-term analysts will miss this market top. They're waiting for overvaluation territory that looks like the levels we reached in 2000. We simply won't get there. Stocks are already stretched beyond most past valuation extremes with the exception of the once-in-a-lifetime cycles' convergence in 1929 and 2000.

Here's some more detail of the Geopolitical Cycle's impact on P/E ratios (we can go back much farther on this cycle, but I think you get the picture):

Figure 12-4: Geopolitical Cycle vs. P/E Ratios

The Impact of Changing Risk Perception!

Years	Direction	CAPE* P/E at Peaks	CAPE P/E at Troughs	Trough Percentage of Peak
1883-1898	Up	21.40		
1899-1914	Down		10.17	47.5%
1915-1929	Up	22.01		
1930-1947	Down		10.68	48.5%
1948-1965	Up	23.69		
1966-1982	Down		8.47	35.7%
1983-2000	Up	37.28		
2001-2019	Down		7.0 Estimate	18.7%
Average 1883-2019	N/A	26.1	9.1	34.8%

*CAPE. Robert Shiller's Cyclically-Adjusted Price-to-Earnings Ratio
Source: Dent Research, www.econ.yale.edu/~shiller/data/ie_data.xls

When crunching the numbers for this table, I measured the P/E ratios at the peak of the projected Geopolitical Cycle, not when the ratios themselves peaked. I did that because investors would be following the model and not be able to guess the exact peaks.

As you can see, we saw P/E ratios ranging from 21.40 to 37.28 at the peaks of the last four Geopolitical Cycles.

Ratios were their strongest between 1999 and 2000, precisely when the massive baby boomer generation was spending at their fastest rate, the Internet was moving mainstream most rapidly on the S- Curve, and the Geopolitical Cycle was at its peak of favorable trends.

But at the bottom of the troughs of the cycle, those ratios range from 8.47 to 10.68, averaging between 19.7% to 48.5% of the peaks. That's a huge difference in how much investors will pay for stocks.

I estimate conservatively that at the bottom of this latest trough we'll see P/E ratios around 7.0 because the next crash will come during the worst of the economic winter season… and crashes and ratios are always horrible during times like that, just like they were in the Great Depression.

For the last four complete cycles (including the estimate for the next trough), the low cycles see P/E ratios 50% lower and often more than that at the peaks. *That's* why this cycle is my #2 in the hierarchy.

Given that stocks have now seen the second highest P/E ratios in this cycle, and the Generational Spending Wave peaked back in late 2007, you don't want to be sitting passively in stocks. Rather, if you must invest, follow any tested and proven trading system like Adam O'Dell's *Cycle 9 Alert* and *Max Profit Alert*, John Del Vecchio's *Forensic Investor*, Rodney Johnson's *Triple Play Strategy* or Lance Gaitan's *Treasury Profits Accelerator* (you'll find some details about all of these and how to sign up at the end of this book).

The Value of Increased Productivity: The Innovation Wave

Now that you've seen what the Generational Spending Wave and the Geopolitical Cycle look like in real life, let's take a look at the Innovation Cycle. It's the longest-term and the broadest one in my hierarchy. It's not as important when forecasting long-term turning points. However, it adds to economic trends by increasing things like productivity by 1% a year in the up cycles, and that makes a big difference when compounded over its 22.5-year uptrend.

Most importantly for investors and businesses, though: when this cycle moves into its plateau, the maturing companies of the past will fade and new sectors will emerge… especially in a downturn. That's how you spot massive new opportunities, which we'll see in spades in the years ahead (I share more details in Chapters 21, 22, 23, and 24).

This cycle entered into its sideways movement in late 2010 and will continue in this direction until mid-2032 (it doesn't turn up between early 2020 and late 2022 like my other long-term cycles). That tells me that while there will be another global boom from 2023 forward, when the Generational Spending Wave and Geopolitical Cycles both turn up again together, it won't be as strong as past positive cycles, especially in the developed world where technology and productivity will be more important than ever with waning demographic trends.

Here's how *this* cycle makes itself felt in real life.

Figure 12-5: The Innovation Cycle

Increasing Productivity

Years	Cycle Direction	Average Annual Growth	
		Patents per Capita	Productivity
1876-mid 1897	Down	0.6%	
Mid 1897-1920	Up	0.8%	
1921-mid 1943	Down	-1.5%	
Mid 1943- 1965	Up	2.2%	2.0%
1966-mid 1988	Down	0.6%	0.8%
Mid 1988-2010	Up	3.8%	1.0%

Source: Dent Research, MeasuringWorth.com, www.econ.yale.edu/~shiller/data/ie_data.xls, Bureau of Labor Statistics, U.S. Patent and Trademark Office

The two strongest correlations for this cycle are:

1. Patent activity, which is far stronger in the positive trend. In the most recent upward movement from mid-1988 through 2010, patents were up 3.8% a year on average compared to only 0.6% during the prior plateau from 1966 through mid-1988.

2. Productivity, which increases sharply as the cycle moves upward. We don't have consistent data on labor productivity before 1947, but the first full cycle saw 2.0% average gains from mid-1943 through 1965 in the uptrend, compared to 0.8% in the downtrend. The last move up from mid-1988 through 2010 was lower than the previous cycle, at 1.0%, but I think that's a result of our rapidly aging society and the Asian and immigrant deflation in wages. I wouldn't be surprised if the current down cycle comes in at closer to zero.

The next upward leg of this cycle will be from mid-2032 through 2055. *That's* when all the great new gee-whiz technologies will have the greatest impact and finally move mainstream. Biotech, as I mentioned earlier, will most likely be the first to break out, followed closely by 3D printing, clean energy, robotics, and last but not least, nanotechnology.

And finally…

The Powerful Leading Indicator in Action

As I said earlier, the Sunspot Cycle lets us see when stock crashes and recessions are most likely to occur. What gives this cycle an edge is that scientists have measured sunspot activity accurately since the mid-1700s, as you can see for yourself:

Figure 12-6: Sunspot Cycles

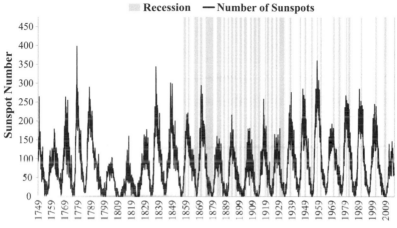

88% of Crashes and Recessions Occur in the Down Cycle

Source: NASA.gov, Dent Research

Dave Okenquist, my research assistant, found data on recessions back to 1850 and added the grey shadings to indicate these on the chart. That shows us that 88% of such recessions occurred in the downward leg of the sunspot cycle. That's an astounding and irrefutable correlation! Anyone who thinks this is too weird to pay attention to does so at their own expense.

In the last Sunspot Cycle, we experienced the tech crash from right at the top in March 2000 into October 2002, exactly within the first three years of the downward trend. Then we had the 2008/09 crash and great recession right into the cycle's bottom in August of 2009. How's that for a forecasting tool?

The most recent cycle was the most extreme in hundreds of years. It stretched out to 13.9 years! It only peaked and began to turn down in February 2014, not the more typical early decade setback we've seen in the past.

This next table lists the major crises as they correlate with downturns in Sunspot Cycles:

Figure 12-7: The Sunspot Cycle

Major Stock Crashes & Crises
in the Cycle Downturns

Depression, Major Recession and/or Major Crash	Downturn Periods (NBER) Recession/Depression	Down Sunspot Cycle Period
Depression	1837-1843	Dec. 1836-Feb. 1843
Depression	Oct. 1873-Apr. 1879	May 1870-Mar. 1880
Depression	Mar. 1882-May 1885	Apr. 1882-Feb. 1890
Depression	Jan. 1893-Jun. 1897	Aug. 1893-Apr.1902
Crash and Recession	May. 1907-Jun. 1908	Feb. 1907-Jun. 1913
Depression	Jan. 1920-Jul.1921	Aug. 1917-Aug. 1923
Depression	Aug. 1929-Mar.1933	Dec.1929-Aug. 1933
Major Crash and Recession	Nov. 1973-Mar. 1975	Mar. 1969-Jul. 1976
Two Recessions	Jan. 1980-Nov. 1982	Sep. 1979-Jun. 1986
Major Crash and Recession	Mar. 2001-Nov. 2001	Jul. 2000-Aug. 2009
Recession	Dec. 2007-Jun. 2009	

Source: Dent Research, NBER.org, NASA.gov

That's 11 out of 11 major financial crises right — a 100% batting average!

Again, that makes this the best cycle I've uncovered since the Generational Spending Wave in 1988.

So what does the current cycle say?

It tells us that the first and greatest danger zone is right ahead into 2017 in the earlier stages of this cycle down, as in 2000-2002 in the last one with the massive tech wreck!

Central banks are fighting this tooth and nail and they may just succeed in delaying a crash a bit longer. But passive investors would be silly to risk staying in this market, especially as it has moved violently sideways for the better part of two years now (since November 2014).

It also tells us that the second danger zone will be around mid-2018 into late 2019/early 2020... exactly when scientists expect sunspot activity to start to bottom again. Then again, they may extend that projection into 2021 or 2022. The best scientists are my secret weapon here, as investors who continue to follow Ned Davis's Decennial Cycle will likely be way off track.

In short: all four of these powerful macroeconomic cycles point down together into early 2020. The most critical demographic cycle does not turn back up until late 2022 forward. Each one represents the most comprehensive, but still simple, view of the dimensions that shape our economy over time, giving you a window into future years.

And what they're all saying is that we'll soon see the sale of a lifetime, when stocks, real estate, businesses, and even gold will be going for pennies on the dollar... and where those who understand what and why it's happening can take advantage!

So let's talk about the 800 pound gorilla in the room...

CHAPTER 13

Bursting Bubbles Make Investors Rich… And You Can Be One of Them

I RECENTLY HEARD SOMEONE say: *"Death… the pause that refreshes."* How true!

What do you do when your computer gets overwhelmed and freezes up? (After giving it a good thump, which occasionally works) — you reboot it!

What happens after an icy winter? Blossoms bloom and everything regrows.

Look at what happened after the 1930s Great Depression. We had the biggest and longest boom in history — at least since the Roman Empire.

Said another way: before we can see real growth after a period of overexpansion, we first need a reboot.

Nothing could be truer today.

After seven years of artificial stimulus, courtesy of the Fed and other central banks, world markets have bloated into more epic bubbles while economies continue to slow.

The only way to reignite growth now is for the global economy and all stock markets to endure a painful burst… to wipe the decks clean… to reset.

And we're due for exactly that.

Hopefully, by the time you're finished reading this book, you'll be ready to pick up the pieces left behind after the reboot. These will turn into your generational wealth!

So let's take a look at what past resets have looked like. This will give us a good idea of what we can expect in the reset heading our way and why we're about to see the sale of a lifetime!

My favorite classical economist today, Lacy Hunt, has a great chart that shows how debt bubbles have built and then collapsed, creating depressions, all through modern history. While his chart only goes back to 1870, I'm sure the times before that look much the same. When debt grows faster than the economy — which is inevitable, thanks to human nature, as I discussed in Chapter 2 — we get economic and financial asset bubbles that always burst.

Figure 13-1: Total U.S. Debt as a Percent of GDP

Source: Courtesy of Hoisington Investment Management, Dent Research

There was a depression from 1873 into 1877, after the first railroad bubble burst. Debt as a percentage of GDP peaked at 164% and then we suffered the consequences of a major deleveraging. For five years (at least) after the railroad bubble had finally fully unwound, opportunities to get positioned for great wealth abounded.

During the Great Depression, debt as a percentage of GDP peaked at 300% and we've all seen the images of the aftermath of that collapse. In fact, the impact of the Great Depression is burned into the American psyche. It's just a pity that the lessons have been lost!

Note that the actual debt bubble peaked in 1929 at 180%. It was the dramatic collapse of GDP into 1933 that caused the ratio to spike even more dramatically. Same for the railroad bubble prior, where stocks peaked in 1873, but the debt ratios with falling GDP peaked in 1875.

As you can see, during the Depression, the opportunities to pick up wealth-building investments lasted from 1933 to 1942... and paid off... all the way up to 1968-1972. Just imagine if you'd been ready and waiting for that moment to invest in stocks or real estate or business. You'd have been smiling all the way to the bank since then!

Now, we're in the midst of the greatest debt bubble in modern history. So far it has peaked at 375% of GDP in the worst year of the last great recession. I believe that we'll see an even greater spike in debt-to-GDP into 2017 or later — towards 450% to 500%-plus — when the worst of the coming depression hits as GPD collapses.

As in every bubble burst that has come before, we will ultimately erase most of this one as the winter economic season draws to a close. Debts will get restructured or written off as real estate and many companies and households fail. And we'll likely see debt-to-GDP fall to 180% or lower by sometime in the early part of the next decade.

All these debt bubbles are similar. And they all end the same: with a stock crash and a financial detox that sees a painful deleveraging in financial assets, ranging from loans to high-yield bonds to stocks to real estate to commodities. The trouble is, with the extreme levels we've reached now, this time's going to be even more excruciating than it would have been without endless QE to extend this bubble...

The thing is, we've seen many bubbles in stocks, like the railroad bubble into the late 1870s, the 1987 bubble and the massive tech stock bubble from late 1994 into March 2000. But those bubbles didn't create the massive resets like the ones we got from 1720 to 1722, 1835 to 1843 and 1929 to 1932... or the one we face ahead. In 1987 we didn't even have a recession, and in 2001 we saw only a minor one.

That's because the major resets take place when there's more to the story than just stock bubbles, which is as much the case today as it was prior to the Great Depression.

While everyone's familiar with the major stock bubble that burst in 1929, very few know the full story. It was, in fact, a pervasive farm bubble in real estate that struck the death blow to the banking system!

It was the same story with the bubble burst in 1835, after the great Midwest expansion in real estate.

And it's the same story today, with the current global real estate bubble unimaginably distorted thanks to the most liberal borrowing policies in history.

Central banks also play a heavy hand in setting us up for great resets. They emerged to stimulate the economy in the early 1700s in Europe. And, with the creation of the Federal Reserve in the U.S. in late 1913 and the advent of QE from central banks globally since late 2008, we've witnessed the creation of the greatest and most global and real-estate-oriented bubble yet!

It was no accident that the greatest bubble burst and resultant depression came after the advent of the Federal Reserve in 1913 on a near 20-year lag!

The thing with depressions (great resets) is *that's* where you get these extreme fire-sale opportunities.

See for yourself...

The 67-Year Bear Market of 1720-1787

John Law was the first central banker in modern history. France and England had finished a long and expensive war and had built up massive government debts. France had acquired the Mississippi land area from the U.S.

John Law decided that the best way to pay back those debts was to sell off that land to the public with government-financed loans at below-market interest rates... Yes! He essentially sold swamp land to the public!

At the same time, England had a monopoly on the South Seas Company for financing trade with India and the Far East. Its government similarly sold shares to the public to pay off its debt at low-cost financing... again, a government-driven financial scheme! That created the first great stock bubble (stocks were first created on a minor scale in 1607... the futures markets first emerged in the mid-1600s, followed shortly by the infamous Tulip Bubble).

These twin bubbles, which I talked about in more detail in Chapter 6, exploded into 1720 from low-cost interest rates, encouraging speculation, courtesy of governments. They then burst, losing more than 90% into 1722. A depression followed and stocks went essentially nowhere into 1787 — that's 67 years!

I hope by now you understand clearly that when a bubble bursts, it's not a gentle affair, but rather a catastrophic collapse. There's *never* a soft landing! But, once that initial lurch has run its course, the markets and economy involved continue to slide more slowly. And for years, they stumble along the bottom. This is where we find those opportunities I'll share with you later.

During those 67 years of depression in the 18th century, many entrepreneurs, businessmen, investors and innovators took advantage of the fire-sale available to them while the majority of people hid in fear, all too aware of the pain the crash had caused. One of the most famous of those successful investors is Benjamin Franklin (1706-1790).

Many view Franklin as "America's first entrepreneur." The son of a candle-maker, he was a popular author, a printer, an inventor and a savvy businessman. Of course, while his invention of the lightning rod, the glass harmonica, the Franklin stove, bifocal glasses and the flexible urinary catheter are all very interesting, they're not the scope of this book.

What is in our scope is that in 1723, just one year after the collapse of the Mississippi Land Bubble and South Seas Bubble, Franklin struck out on his own. He moved to Philadelphia and started an enormously successful printing business while the majority of his fellow citizens were still licking their wounds and worrying about the bleak future they saw. This proved so lucrative that he was able to retire at just 45 years of age.

While it is never explicitly stated that he was taking advantage of the fire-sale presented to him after the bubble burst, his actions prove that he was smart and courageous enough to take advantage of the opportunities in that environment. As he himself said: *"Opportunity is a great bawd."* In short, he took calculated risks… and they paid off handsomely!

In 1733 he began publishing *Poor Richard's Almanac*, which he wrote under the guise of Richard Saunders, a poor man who needed money to take care of his nagging wife. This is where many of his infamous quotes come from.

He helped launch the Library Company in 1731, during a time when books were scarce and expensive. He rationalized that by pooling together resources, they could afford to buy books from England. And he, together with Dr. Thomas Bond, founded the Pennsylvania Hospital in 1751.

Both the library and the hospital still exist today, more than 285 years later!

Mayer Amschel Rothschild is another example of someone who grabbed at the opportunities the 67 year depression presented to him.

He created the Rothschild banking dynasty, which is believed to have become the wealthiest family in history. In fact, in 2005, Forbes magazine ranked him seventh on the list of "The Twenty Most Influential Businessmen of All Time." Remember what we quoted him as saying earlier: "I always sold a little early."

Josiah Wedgwood and Matthew Boulton also made it into the history books as highly successful entrepreneurs and businessmen of that era.

The depression of 1835 to 1843 saw the likes of Frederick Douglas, Abraham Lincoln, P.T. Barnum, and Cyrus McCormick find their fame and fortunes.

Douglas escaped from slavery when the depression was already three years old. He went on to become a great orator, bestselling author and newspaper publisher.

Barnum started his "Barnum's Grand Scientific and Musical Theater" just one year before the collapse and his circus was eventually bought by the Ringling brothers in 1907! Besides that, he too was a small business owner and newspaper publisher.

McCormick, founder of the McCormick Harvesting Machine Company, almost lost everything in the Panic of 1837. But he persisted, took risks when others were too afraid, made the most of the opportunities he could see, and the rest is history.

The railroad depression from 1873-1877 gave the likes of John D. Rockefeller (the richest man in American history), Andrew Carnegie, J.P. Morgan, and Edward Harriman their great breaks.

Rockefeller's business plan was simple: obsessively increase the efficiency of his refineries and pressure railroad companies for discounted shipping so he could undercut and then buy the competition. Much of this he did at a time when businesses where barely able to stay open under the pressures of the depression.

Carnegie religiously saved his money and reinvested it in the railroad business (later he moved into building and investing in ironworks).

And Harriman was a "railroad investor extraordinaire." He snatched up underperforming railroads and poured money into them to make them more efficient and profitable, as the story goes.

Talk about taking advantage of sales of a lifetime!

It's no coincidence that men like this made their fortunes in the railroad industry. They all took advantage of the opportunities the railroad depression presented to them. These were not people who came from wealthy families. These were self-made men.

And the long aftermath of the Great Depression, from 1929-1942, presented people like Ross Perot (founder of EDS), Ray Kroc (who made McDonald's what it is today), Sam Walton (founder of Wal-Mart), Harry Truman, Ronald Regan, Walt Disney, John Sperling (founder of the University of Phoenix), Amadeo Giannini (founder of the Bank of America), Charles Merrill (co-founder of Merrill Lynch), Estee Lauder and John Templeton (who is said to have "bought low during the Great Depression and sold high during the Internet bubble") with the feeding grounds to become some of the wealthiest and most well-known businessmen and investors today.

The Great Debt and Asset Bubble of 1995-2015

The Federal Reserve has kept right on with its mission to keep growth chugging along with artificially low interest rates and stimulus after the great inflation and recession of the 1970s… gaining the company of other central banks along the way.

From 1983 to 2008, total U.S. private and government debt grew at 2.54 times GDP. It grew at similar rates around the world, except in China — but that should never happen in an emerging country with much lower incomes and credit capacity. Any economist that doesn't see this as the problem it is shouldn't call themselves an economist.

Most of them missed it!

Even the recession didn't stop this bubble and it's continued to inflate to monstrous levels. Here is what it looks like now:

Figure 13-2: U.S. Debt vs. GDP Growth

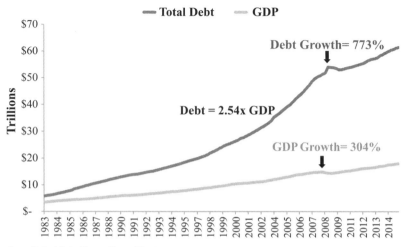

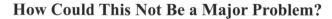

Source: St. Louis Federal Reserve, Treasury Direct

But here is where something happened like never before...

Central banks around the world decided they wouldn't allow the next great reset to happen. They opted to prevent the debt and financial asset bubble burst.

To do so, they printed over $8 trillion (with more promised) — more than $3.5 trillion of that is in the U.S. alone — to provide liquidity to banks and so prevent them from collapsing like they did in the 1930s.

Figure 13-3 shows this explosion in money created out of thin air and used to buy government and mortgage bonds.

This doesn't include the explosion in government-backed debt in China that has grown $23 trillion just since 2008. That has been the greatest stimulus and free lunch of all. China largely uses this debt to build infrastructures, industrial plants and real estate for nobody.

And they dismissed "mark to market" rules for banks so they didn't have to declare their real estate and loan losses.

Figure 13-3: Balance Sheets of Major Central Banks

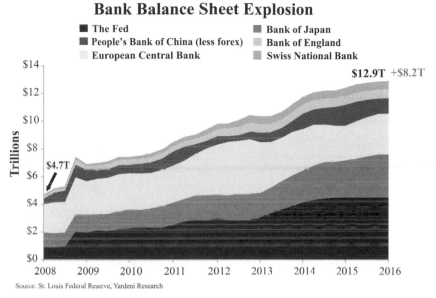

The Post-Crisis Central Bank Balance Sheet Explosion

- The Fed
- People's Bank of China (less forex)
- European Central Bank
- Bank of Japan
- Bank of England
- Swiss National Bank

$12.9T +$8.2T

$4.7T

Source: St. Louis Federal Reserve, Yardeni Research

With central banks involved, far fewer banks have failed than should have. Very little past debt has yet been detoxed with much more new government and corporate debt created to stimulate the economy.

Japan has applied this same policy since 1997 and has been in a "coma" ever since. Its population is aging and its economy is on life support. Its future is in serious doubt… and we're heading in the same direction.

If you have a debt and asset-price bubble and don't detox or deleverage, then you don't ever come out of the economic winter season. You don't clear the decks and make way for new growth. Japan is the living example of this. And we most certainly don't want to turn out like them!

Mainstream analysts like Ron Insana call the Fed's approach a new, "enlightened economics." I call it insanity. It is denial, plain and simple, and it will ruin us if we keep it up!

So where do we go from here?

The Great Depression of 2016-2022

How long can you keep a bubble going with free money and endless QE?

Certainly not forever… and at this point, not much longer!

Can you really get something for nothing?

Absolutely not!

Stocks have continued to rise in an economy barely able to eke out 2% growth, despite the endless QE. And that's only in the United States. Economic growth in the Eurozone is even worse!

Debt is a financial drug. It enhances short-term performance at the expense of long-term degradation and costs.

Keeping this debt and asset bubble going after its natural peak in 2007 has been like taking more of a drug to keep from coming down. Now, like any real-life addictions, the detox is only going to be harder.

We haven't escaped the detox. We've just made it worse, with a greater debt bubble that will burst and deleverage.

The now totally artificial stock market bubble in the U.S. has gone nowhere since late 2014. It's a "market on crack" and it's finally fading, despite the stimulus.

From March 2009 into the apparent peak in May 2015, the market would rise dramatically to new highs as highly leveraged traders and hedge funds bought on every dip. But since that peak, these rallies have been failing at lower highs.

And there's been a classic divergence: the dumb money is buying in leading large-cap stocks while the smart money is exiting, especially in small-cap stocks. For many reasons, which I've explained in detail in previous chapters, this bubble is over.

Mark my words here: later 2016 and 2017 will see the worst stock decline since 1930-1932 (and 1973-1974) and this next Great

Depression will last into the end of the demographically based down season, around late 2022. We'll see the worst coming into early 2020, when all four of my key macroeconomic cycles are still pointing down together. It will be brutal, especially after such unprecedented monetary policies.

I expect stocks to see levels as low as 5,500 on the Dow Jones Industrial Average before we ring in 2018.

To erase the bubble that began in late 1994, we could see stocks drop as much as 80%-plus, down to between 3,300 and 3,800 on the Dow before the trends turn back up between early 2020 and late 2022.

Figure 13-4: Dow Megaphone Pattern

The Greatest Crash of Our Lifetime Has Begun

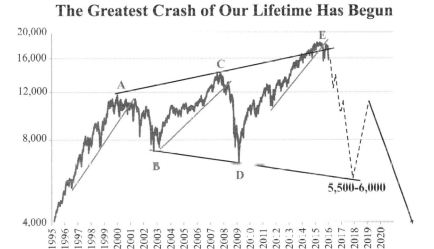

Source: Yahoo! Finance

And because of our bubble blindness, most people haven't yet acknowledged the bubble we've inflated, let alone begun preparing for the crash. They'll also be caught wrong-footed when the investment and business markets are flooded with the opportunities that always follow such great resets!

Thankfully, you're reading this book, so not only can you now see the extent of the bubble we're in, but you'll soon be ready to embark on the kind of wealth-building that made Rockefeller, Templeton, and Merrill household names. I'll give you all the details I can in Part III.

But before we wrap up Part II and move onto exploring the greatest bubble of our lifetime, I want to point out that after this detox, we will enjoy real growth again... but we'll never see a boom like we enjoyed from 1983 into 2007. Rather, emerging countries will lead the next global boom.

Sure, the U.S. will do well again, but our demographic trends move sideways for decades to come, and that will limit the extent of the next boom.

Before we can get there, though, we must first detox... so let's move on to what that will most likely look like...

PART IV

The Greatest Bubble and Reset of Our Lifetime

CHAPTER 14

The Single Greatest Economic Force the World Has Ever Seen

I'LL GO INTO every detail of the greatest debt and financial bubble of our lifetime — and the fire-sale opportunities it will hand us — soon. But before I do, there's another important bubble that we must consider. Ultimately, it has played the instrumental role in leading us to the point where we now find ourselves. Of course, I'm talking about the baby boomers.

They have proved, without a shadow of doubt, that consumers drive economies and markets, not "sentiment" or the government, not interest rates... inflation... or the price of oil, not the Fed or the president, not the weather or even wars, past a point. Sure, all those things have an impact, but the most powerful force in the economy is people, and this became obvious to me from the larger-than-normal impact of the baby boomers — that "pig moving through a python."

They have proved to be a group so powerful they have affected everything that Americans (and the world) eat, drink and do today. They quite literally changed the world. And they will continue to do so for a few more decades.

I explained earlier that I refer to the baby boomers as the largest generation. While there are numerically more millennials and echo boomers, the former is far more impactful because of their much more rapid increase over a shorter timeframe. Like I've said, they're a pig moving through a python.

It would be useful at this point to also explain how I calculate the size of the generation. It's not the more commonly practiced method.

You see, most people will tell you that the baby boomers were born between the years 1946 and 1964, adding 76 million people to the population. That's the generally accepted view, but it misses the true enormity and influence of this generation.

A marketer coined the term "baby boomer" — which first appeared in *The Washington Post* in 1970. He was creating a *social* classification that referred to how those born *after* World War II viewed the world. Between 1946 and 1964, the general environment was one of growth and prosperity.

The problem with that classification is, of course, that it's highly subjective and nebulous. It was based on higher-than-average birth rates by sociologists — who, like economists, rarely have sex or run a business.

I measure the baby boomers differently... more accurately... scientifically, if you will... so that I can harness the predictive power of this cohort. I'm interested in the rising and falling wave of births.

Rather than considering the social environment, I want to look simply at the numbers: when was the lowest number of births on the National Birth Index... and when was the highest?

And as the numbers show, in reality, the generation began in 1934 (after the bottom in births in 1933) and peaked in 1961, as you can see:

Figure 14-1: U.S. Births Adjusted for Immigration

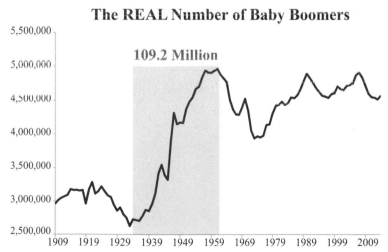

The REAL Number of Baby Boomers

109.2 Million

Source: U.S. Census Bureau, National Center for Health Statistics, Dent Research

Counting the baby boomers *this* way gives us a generation that's not only a whopping 109.2 million people strong (when I add in the predictable births of immigrants that now live here) but also highly predictable because, no matter what your social environment is like, you'll still go so school at a predictable age... get married and have kids at a predictable age... retire at a predictable age...

Like I've said: a pig moving through a python from the start.

And the generation has distorted the snake beyond recognition. As it passed through the school system between 1952 and 1979, it drove enrollment percentages up to near a hundred! More schools had to be built, more teachers trained.

Figure 14-2: U.S. K-12 Public School Teachers

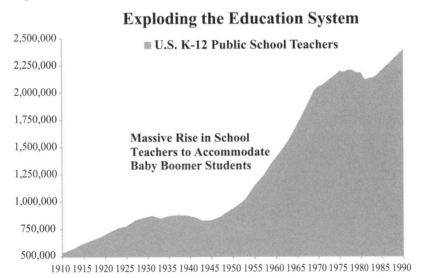

Exploding the Education System

The lag on the immigration-adjusted birth index for graduation from high school at age 18 would have seen the secondary school education bubble peak in 1979, and yes, the real bubble did peak there.

As it entered the workforce, the generation not only inflated the size of the pool, but blew up inflation as well, as I explained in Chapter 9. This occurred on a 20-year lag for workforce entry, causing the highest growth rates between 1977 and 1981 as the peak of the 1957–1961 births hit.

Figure 14-3: Labor Force Growth and Forecast

Exploding the Labor Force

Source: Bureau of Labor Statistics, Dent Research

Baby boomers embraced the American dream of owning a home, taking home-ownership rates from 63% to an all-time high of 69% between 1965 and 2005. This occurred on a 31-year lag for starter home buying.

Figure 14-4: U.S. Homeownership Rate

Source: St. Louis Federal Reserve

And talk about a bubble and crash… look at new home sales that skyrocketed into early 2006 and crashed and burned ever since.

Figure 14-5: U.S. New Home Sales

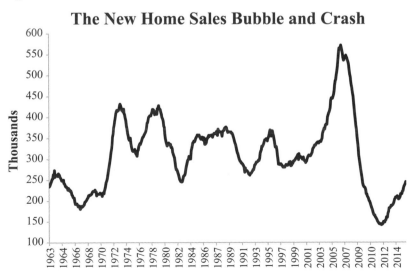

Source: St. Louis Federal Reserve

In the process, we amassed nearly $11 trillion in mortgage debt by 2008 and another $3 trillion in consumer debt — another record.

Figure 14-6: U.S. Consumer Debt

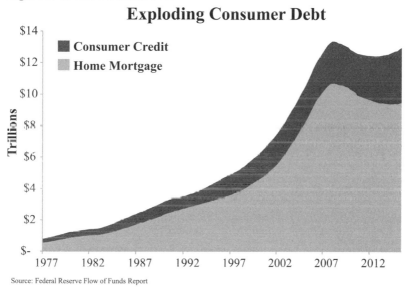

Source: Federal Reserve Flow of Funds Report

But the generation didn't stop there. They also drove technology into the mainstream...

Baby boomer Dr. Robert Jarvik brought the world the artificial heart, transforming health and extending lifespans.

Baby boomer Sir Tim Berners-Lee gave us the Internet, revolutionizing how we communicate, learn and do business.

Baby boomers Sir Alec Jeffreys and Dr. Gill Samuels gave us DNA fingerprinting and Viagra, altering how we fight crime and age.

In short, we wouldn't have seen all the advances in health, entertainment, sports, music, science, technology, business, art, fashion, communication, or education that have made the world what it is today if it weren't for the baby boomer generation.

They made convenience vital, communication universal and health care a right, not a privilege.

Speaking of health care, they continue to distort this sector as they move through it, making it the greatest growth sector in public spending on health care.

Health care insurance and costs have also been the second fastest growing inflation sector only after education costs.

Health care will continue to rise towards 20% of GDP in the decades ahead — it has never been anywhere near that in history.

Figure 14-7: Medicare and Medicaid Spending vs. All Other as a Percent of GDP

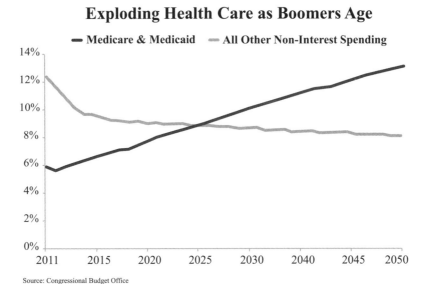

Exploding Health Care as Boomers Age

Source: Congressional Budget Office

They're even the initial driving force behind the new technologies that will leap into the mainstream when my Innovation Wave turns positive again in 2033…

Dr. Paul Morris, a research training fellow at the British Heart Foundation, is creating personalized "virtual arteries" using images of a patient's actual heart, which can accurately predict how effective an operation might be.

Already, a scientist at the University of Pennsylvania has reversed muscle decline in rats by injecting them with extra copies of the gene that develops muscle mass.

A researcher at Southern Illinois University has genetically engineered mice that live to an age equivalent of 180 human years.

J. Craig Venter, the man who raced the U.S. government to sequence the first human genome, has a new goal: to help everyone live to 100, in good health.

In a cloning first in 2014, scientists moved a step closer to the goal of creating stem cells perfectly matched to a patient's DNA to better treat diseases.

And even super-small robots called MagnetoSperm are under development (and they have nothing to do with reproduction). One day they'll swim around inside us to deliver medicines to otherwise unnavigable parts of our bodies.

These technologies are still decades away from going mainstream, but when they do, they'll alter our reality again.

And Then There's the Fed

Baby boomers have done a lot of good throughout their lives. They've also done some harm.

As you can see, the generation has a penchant for inflating massive bubbles. That's what happens when a pig moves through a python.

But perhaps the most damage they've done is in their leading central banks on an impossible quest to stop the unstoppable... after all, they are termed the "Idealists" by William Strauss and Neil Howe in their book *Generations* (1989). Since the massive Spending Wave of the baby boomers peaked in late 2007, as I forecasted it would all the way back in 1988, and its debt bubble peaked with it, the Fed has been feverishly printing money to try to fill the gap. It's a battle they simply won't and can't win because the demographic slide is the worst by far from 2016 into 2020... and don't even get me started on the demographic outlook for Germany and Southern Europe!

There have been endless bubbles in baby food, jeans, drugs, social change, rock music, health food, Harley Davidson motorcycles... all thanks to just one generation — the baby boomers.

Next up will be a bubble in things like cruise ships, funeral homes and then nursing homes. I would prefer the funeral home business. Dead people are easier to manage than cruise ship passengers or nursing home patients.

This was a bubble generation from the beginning and it will continue to be the game changer in the sectors it invades as it ages.

Retirement will never be the same. Baby boomers claim they won't retire, or at least not fully... that's good because they'll have to keep working as the economy slows ahead.

Politics and social change will also accelerate in the "power cycle" of the baby boomers, which peaks around 2026. The next two to three administrations will be like the FDR 1930s period of nonstop reforms.

That leads me on to the next chapter: the greatest debt bubble in history (1983 to 2016/17, especially 2000-2008).

CHAPTER 15

The Greatest Debt and Financial Bubble in History

REMEMBER, BUBBLES ALWAYS go to extremes and very few ever recognize them. This latest stock market bubble is just another example in a long line... as is the debt and financial bubble that has already begun to deleverage.

Really, it shocks me that so many can be so blind to what's so obvious...

Figure 15-1: Dow, Late 1994 — Early 2000 vs. Early 2009 — Mid-2015

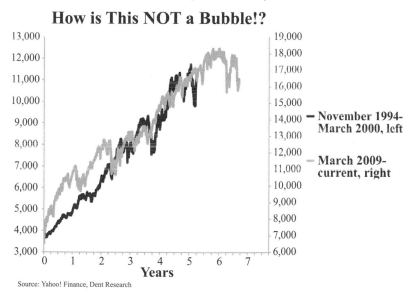

How is This NOT a Bubble!?

Source: Yahoo! Finance, Dent Research

As I've explained in previous chapters, we have the Federal Reserve (and central banks around the globe) to thank for this bubble about to unwind... the pain investors and the economy will experience... and ultimately the sale of a lifetime that you and I will get to enjoy.

Ultra-low interest rates have pushed up stocks or bonds to overvalued and unaffordable levels (and they continue to do so). When interest rates fall the value of bonds, especially longer-term ones, rise. Stocks are not just valued on 10 years' forecast of earnings. Those earnings are discounted back to present-day value through the risk-free, 10-Year Treasury bond rate. So the lower the rate, the higher today's value of those future earnings... and the higher the value of stocks. Does this sound like something for nothing to you?

See how central banks printing money to buy their own bonds to push long-term rates down would cause a bubble in bonds and stocks (and housing, which benefits from lower mortgage rates; and car sales, which benefit from lower rates as well)?

The near-zero, short-term rates allow major financial institutions and hedge funds to leverage up at massively lower costs. From this position they speculate and dominate the markets more and more — it's an all-around free lunch for the greedy bastards!

A big freeze can destroy most of an orange crop, but then prices will spike until consumers start drinking something else. All types of natural disasters destroy resources and make them temporarily scarce and expensive. But bubbles always cure themselves. Without exception. This is a natural mechanism of life and free markets, allowing us to always adapt to anything, rebalance and grow again.

Yet, people don't get it. They just don't see it. And when I try to convince them we're at the end of the greatest bubble known to modern man, they argue with me. I can't tell you how many times I've heard: "Stocks aren't yet as highly valued as they were at the top of the tech bubble in early 2000."

No. They're not. But then we're also not in a positive geopolitical trend where the world is easy-go-lucky and news of terrorist attacks and brutal civil wars are uncommon.

Take my Geopolitical Cycle (as well as the other three in my hierarchy — the Generational Spending Wave, the Innovation Cycle and the Boom/Bust (Sunspot) Cycle) and it's clear that the 2008-2016 stock bubble is nearly as high, if not higher, than all of the major tops over the last century, including 1929, 1937, 1965, 1987 and 2007. Only 2000 went to substantially higher extremes in valuations.

Look at the best model for stock valuation from Robert Shiller in Figure 15-2. It's the classic P/E (price to earnings) ratio, except that Shiller adjusted for the extreme volatility in earnings by using a 10-year moving average — a great improvement.

Figure 15-2: Cyclically-Adjusted Price/Earnings Ratio

Higher Than Most Major Tops

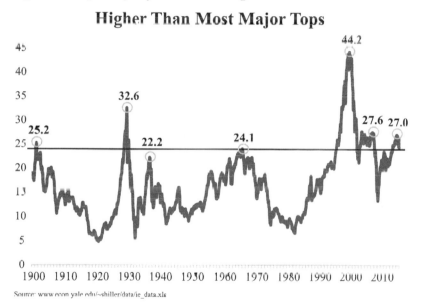

Source: www.econ.yale.edu/~shiller/data/ie_data.xls

As you can see, the 1929 bubble was slightly more extreme than this one. Only the 2000 bubble was substantially higher — the highest in 250 years. Using that tech bubble as a benchmark is just plain stupid, given the strongest confluence of demographic, technology and favorable geopolitical trends in all of U.S. history, as I explained in Chapter 10.

The trouble is, central banks are desperate to avoid a massive reset on their watch. That's why they're the loudest voices in the "no-bubble" chorus. It's also why they've gone to extremes to prevent the inevitable.

Starting way back in 1987, and accelerating their efforts from late 2008 onward, central banks have hijacked the free market by controlling interest rates and injecting trillions of dollars to save the financial institutions.

Instead of the once-in-a-lifetime bubble peaking as it should have been in late 2007, we are now in a rare time in history where we have seen three major stock bubbles in a row.

Look how ominous this is:

Figure 15-3: Dow Megaphone Pattern

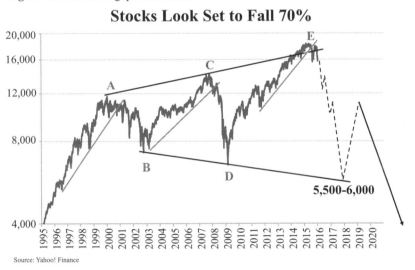

Source: Yahoo! Finance

This is one of the most obvious stock patterns I have ever seen, but almost no one has talked about it in the financial media, except Robert McHugh from Australia and thestreet.com.

Why not? Because the whole country has been in bubble denial, as usual. Politicians, economists, stock analysts, media anchors, investors… the whole lot of them.

Figure 15-3 (which I've presented to you several times throughout this book) clearly shows how each bubble has taken us to new highs and how each crash has taken us to new lows — and each bubble is over once the steep bottom trend line is finally broken, as occurred again in August of 2015.

A similar pattern of three new highs and three lower lows occurred at the last major long-term peak in stocks between 1965 and 1972. In that case, the most devastating crash happened after the third peak in late 1972. In fact, the worst crash since the Great Depression occurred from 1973 through 1974.

But the Bob Hope generation boom from 1942 to 1968 was not a bubble boom like the baby boom expansion from 1983 to 2007. Stocks went up only about 10% a year and the worst corrections were only 20%. So that crash was less than what we saw in the early 1930s… and it's less that what we'll see over the next few years.

The crash from late 2007 into early 2009 saw a crushing drop of 57%. The next crash, I believe, will suffer closer to a 70% loss.

Yes, that means a decline from an 18,350 Dow top to a 5,500 — 6,000 bottom by late 2017.

And like the crash of 1973-1974, that won't be the end of the long decline after a long boom. It will just be the worst of it. Stocks and the economy didn't turn around until late 1982, with the rising baby boom demographic spending trends. They won't turn around again now until at least mid- to late 2022.

Remember, bubbles burst at least twice as fast as they build. The typical stock bubble takes five years to build and 2.5 years to crash. And when that bubble bursts in a great reset, like what we face now, it takes years longer for the shakeout to run its course. It's during this time that we find those sales of a lifetime!

Cuffing the Weight to Our Ankle

Have you seen the most popular commercials in 2015/16? The ones for reverse mortgages?

Don't they just make them seem like a no-brainer?

You get tax-free cash... your mortgage payment disappears... and you still own your home.

The mortgage is only paid off when the last owner dies.

Why the hell isn't every baby boomer scrambling to sign up?

Because there's a catch. There's always a catch!

You must pay a higher interest rate than a normal mortgage to compensate the lender for taking such a long-term risk on your home value. That means much higher costs until you die.

Yes, you will have a better retirement even if your house is under-water (as I would suggest) when you do finally die.

But your children will pay the price when they inherit a house worth nothing.

I mention this because it speaks to the heart of our biggest problem: debt and the burdens we aging baby boomers are putting on the young millennials for the decades ahead.

We're drowning in it and the tap is still open full force.

NINJA (No Income, No Job, No Assets) and no-document loans... lower-than-market mortgage rates, backed by the U.S. government... home equity lines of credit... all of this allowed people to buy more home than they could afford, fueling the housing bubble that burst in 2006. That collapse crippled millions of households.

Apparently, we didn't learn from those mistakes. Instead, we stepped up the ante and took the game global.

In short, we've created the greatest debt bubble ever seen...

Figure 15-4: Total U.S. Debt Growth vs. GDP Growth

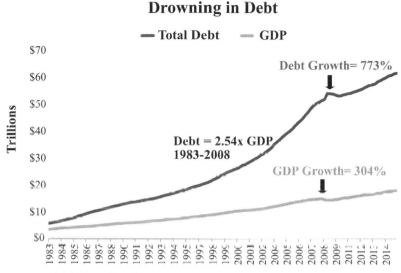

Drowning in Debt

Source: St. Louis Federal Reserve, Treasury Direct

In the last great boom and bubble (from 1983 to 2008), total debt — government and private — grew at 2.54 times GDP. Private debt is two to three times government debt in most developed countries. Some of that larger private debt was natural with baby boomers raising their kids and borrowing to buy houses and cars. But 2.54 times for 26 years!?

Any economist that doesn't see this level of growth as the problem it is shouldn't be an economist!

In China, total debt has grown at similar rates since 2000 and that is extreme for a still poor emerging country with much less credit quality.

In the UK, it has grown 3.5 times since 1983.

These are insane numbers!

The last debt bubble anywhere close to this developed from 1914 into 1929 in the U.S. when we were the emerging country of that era.

And guess what we got?

The Great Depression.

The greatest financial "detox" or deleveraging of debt and inflated financial assets in modern history.

Recall that the Dow Jones Industrial Average crashed 89% in less than three years when that bubble finally began to burst. The first wave down saw 42% disappear in just 2.5 months.

What we now face is so much worse than that. Let me show you…

Good Riddance… Only, it's Too Late

Some say quantitative easing, the Federal Reserve's six-year-old plan to save the U.S. economy and stock markets, ended as a magnificent success. A vindication of monetary-crutch policy at its best.

"Just look at the numbers," they say. "The stock market has been hitting one record high after another into mid-2015," they say. "America has been returned to its rightful place as the engine of global economic growth, albeit at 2% growth and not 4%," they say.

There is only one problem: it's all set to crash and burn as it was all funded by free money created out of thin air. Last time I looked, you just don't get something for nothing in this world.

And the truth is that QE has done nothing more than re-inflate the largest bubble of the century, while unsurprisingly failing to overcome the underlying forces of declining demographics and deflation waiting in the wings.

Said another way: it's dragged us back to above the rapids and left us without a paddle.

From the moment the Fed began printing in late November of 2008 until it ended QE on October 27, 2015, it was doomed to fail. It pumped $5.44 trillion into the economy during those seven years. This number is higher than the total balance sheet I showed you in Chapter 13 because the Fed has had to replace bonds that have matured. But this free money has only delayed the inevitable… and worsened the ultimate outcome. It has also totally perverted the bond and stock markets.

Despite the widespread fear of inflation — and hyperinflation many worried so desperately about — the country has been able to eke out only 2% growth, with the first quarter of 2016 plunging down to 0.5%. Looks to me like we're heading into a recession again, as we forecast.

All of that money didn't lead to inflation because it's been fighting deflation. Now that the Fed has stopped printing, the deflation so typical of the economic winter season will begin to accelerate again into 2017-plus.

That's because we face massive — astronomical — deleveraging ahead.

Deleveraging? What Deleveraging?

The 16th Geneva Report on the world economy raised an interesting question. It also just so happened to supports our views on the global debt situation. That is: it's completely out of control!

The report asks: "Deleveraging? What Deleveraging?"

As much as it's needed, there's been very little debt deleveraging around the globe since the last global debt crisis, and that makes the coming years extremely dangerous.

Since 2008, deleveraging, or the process of reducing the level of your debt by restructuring or writing it off, was limited to the private sector. Governments, on the other hand, didn't get the memo. They've racked up an unimaginable mountain of debt — more than they did at the peak of the last debt bubble in late 2008.

Thanks to the adoption and implementation of Keynesian policies, they've used fiscal deficits and monetary injections as stimulus to offset what would have been the next great depression.

Japan continues to use such policies, tripling down its QE efforts from early 2013 forward. It moved to negative short-term rates because zero wasn't enough to keep its coma economy from falling back into recession over and over again. And right before we went to print with this book, it promised a new, massive stimulus effort for later this year (2016).

Why they do it is obvious...

No president or premier or central banker wants to have debt deleveraging and a great depression on their watch. So they've done (and continue to do) everything in their power to prevent it, regardless of the damage they're causing to their economies and citizens longer-term through mal-investment and speculation.

What they fail to realize is that allowing the economy to move through the winter economic season — as painful as it is — is the only way to grow again when the spring economic season rolls around.

Deleveraging and deflation helps clear the decks.

It presents challenges that inspire people to innovate.

It sheds the dead weight of debt and excess capacity, making companies more efficient and prices more affordable to consumers. It makes room for the new, lean and agile.

Without it, we will never take the next step to greatness. Just ask Japan. Its economy is still comatose 26 years after its peak thanks to endless monetary and fiscal stimulus that has prevented deleveraging. Japan's been doing QE since 1997, when its demographic trends predictably worsened on a 47-year birth lag. The situation *still* looks grim over there while debt keeps piling on... a retirement community in hock!

Global Financial Assets Are Massive... And Still Rising

All of this Keynesian economics has created an extreme debt and financial asset bubble. According to that 16th annual Geneva Report, financial assets in the developed countries were at $184 trillion in 2013, a full 10% higher than they were in 2008. They were nearly $200 trillion in early 2016.

Figure 15-5: Financial Assets in Developed Countries

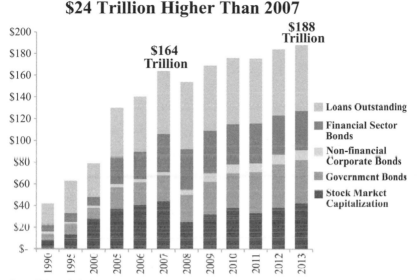

Source: "Deleveraging? What Deleveraging?" Geneva Reports on the World Economy 16, Luigi Buttiglione, Philip R. Lane, Lucrezia Reichlin and Vincent Reinhart, St. Louis Fed

This is the work of central banks. They have created the largest financial assets bubble this century with all of their money printing.

That money hasn't gone to those who need it most — consumers. Instead, it's ended up in the hands of speculators who have leveraged their bets and taken advantage of ultra-low interest rates and corporations who buy back their own stocks and fund endless mergers and acquisitions to financially engineer their earnings short term rather than make real investments that would grow them longer term.

As you can see in Figure 15-5 above, the Geneva report broke down financial assets into several groups. The ones to pay particular attention to are stocks, financial sector bonds, and loans. They are the most vulnerable to deleveraging.

(Note that real estate is not included in this chart, but the large rise in loans does reflect that to a substantial degree through mortgages.)

Just those three groups — stocks, financial sector bonds, and loans — total $125 trillion in financial assets at last count (they're no doubt much more by now).

I expect us to see at least half of that disappear over the next several years. I'm talking $62.5 trillion to $70 trillion just gone!

That dwarfs the total money printed globally by central banks — at the time of writing that was more than $8 trillion — by eight to one.

So are central banks going to print $70 trillion this time around to save the financial institutions?

Will they have any credibility when the first $8 trillion ended up succeeding only in inflating bigger bubbles that burst even harder with an even deeper economic collapse?

I don't think so.

This is how deleveraging and the resultant deflation outstrip money printing efforts and government deficits. It's what makes central bank attempts to save their countries (or zones) futile.

It's what happened in the 1930s. And it's what's going to happen again — on a much larger scale — into around 2022/2023.

Whoever gets elected president in 2016 will likely wish they hadn't. The lucky one will be who gets elected in 2020 (like Reagan in 1980 or FDR in 1932) because, by then, most of the deleveraging and crash will be done and the economy will finally start to turn around in the last two years of their first, four-year term.

Remember, when major bubbles peak, like stocks did in 1929, and then burst, it takes decades to recover the losses.

It took 24 years for the Dow Jones to get back to its late-1929 high and 25 years to get back to its late-1968 high, adjusted for inflation.

If you had retired in 1929, you would most likely have been dead before your stocks broke even.

Many companies and investors never recover from shocks like that, especially the investors who sell near the bottom and don't get back in for many years.

Of course, there is also the $47 trillion in financial assets in emerging countries to add to the camel's back. Take a look…

Figure 15-6: Financial Assets in Emerging Countries

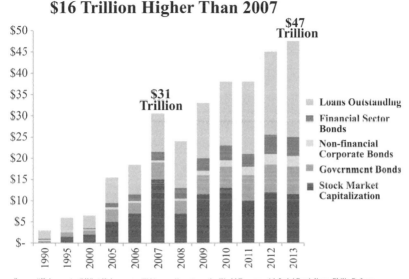

$16 Trillion Higher Than 2007

Source: "Deleveraging? What Deleveraging?" Geneva Reports on the World Economy 16, Luigi Buttiglione, Philip R. Lane, Lucrezia Reichlin and Vincent Reinhart, St. Louis Fed

These have risen by 104% since the drop in 2008, much more than in the developed countries. This number is closer to $55 trillion at the time of writing.

These assets tend to be even more vulnerable to crises than those of developed nations.

When I add the two together, we see that total global financial assets equal $231 trillion at last count. As I write this, they're probably closer to $255 trillion.

The numbers really are almost unfathomable.

I expect we'll see another $25 trillion to $30 trillion disappear from the developing world.

That means, at a minimum, $87.5 trillion to $100 trillion is just going to disappear in the next several years, much of it in short order.

You don't need to be a genius to know that's going to hurt!

Another report worth noting is the *Global Shadow Banking Monitoring Report 2014* from the Financial Stability Board. It focuses on financial assets in 20 major countries and the Eurozone, but with more emphasis on shadow bank financial assets around the world. This sector tends to lend to the riskiest projects, have the greatest leverage and hence deleverage the fastest. They're also less likely to receive government assistance during a crisis.

Financial Assets Are Out of Control

Figure 15-7 shows you total global financial assets by sector. When we total all five sectors, we get $304 trillion in financial assets. That's more than the Geneva Report's $230 trillion, and likely more accurate.

It suggests even more potential for financial deleveraging that will dwarf the money printing of the last seven years.

Figure 15-7: Total Global Financial Assets by Sector

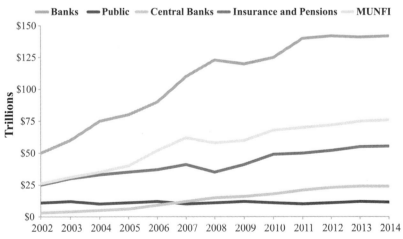

Source: Financial Stability Board

The largest financial asset sector is still banking at nearly $140 trillion. But that sector has been flat since 2011, as has the smallest sector of public financial institutions, which is about $12 trillion.

The fastest rising sectors — those of most concern — have been:

1. Shadow banking, now at $75 trillion and 120% of global GDP;

2. Insurance and pension funds, at $53 trillion; and

3. Central banks, at $24 trillion.

This group — the most vulnerable of the lot — totaled $152 trillion in 2013. It's closer to $170 trillion by now.

Central banks hold only 7.9% of the total global financial assets, which means they don't have nearly the power they claim.

Even if they *doubled* their assets in an attempt to fight this coming round of deleveraging and deflation, it wouldn't even scratch the surface of the other $280 trillion worth of financial assets out there.

In fact, just a 10% deleveraging in the private sectors would offset all central bank money printing and assets around the world.

Scaling down from the global to the local view, the outlook doesn't improve any.

CHAPTER 16

Total U.S. Debt Is at Crushing Heights

LOANS AND FINANCIAL SECURITIES make up the total financial assets we looked at in the previous chapter. That's because greater debt and lending serves to augment economic growth and the value of financial assets.

But when the whole bubble finally bursts and economic growth slows dramatically, loans will fail or get restructured and financial assets will crash, often taking decades to regain their former levels of glory.

In both cases money and wealth will be destroyed. It will just disappear.

I like to compare bubbles to magic. They create money and wealth out of thin air. And then all that artificial money and wealth disappears in the blink of an eye.

"Now you see it, now you don't!"

The banking system does the same on a much larger scale than the recent central bank money printing by lending against a small fraction (typically 10%) of their deposits (actually your deposits) and their capital. They do this to absorb losses. When loans go bad, all the money created disappears, including your deposits. It happened in the great deflation of the early 1930s. It will happen again in this next great deflation from 2017 to 2023.

Let's look at debt in the U.S. as an example of how the bubble built and how tens of trillions could disappear in just this one sector of financial assets.

Total U.S. debt at the end of 2015 was $67.5 trillion, 15.8% higher than it was in early 2009. That number was just around $5 trillion at the beginning of the boom in 1983. By 2008, at the top of the bubble, it was 11 times greater, reaching $56 trillion. To reach that level, debt grew at 2.54 times GDP for 26 years. Now, it's 13.5 times greater than when the boom started in 1983! That is how a debt bubble is created... and again, what deleveraging?

Figure 16-1: Total U.S. Debt

$9.2 Trillion Higher Than First Bubble Peak

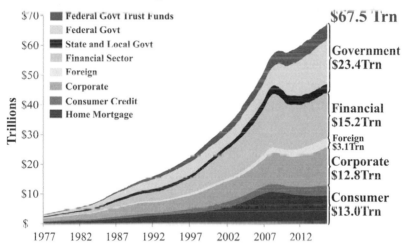

Source. Federal Reserve Flow of Funds Report, Treasury Direct

2008 should have been the end of the debt bubble. Unfortunately, massive monetary and fiscal stimulus didn't allow that. Instead, they spooned more cocaine to the crack addict by the shovel full.

The largest debt increase since 2009 has been in the government sector, which has risen a whopping 48% (and it is still rising, albeit at a slower rate)! In the downturn we're moving into, that debt will rise rapidly again with $2 trillion-plus deficits at times.

Corporate debt rose by 10.4%, as companies have borrowed $3 trillion since 2009 to buy back their stocks and artificially inflate their earnings per share with nearly free money courtesy of the Fed.

On the other hand, financial sector debt declined the most over the last six years, losing 19.3% from its peak in late 2008 to its bottom in mid-2012, while consumer debt fell by 7.0%.

Clearly there is massive room for deleveraging.

We can also drill down into the consumer sector's assets, liabilities and net worth, which you can see in the next Figure 16-2.

Figure 16-2: U.S. Household Balance Sheet

$26+ Trillion Loss Just Ahead

	2013	Percent Change	2017 (estimate)	Dollar Change
Assets, billions				
Real Estate	$22,070	-40%	$13,242	-$8,828
Consumer Durables	$5,011	-20%	$4,009	-$1,002
Financial Assets	$66,498	-40%	$39,899	-$26,599
Total Assets	$94,042	-39%	$57,150	-$36,892
Liabilities, billions				
Home Mortgages	$9,386	-50%	$4,693	-$4,693
Consumer Credit	$3,098	-50%	$1,549	-$3,098
Total Liabilities	$13,768	-50%	$6,242	-$7,526
Net Worth, billions	$80,274	-37%	$50,908	-$26,366

Source: Federal Reserve, Dent Research

In the last crash, consumers lost $16 trillion in net worth, but the Fed quickly re-inflated the bubble.

When this bubble finally bursts, as all bubbles do, everyone will be able to see all of this magical money printing for what it is: ineffective and destructive. As such, the Fed very likely won't have the credibility to keep doubling down on more quantitative easing when the economy fails again.

When the next downturn arrives, during late 2016, I reasonably expect to see 40% declines in real estate and financial assets and a

50% decline in consumer debt, which consists mostly of mortgages. We could see 70% to 80% declines in the stock market early into the next decade, with most of that likely coming in the next few years.

That means U.S. households face losing $36.9 trillion, but with $7.5 trillion of that offset with debt relief. That's wealth that disappears and doesn't come back anywhere near as quickly as it did after the 2008/09 crash.

How it All Ends

The bottom line is that the U.S. and global economy is facing a period of very painful deleveraging. Clearly financial assets, and the debt used to fuel them, are in bubble territory and the slightest trigger could crumble everything.

The next Figure, from the 16th Geneva Report, summarizes best how debt bubbles build, deleverage and are always followed by deflation, not inflation. History is crystal clear on this. See for yourself:

Figure 16-3: Total U.S. Debt as a Percent of GDP

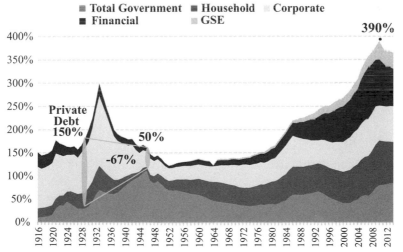

U.S. Private Debt as % of GDP Fell From 150% to 50% After 1929

Source: "Deleveraging? What Deleveraging?" Geneva Reports on the World Economy 16, Luigi Buttiglione, Philip R. Lane, Lucrezia Reichlin and Vincent Reinhart, St. Louis Fed

Figure 16-3 shows a breakdown of total debt in the U.S. into the four key sectors: financial, corporate, household and government. Clearly we're in a massive bubble. Just look at how it compares to the one that peaked into the Great Depression.

But there's something else I want you to pay particular attention to in this chart. It's what I've been trying to explain, and what I discussed in Chapter 1. That is, major debt bubbles peak and then burst about once in a lifetime.

Debt grows much faster than the economy, so debt-to-GDP rises accordingly. Eventually, that debt becomes too large for the economy to carry.

The last debt bubble peak was in 1933, at 290% of GDP. Just prior to that, the real bubble peaked in late 1929 at around 180% of GDP (the surge after that was due to GDP falling like a rock).

The present bubble has peaked at 390% of GDP, more than double the 1929 peak, and that will go much higher when GDP falls dramatically ahead. I'm talking as high as 500% in the next few years.

Of course, every debt bubble is larger than the preceding one because income and wealth increase as we get more productive and affluent over time. That allows each generation to borrow more than the last. But that doesn't change the fact that this bubble is much larger than ever and going to burst!

When this all goes belly up, private debt deleverages first. Government deficits and debt tend to go up during the first stages of a crisis.

Private debt in late 1929 was around 150% of GDP. Just after World War II it shrunk down to 50% of GDP. That's a two-thirds haircut!

When debts are written off or written down as banks, households and companies fail, the money that was largely created out of thin air through our fractional reserve banking system disappears forever.

Now you see it.

Now you don't.

Remember, banks don't lend real money to people that they raise from investors. They pledge 10% of their deposits against those loans and they tend to have around 10% in capital to back those 10% deposit pledges up. That's not much when real estate can fall by 26%, as it did in the U.S. in the early 1930s, or by 65%, is it did in Japan in recent decades. That's not much when other financial assets can fall even more, like U.S. stocks plunging 89% into 1932 and 80% in Japan at the early-2009 lows.

That's how banks suddenly become insolvent. Their losses eat up their deposits after their small capital base is exhausted and they suddenly can't give people their money back.

Deflation Always Follows Deleveraging

There have been three major debt and financial asset bubbles since the early 1800s and resultant depressions and periods of significant deflation in prices: 1835 to 1844, 1873 to 1877, and 1930 to 1939. Now we're about to experience the fourth, from 2016 to 2022-2023.

Debt bubbles create deflation when they finally deleverage. Money and wealth are destroyed, leaving fewer dollars to chase the same goods. That is the textbook definition of deflation and what the gold bugs that call for hyperinflation from unprecedented money printing don't understand. And it's why we only managed to eke out 2% inflation on average since 2009, despite the trillions in Fed stimulus.

So when the economy crashes again in the next couple of years, expect to see as much as $21 trillion (if not more) simply disappearing in a first round in the U.S. alone. That is simply the amount of private debt that was created between 2000 and 2008 in the original bubble. A lot more will vanish as the bubble unwinds, and globally.

The next Figure shows how we actually got a brief bout of deflation between 2009 and early 2010, before the massive money-printing (QE) program brought it to a halt.

Figure 16-4: M3 Money Supply

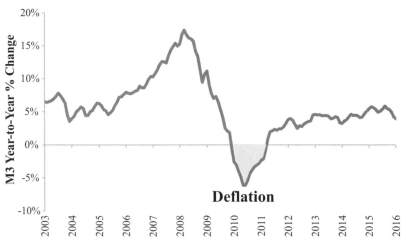

Source: St. Louis Fed, Shadow Stats

The broadest definition of the money supply, M3, declined 6%, before turning around as you can see. It's been at low levels of growth ever since, after getting as high as 17% at the top of the bubble.

I expect M3 to decline 10%, or even 20%, in the next crisis.

That's because deflation is the natural trend when debt and financial assets deleverage, unless governments go to extreme lengths to counter it, which they have thus far.

However, I don't believe that the government (U.S. or otherwise) can keep this bubble going forever. The Fed is out of ammunition and the move to stop printing has put it on the back foot for the next crisis.

Besides, the Fed's efforts to stop the inevitable crash have only made the situation worse. The longer you keep a bubble going, the greater the imbalances in mal-investment, financial assets and income inequality you create and the worse the deleveraging and hangover to follow.

In short, the next financial crisis and stock crash will be far worse than the one we saw in 2008.

We'll endure deflation instead of low inflation.

But I get it. You're wondering how I can be so adamant that deflation is in our future… how I can say that we've even had deflation on and off over the last few years. You walk into the grocery store and you walk out wondering what the hell just happened!

My health care insurance didn't just go up the normal 10% to 15% in the last year. It went up 65%. Granted, that's more of a one-time adjustment for Obamacare than anything else. I can't imagine another increase of that size happening again. But still…

It's hard to see and feel the deflation because, to this point, it's been in pockets throughout our economy. And, as human beings, we have the tendency to be more aware of the pains we feel from day to day than anything else. You could think of deflation like a cancer in the economy. It eats away at the systems and infrastructure slowly, killing the economy from within. But, more often than not, cancer patients aren't even aware they have the horrible disease until they begin to feel the effects of its destruction.

So while we're paying more at the grocery store and on health care, there are areas where we're paying less.

Just the other day I bought a laptop for $279. A few years ago, that would've cost me $1,500. And the 27-inch HD TV I bought in 2002 for $5,000 is now going for $200! And mortgages are much lower in cost.

So which is it?

Do We Have Inflation or Deflation?

This is perhaps the one question I get most frequently. In fact, it's *the* biggest debate I have, typically with gold bugs like Peter Schiff, Jeff Clark and Porter Stansberry.

The answer is: both. We have inflation bubbles in some areas and deflationary trends in others. As the economic winter season progresses, and when this global debt and financial asset bubble bursts, deflation will become the dominant force.

Despite the inflation we feel from day to day, all the money printing and stimulus we've seen around the world has been a fight against deflation. Economists and politicians are petrified of *deflation* — not inflation. They believe it's the single greatest threat to the economy, and they're right.

The extreme deflationary 1930s was way worse than the equally extreme inflationary 1970s. It's the difference between 25% unemployment and 10%, just by one measure. And don't even talk about bank and business failures!

But through an unprecedented effort to fight deflation, our monetary "wizards" have dragged the debt bubble out longer than it was ever meant to go. In fact, it has made the bubble so much worse than it was before they got involved. In their efforts to fight the tide, they've created a monster.

Inflation in certain areas is simply a byproduct of this over-extended debt bubble.

The Three Inflation Bubbles

Health care has become obscenely expensive. It's to the point where I'd almost rather not *have* health care.

But it's not even the worst.

The highest inflation has occurred in higher education costs for college. These institutions have had parents by the balls for a long time. For most parents, giving your kids the best education you can is the ultimate goal, and universities have absolutely taken advantage of that.

And as the demand has increased, the competition has grown fierce. The top schools compete to have the best campus and facilities, so costs have just gotten more expensive.

The irony is that the professors who teach your kids don't see the bulk of that money, although they tend to have very generous tenure and retirements. It goes toward adding a bunch of non-teaching faculty and elaborate construction projects. So the price just keeps going up and up. It's outstripped health care inflation by a mile!

I repeat this Figure from Chapter 3 here, with one addition for childcare, because it shows clearly how insane this inflation in these three sectors has been.

Figure 16-5: College, Health Care and Childcare Costs vs. Consumer Price Index

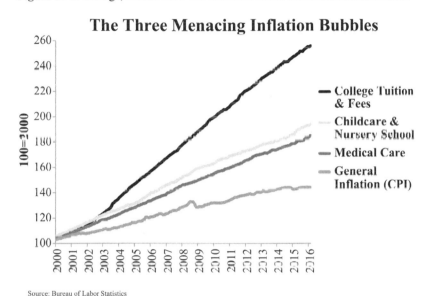

The Three Menacing Inflation Bubbles

Source: Bureau of Labor Statistics

It's completely nuts!

At some point, prices got so high that even more affluent parents couldn't afford them. So, government stepped in and backed student loans… anything to keep that bubble going. Now, college graduates come out with $30,000, or $60,000, or even $200,000 in student loans.

So much for buying a house or having kids or even breathing! If we wanted to find the best way to cripple the rising generation financially, we found it.

Of course, childcare costs have also outpaced core price inflation by a long shot, though nowhere near the extent of higher education.

One of the reasons is that demand for these services has ballooned in recent decades. U.S. Census Bureau figures show that there were 262,511 childcare facilities in 1987. By 2007, that number had shot up to 766,401 — a 192% increase!

It's Worse If You're Rich

So far, I've mentioned things that all people need, like health care and childcare. When it comes to luxury goods, inflation is off the charts.

$5,000 per square foot for an upscale condo in Manhattan (and as high as $13,000)…

$5,000 for a 1961 Haut Brion wine…

$300,000 or more for the latest Ferrari, assuming you can even get on the waiting list…

$5,000 minimum for a Brioni suit…

Watches? Forget about it!

From its bottom in early 2009 to its top in the summer of 2014, the S&P Global Luxury Index shot up some 371%. And it's finally falling.

Figure 16-6: S&P Global Luxury Stock Index

The problem in this sector was that there were simply too many rich people chasing the same, often limited, goods, and that's not sustainable, either — not the exponential rise in the top 0.1% to 10%, or the prices.

What's the point of busting your ass and taking huge risks to be rich if you have to pay $20 million to get a reasonable-size house, in an exclusive neighborhood full of other people just as stressed as you who never have a backyard barbecue to even socialize!?

But now we're witnessing deflationary pressures exert their influence. From its 2014 high, the luxury index was recently down 26%. And that's just the beginning. Prices for these products will also decline as demand falls — another "sale of a lifetime" ahead. At the bottom of the 2008/2009 crash I bought a Maserati at factory cost — that means no dealer or factory mark-up.

So that's some of the inflation we live with from day to day. It's painful, and we're acutely aware of it because it's draining our pockets dry.

What we're less aware of is the deflation we're already seeing in some sectors. For now, it doesn't hurt us when we pay less, so we don't give it a second thought…

Mark my words: it won't be too long before these inflationary bubbles in college tuition, health care and childcare follow luxury goods over the edge of the deflationary cliff. And they'll have company.

My last car lease charged an interest rate of 2.2%, and car prices have not gone up as much as inflation.

And then there's the largest cost of living — your house and mortgage!

Mortgage rates are 3% to 4% today, versus 6%-plus just a few years ago. And home prices fell 34% between 2006 and 2012 for the first time since the Great Depression. While they've risen again since then, there are clear signs that the property market is facing increasing pressure. I expect we'll see prices drop again and more sharply.

Of course, we haven't even touched on the greatest evidence that we're already in the grips of deflation.

The Great Commodity Bust

The global collapse in commodity prices started in 2008 and accelerated after 2011.

The CRB Index that best measures all commodities is down 70% since its peak in mid-2008 and 56% from its secondary peak in early 2011. Industrial commodities and energy have been especially hit.

Figure 16-7: CRB Index Is Down on a Predictable 30-Year Cycle

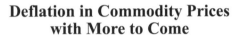

Source: Bloomberg

While these commodities account for only a small portion of our budgets in developed countries, we're still paying less for items like gas and jewelry. That's deflation happening now!

But in emerging countries like India or China, such commodities are a much larger portion of their spending, with a larger impact globally. And that commodity deflation is killing the export industries of most emerging countries, which is why their stock markets and economies are much weaker than ours, despite their stronger demographic trends.

So housing and mortgage costs have fallen, as have many commodity costs like gasoline, as well as computer-related appliances that have even further to fall.

Deflation is happening right now… and it will only accelerate in the years ahead!

We've seen fire (inflation) and we've seen rain (deflation) But these inflationary bubbles are just that — bubbles… and bubbles always burst.

Deflation is the trend going forward, not inflation. It has always been the hallmark of the winter economic season.

As the baby boomers age and the economy collapses (locally and globally), removing excess capacity in all of these bubble sectors, *deflation* will set us on a more sustainable path. And the millennial generation will benefit the most from downward pressure on prices for housing, education and childcare.

The Winter of 2016-2022

This is where the big picture of demographic trends and the four season, 80-Year New Economic Cycle comes in.

The reason that unprecedented QE and ZIRP policies have not created inflation is that governments are fighting the natural and painful deflationary trends of the economic winter season. That season started in 2008, just as I forecast decades ago would happen as the baby boomers peaked in spending, and that unsustainable debt trends would come home to roost.

The best chart to explain why we've had so little inflation despite massive money printing is Figure 16-8:

Figure 16-8: Money Velocity

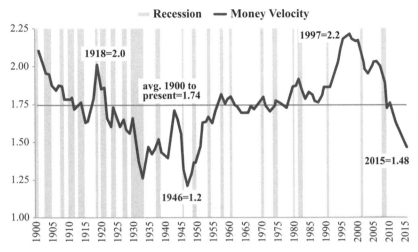

Source: St. Louis Federal Reserve, Hoisington Investment Management

This chart is from Lacy Hunt, who speaks at our Irrational Economic Summits. It shows you that the amount of money the Fed actually created is only a small fraction of our economy. The turnover of this money, how quickly it is spent and expanded through fractional reserve bank lending and capital investment is much more critical.

Lacy explains this chart very simply and elegantly so I'll paraphrase him: when money velocity is above average (the horizontal line through the middle of this chart) and growing, money is being invested in productive assets that help the economy grow. Productive investments create higher income for businesses and workers, who can then spend and invest more.

When money velocity is still positive, but starts to fall, as it did in 1919 and 1998 forward, then the money is going more into unsustainable speculation. Speculation doesn't create productive assets. Debt and financial asset bubbles build in this stage — like the Roaring 20s and 2000s. Investors increasingly gamble on bubbles in stocks or real estate (flippers), and businesses focus more on stock buybacks and increasing dividends — both are not investments in productive capacity.

Finally, money velocity slows below average. That is when you see deleveraging and deflation start to set in.

This chart from Lacy Hunt clearly warns of a deflationary phase already in the making, despite governments' best efforts to counter it with ever more money printing and something-for-nothing stimulus. We are about where we were in early 1930 as the Great Depression was unfolding and the worst stock slide was beginning after an initial decline in late 1929.

The Fed increased interest rates to 0.25% at the end of 2015. It has said it would have at least a few more increases in 2016. I'm skeptical and think at most we'll get one more in mid-2016. They'll find themselves on the back foot when the next crisis hits. They've backed themselves into a corner and anything they do now will just result in their losing credibility.

The big question now is when we'll see this deflation. It takes time, between nine and 18 months for stimulus to move through the economy. That means the declining levels of stimulus through October 2014 will hit the economy in late 2015 and 2016, just as the baby boom moves into its steepest demographic slide after reaching age 54 in 2015.

And should the Fed react to any new crisis by stimulating again, we won't feel those effects fully until well into 2017. So watch out for deflation to accelerate throughout 2016 and most of 2017 into at least early 2018, right alongside major market crashes.

All we need is a trigger… and there are many candidates vying for that honor…

Biggest of the lot is the unprecedented global debt and financial asset bubble that has already begun to unwind.

Second is the Red Dragon, which I will discuss in more detail in Chapter 18.

And then there's the Eurozone. Germany is in the midst of a major demographic drop — worse that what Japan saw in the 1990s — and it will increasingly feel the effects of that between now and 2022, while Italy is looking like the next Greece with rising bad loans… and it's simply too big to bail out.

Whichever trigger turns out to be the BIG one, watch out for a more serious downturn by the summer of 2016 and late 2016 at the latest. This will cause sharp defaults in student loans and subprime auto loans ahead, which have both bubbled up. Fracking bonds will default like crazy. It will cause a second and deeper decline in real estate, putting more homes underwater in the years ahead than ever before. Companies will go bankrupt. Banks will be shaken to their core again.

It'll be nothing short of an implosion. And when it's done, we'll be ready to snap up the sales opportunities of a lifetime!

CHAPTER 17

The Great China Bubble

DIDN'T WE LEARN ANYTHING during the great battle between communist and capitalist economies from the 1960s through the 1980s, or the Cold War?

When the Berlin Wall finally fell in 1989, it was clear to the world that the Soviet Union couldn't compete with the U.S. and other western countries that thrived on a combination of free-market capitalism and democracy.

Yet, clueless economists are now increasingly touting the Chinese model of state-driven capitalism as the new model for the future. Seriously!?

The Chinese, just like the Soviets before them, are not performing many of the essential functions for which a state should be responsible. They're not representing the people and making sure that gains from capitalism pass down appropriately to the populace. They're not setting rules for the game of capitalism. They're not providing a legal system to enforce such rules, regulations and fair play. They're not regulating things that can't be taken into account by the free markets, like pollution (except just recently as they've been choking to death). They're not doing a lot of important things. And where they are providing infrastructures for expansion, they are way overdoing that!

Instead, they're doing some very harmful things. And in so doing, they've created a bubble so big it could be the primary trigger that brings the world to its knees.

While extremely dangerous, it too is helping to make possible those once-in-a-lifetime opportunities we'll be able to pick up, a dime for a dozen, over the next few years.

Urbanization on Steroids

Let's start this conversation with a simple reality: even though China's economy only contracted from 12% growth to 6% growth during the 2008 global crash, that stock drop represented one of the biggest plunges.

The Shanghai Composite (shown in Figure 17-1) saw one of the fastest inflating bubbles between 2005 and 2007… and then one of the fastest collapses, losing 72% in one year!

Then it did it all again in 2015, with much more to come!

Figure 17-1: Shanghai Composite

The Perfect Example of Bubbles

Source: Yahoo! Finance

This is a classic bubble! Such a bubble peak is not likely to see new highs for decades.

The first insight here is that China's market took the biggest plunge because it had the greatest bubble! Remember, bubbles tend to return to where they started (or a bit lower), as the chart shows... and as I keep saying.

But more importantly, China's rebound after the first crisis was the feeblest and shortest lasting, despite some of the world's strongest growth rates. It limped into February of 2010 with the smallest gains of any major country and then saw stocks fall back to near its late-2008 lows. Meanwhile, the U.S., Germany, the UK and many other countries saw new highs.

How could China's stock market be so weak when it was the second largest and fastest growing country in the world?

The answer is its government's policy of overbuilding capacity in everything in an effort to accelerate growth and urbanization (i.e., a B.S. economy driven by top-down central planning).

Overbuilding creates excess capacity with high fixed costs and debt service. That kills profits and that is what the stock market values most, not GDP growth.

So, let's look at the economic realities in China's growth over the last few decades.

First, it isn't fueled by consumer income and spending, as is the case in all other developed countries. Instead, it's largely government-driven. Consumer, or personal, consumption as a percentage of GDP declined from near 70% in 1986 to 35% in 2015, as you can see in Figure 17-2.

Figure 17-2: Personal Consumption as a Percentage of GDP

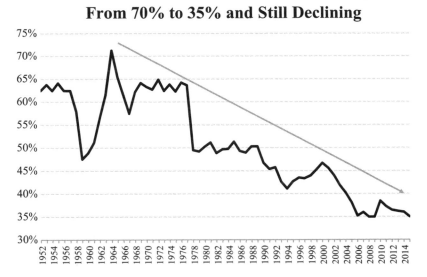

From 70% to 35% and Still Declining

Source: *The Economist,* "One-Track Bind." 9/24/2011; World Bank

Compare that to a healthier and sustainable economic system like the U.S. Personal consumption as a percentage of GDP in the U.S. is around 70% today.

Figure 17-3 shows changes in government, export and consumer spending.

The huge swing you see from the left pie chart to the right one represents government investment shifting from 26% to 56% — almost double.

Net exports decreased from 16% to 7% and consumer spending dropped from 58% to 35%.

Figure 17-3: China, Percentage of GDP by Sector

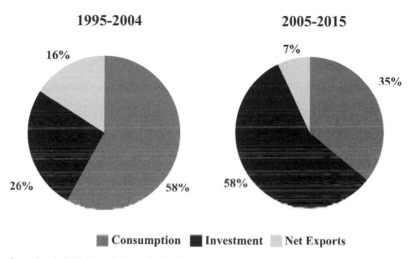

A Capital Investment-Driven Economy

1995-2004   2005-2015

■ Consumption ■ Investment ▨ Net Exports

Source: Organization for Economic Co-operative Development

There is no way you can call that healthy. The government has simply taken over the economy and is dictating its growth... oh, that could turn out well!

Of course, I understand it's natural for emerging countries to have more government involvement at first. It's like a parent raising its children. Governments need to invest in the infrastructures that will allow increasing urbanization. This is the greatest leverage to income growth, productivity and growing consumer demand — but the consumer demand comes last. So, targeting export industries that can help fuel such urbanization and job growth is also critical to fueling such consumer growth in incomes and demand. This is all natural.

That's why China's government investment and net exports have increasingly driven its growth in the last decade or so.

But why has consumer demand not risen yet, even on a lag, as it should? And no other emerging country has taken capital investment to such extremes.

It's because of the long tail of corruption in a top-down communist (I prefer the word "mafia") government. But before I get to that, let's look at Figure 17-4.

Figure 17-4: Capital Spending as a Percent of GDP

Twice the Intensity and Duration

Source: IMF, Pivot

In this chart, you can see that China's government-driven investment boom has been more exaggerated and has lasted much longer than the export-driven expansions in Japan, South Korea and Germany. In fact, it has grown twice the intensity for twice as long!

The last such surge in Southeast Asia and South Korea ended up in a major financial crisis and currency devaluation during 1997 and 1998, which continued off and on into late 2002.

China will suffer the same fate, only much worse and for longer.

I can't stress this enough: any bubble or major expansion will see a peak at some point and then a contraction. That will stimulate new innovations and drive growth again, especially when the next generation comes into its spending cycle… except that China doesn't have an echo boom generation.

China's government-driven expansion model is extreme when we compare it to its neighboring countries. This isn't good because almost any government will over-expand to create jobs and please the people, especially an un-elected one.

The Middle Kingdom, like most emerging countries throughout history, has overinvested dramatically. That forebodes a crisis ahead, just like the one we saw in Southeast Asia from late 1997 into late 2002.

But China's overinvestment bubble is the greatest in modern history. As such, when it bursts it will be devastating, not only locally, but globally as well. And all investment bubbles burst, especially when debt and asset bubbles get so high they're crushed by their own weight. It's like adding grains of sand to a mound until one grain finally causes an avalanche!

Then there's China's demographic problem...

A Population Aging Faster Than You'd Think

China is the only emerging country that peaked in 2011 in workforce or demographic spending growth for decades ahead. It will decline more rapidly after 2025. After that, it will age faster than most *developed* countries, including the U.S., while its fellow emerging countries continue growing.

Latin America and Southeast Asia should peak around 2040 to 2050, India and South Asia between 2055 and 2065, the Middle East and North Africa around 2070, and Sub Saharan Africa around 2100.

Why the big difference?

It's thanks to China's one-child policy, which started informally during the mid-1960s, became formal policy in the 1970s and is just now starting to impact peak spending on a four-decade lag.

The country's birth rate per 1,000 women dropped from around 6.0 in the mid-1960s to about 1.8 — well below the replacement rate of 2.3 — in 2000, where it remains today. That should have been predictable with rising urbanization and income. And then such falling birth rates make it easy to project demographic trends like workforce and population growth. Yet so few saw it coming, and even fewer said anything about it.

The government estimates that the country saw 400 million fewer births — or about one-third of the population — as a result of this policy.

So, late in 2013, it relaxed the policy slightly. It allowed couples who were both only children to have an additional child. They expected to add two million births per year as a result, but, as of September 2015, only 1.76 million permits — about 850,000 per year — had been applied for. Those were only the requests. There is no official count of how many additional births have actually occurred.

Then why is China investing so heavily for a workforce that is slowing?

Quite simply, for urbanization and the huge payoff that brings in GDP per capita.

Rising urbanization tends to nearly triple incomes and spending as long as there are viable jobs. But China is putting the cart before the horse… it's moving people first.

A more free-market model would be to create growth in the economy and exports and then attract rural people into urban areas to fulfill those new jobs. China's government-driven model is to build the urban areas first, then move people in from rural areas and hope to create jobs afterward so that the newly relocated people can become growing consumers.

In other words, these new consumers are supposed to create the jobs for themselves by building stuff for no one and spending the cash they make.

Would a venture capitalist invest in this model? Absolutely not! Would normal investors buy condos for investment when so many are empty?

What if the jobs don't flow fast enough to keep pace with the influx of people? That's a one-way ticket to civil unrest.

And let's not even talk about the fact that most of these people have no skills to even get a job in the first place.

Still, none of these realities has stopped the Chinese government.

Between 2000 and 2012, the country's urbanization took a giant leap from 38% to 53%. That's over 200 million people moving from rural areas into cities in just 12 years. Can you imagine moving the equivalent of two-thirds of the U.S. population from farms to cities in just over a decade?

And where are these people now? I'll get to that later, but I think you can guess.

In the meantime, there is a bigger crisis ahead as the global economy continues to slow, despite desperate and continuous stimulus policies. It's third only to the unprecedented debt and financial assets bubble and China's debt and infrastructure bubble...

CHAPTER 18

China's Unprecedented Real Estate Bubble

DO YOU THINK the real estate bubbles in Japan (1990s), or the U.S. (early 2000s), or Ireland or Spain (late 2000s) were bad? They have already burst or have at least started to.

Or what about the ongoing bubbles in England, France, Canada, Scandinavia, Australia and most of East Asia? These are still inflating, having only suffered a minor correction (hardly worth mentioning) during the Great Recession.

Well, look at China, my friend!

There has never been a bubble this large in any major country in modern history. Why? Because it's being driven by unprecedented overinvestment by the unaccountable Chinese government and the very high savings rates by the Chinese populace, especially the more affluent. They love real estate and shun stocks and bonds. They get an A+ for savings, but an F- for asset allocation. This will kill them in the great deflation ahead.

Take rapidly growing urbanization, growing GDP, growing savings, growing real estate investment and you get a massive bubble, despite growing vacancies and massive overbuilding. Talk about a paradox!

When I spoke at conferences in Dubai in late 2006 and late 2007, local condo prices were going up between 30% and 40% a year, compared to increases of between 15% and 20% back in Miami, which was clearly in a bubble. At that time, most of the building cranes in the world were in Dubai, so what does that tell you?

I told the people there: "This is a bubble that is ready to burst."

They replied: "Harry, you don't understand. The government is supporting this bubble. It won't let it burst. It will buy when consumers and businesses don't."

"Now I am *more* worried," I retorted.

As I had warned, that Dubai bubble started bursting in 2008, just as the tallest building in the world, the Burj Khalifa, was going up. I don't point this out as mere coincidence. In the last century of high-rise cities, the tallest buildings in leading edge growth regions were completed right near the top of the greatest 30- to 40-year, long-term real estate and economic booms.

And I don't think the real estate bust in Dubai is over yet, so look for further declines ahead, especially if oil moves closer to $10 a barrel as I expect it will in the next several years.

The Chrysler Building, Empire State Building, and 40 Wall Street were completed right around the 1929 stock market peak.

Similarly, the Sears Tower in Chicago and the Twin Towers in New York were completed just before the 1970s crash and downturn.

The Petronas Towers in Kuala Lumpur were completed in 1997 just as that crisis set in, and I've already talked about the Burj Khalifa in Dubai.

So where are most of the building cranes in the world today?

You guessed it! China.

Where are the tallest skyscrapers going up today?

You guessed it again! China.

Not only that, China is now taking the stage for building more of the tallest buildings in the world at the fastest rate, as you can see in Figure 18-1.

Figure 18-1: Skyscraper Completions

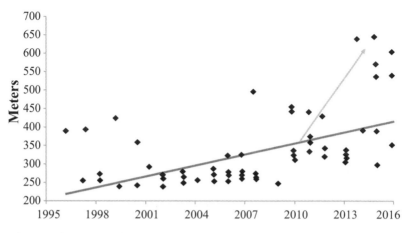

China's Skyscraper Bubble

Pay particularly close attention to building balloons between late 2009 and 2015, mostly after the financial crisis of 2008. That is sheer madness!

This is undoubtedly a skyscraper-building bubble… a symptom of the overbuilding in China at all levels: residential, commercial, infrastructures and industrial capacity.

So, let's see how China's real estate bubble compares to others.

Figure 18-2 shows real estate valuations in price-to-income ratios for major cities around the world, including emerging and developed countries.

Figure 18-2: Price-to-Income Ratios for Major Global Cities

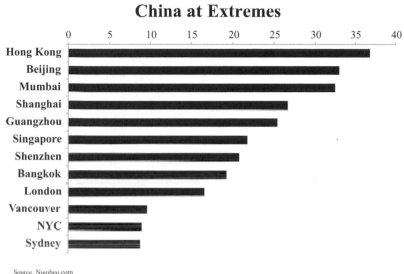

China at Extremes

Source: Numbeo.com

Just look at that!

Four of the top five major cities are all in China. Hong Kong is nearly 37 times price to income. Beijing is 33 times, Shanghai is just under 27 times and Guangzhou is over 25 times.

That's greater than other pricy emerging world cities like Singapore at 22 times price to income, or Bangkok at 20 times.

The highest price city in the western world is London at only 16 times price to income, then Vancouver at nearly 10 times, Sydney at nine times (as high as 10 times in other indicators I watch), and finally San Francisco and Los Angeles above eight times.

The average price-to-income for housing in China, including less expensive rural and smaller cities, is 15.7 times, still more expensive on a relative basis than London.

Let me give you another "concrete" example of the real estate bubble in China.

This next chart, Figure 18-3 looks at cement consumption per capita in four countries with major real estate bubbles.

Spain was the most extreme in Europe. It went up to 1,600 metric tons of cement at its peak in 2007.

The U.S. hit its peak at a mere 600 tons in 2005, before dropping off.

China's consumption is still rising, even after hitting 2,000 metric tons. In fact, between 2011 and 2013, China produced more cement than the U.S. did in the entire 20th century!

Figure 18-3: Cement Consumption per Capita

China's Gone Ballistic

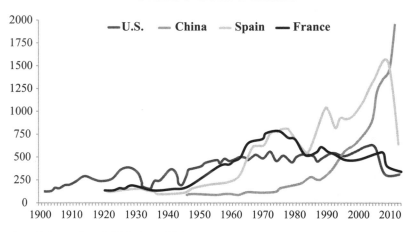

Source: SG Cross Asset Research, USGS, Italcementi, Metric Tons

And this is for a country not nearly as rich as the U.S. and Spain!

And it's not just real estate. It's bridges, railways, roads, shopping centers, office buildings and industrial capacity. Professor Larry Lang at the University of Hong Kong estimates that China has excess capacity of 50% in electrolytic capacitors, 40% in solar batteries, 35% in steel, 30% in flat screens and 17% in copper. Aluminum overcapacity is considered to be the greatest, likely at 50%-plus.

The extremes in Spain and China reflect very high home owner-ship, high foreign investment and strong commercial and residential expansion.

The only way this will continue is with the help of the top 1% to 10% of affluent buyers in these Chinese cities and, to a larger extent, by their foreign buying in key cities globally. But foreign buyers are the kiss of death to a fragile economy because they don't actually live in the local market and they pull out their money as soon as the party is over.

Surveys show that over half of the millionaires in China are considering emigrating to protect their wealth. And for the top 1% to 10% in the rest of the world's richest cities… they are toast as soon as this endless bubble peaks because they own most of the highest-valued businesses, stocks, real estate and other assets.

Remember Ted Turner crying over how his dreams for changing the world were decimated when his net worth went from $10 billion to $1 billion during the tech wreck? Well there will be a lot more Ted Turner's in the years ahead. The only difference is they will be the ones who spent $95 million for condos in New York City, whereas Ted Turner actually did some really cool things with his wealth.

Any way you look at it, real estate prices in China are more over-valued than anywhere else in the world. While developed countries are printing money, China's printing condos!

The scary part is that they're not done. They're doubling down on their steroid urbanization policy and have committed to moving another 250 million people from rural to urban areas between now and 2025. That's crazy!

At this point, as much as 24% of condos and houses in major Chinese cities are vacant. And that's not even the worst of it. There are a number of newly constructed cities across China, some big enough to house one million people, that are almost entirely empty.

The largest mall and building complex in the world, New Century Global Center in Chengdu, is almost totally vacant. Under its roof, there's an amusement park and ocean beaches, but now China is designating it as a tourist area because it can't attract any tenants. Talk about The Disneyland of Overbuilding.

The Changsha Sky City dream, which was meant to become the world's tallest building at 2,749 feet (202 stories) built in the shortest time — about 90 days — is now a fishing hole. Two years after construction was halted because of safety concerns, the building's 2.6-hectare foundations are filled with water and villagers are using the area to raise fish.

Finally, there is Tianducheng in Hangzhou. This government-constructed city was designed to look like Paris with, of course, a 354-foot Eiffel Tower replica at its center. Hangzhou also has replicas of Venice and other famous cities. Even though this concept city has been a total failure (it has been abandoned), the communist government has already begun building a whole new city, Guangzhou, just south of there.

All in all, China now boasts 470 skyscrapers taller than 498 feet, with another 332 under construction and 516 more planned but not confirmed. China is taking the Field of Dreams approach: "If you build it, they will come."

Wouldn't it be nice if business people could just build what they wanted, scrape off short-term profits and be insured that they wouldn't fail long-term because the government has their back?

Come to think of it, we have many large banks and companies here in the U.S. that are deemed too big to fail, and many of them got big, fat government bailouts. So maybe we're not that different after all.

The biggest problem is that China's demographic trends have peaked, so now it will be the first emerging country to feel the effects of an aging populace and a declining workforce. It has already slowed since 2011 and will slow much faster from 2025 forward.

And China's top-down communist government has no accountability. It's been pushing urbanization at the fastest and most intensive growth rates in history. The U.S. was an emerging country in the 1800s and early 1900s, but even then we only grew at real GDP rates of 5% to 6% compared to 8% to 12% in China during the last few decades.

In fact, there are many parallels between the rise of the U.S. from the early 1900s forward to China in the last few decades. But there are also some stark differences.

China: The U.S. of the 21st Century

In the early 1900s, the U.S. was a rising emerging country, mostly thanks to innovation and a massive influx of immigrants. It dominated many radical inventions from electricity to phones to phonographs to the Model T. Henry Ford's assembly line (one of the greatest developments of the last century) catapulted the everyday person into the new middle class during the decades to follow.

When Europe's industries switched over to wartime production at the start of World War I, the U.S. became the prime supplier of industrial and agricultural goods. That was the "tipping point" for the U.S. We started running massive trade surpluses until the war ended and Europe's agricultural and industrial capacities came back online. That caused an oversupply condition, which led to a global economic collapse and mini depression from 1920 into 1921. Yes, building stuff for no one does have consequences! But most economists don't talk about it.

Fueled by the falling prices and interest rates of a debt bubble, as well as the emergence of powerful new technologies (e.g., cars, electricity, phones and radios), the U.S. accelerated faster than ever during the Roaring '20s, even though European industrial and agricultural capacity came back on line to compete. So, we all over-expanded with rising low cost debt in the Roaring '20s. This was the epitome of the economic fall season bubble boom in the last long-term economic cycle, similar to the one we saw from 1983 to 2007.

But such fall season bubbles always end up having to endure a brutal economic winter season of deflation and deleveraging of the excesses of debt, overexpansion and cronyism. This is a very good thing in the long-term, but it's painful in the short-term.

We get addicted to the technologies, processes and lifestyles of the past, and we don't want to give them up if we don't have to. The winter season, deflationary cycle forces us to give up the past. It forces us to face and accept the new reality at all levels: consumer, business and government. When something begins to look like garbage, you're finally willing to throw it away!

From the 1870s, when we surpassed Great Britain in innovation, the U.S. was the up-and-coming emerging country. Our population was only about 50% urban in 1929, at the top of that great boom and debt bubble. We had trade surpluses and budget surpluses. Just like Japan in 1989 and China today, but not quite as extreme.

But as the fastest-growth emerging country, we took the biggest fall when everything crashed after 1929.

As by now I hope you know, this has happened consistently throughout history. The greater the bubble, the greater the burst.

China has been the largest and fastest-growing emerging country since 1980. It's now the largest manufacturer and exporter in the world, given its huge trade surpluses. It's also the second largest economy in the world, albeit with 4.4 times the U.S. population. But its purchasing power (GDP per capita) is only about 20% of the U.S. and its actual U.S. dollar GDP per capita is only $5,000, barely 10% of the U.S. That's why its overall GDP is just over half of ours.

And it has the greatest bubbles today in GDP growth, stocks and real estate.

In fact, China has significantly more debt than the U.S. did at its 1929 bubble peak and its GDP-per-capita rate is not advancing enough to suggest it will become a developed country like the U.S. did from the 1920s into the 1960s.

Besides, it still doesn't have a democratic government or a free-market system necessary to achieve such developed-country status.

Most important, the U.S. had the strong tailwinds of heavy immigration and the baby boom driving it for decades. China has virtually no immigration and its birth rates have been falling for 50 years.

How Soon and by How Much?

The Chinese real estate bubble has gotten so extreme that even the government tried to cool it off by requiring very high down payments on second homes and implementing a new capital gains tax of 20%, among other things. So, rich people began to flee. They see the bubble, so they're getting out of dodge as fast as they can.

The question at this point is: how soon could this bubble burst and by how much?

To find the answer, you must understand the workings of China's communist/capitalist system…

The Chinese central government wants to grow rapidly. It funnels money to local communist governments to achieve this goal. It also stands behind local government and corporate debt so they can borrow much more and at lower costs to fund infrastructure projects in their respective areas. Those local governments naturally have a group of crony businesses and developers that they favor.

The Chinese government also holds down interest rates paid on bank and savings deposits to support the banks and encourage lending and building. But this has caused a shadow banking system to grow on the private side, much like the one that helped create the subprime lending crisis in the U.S.

Wealth management firms take money from investors and put it into funds that lend against real estate and infrastructure projects at higher yields than investors can get in banks.

Just look at how China's shadow banking sector has accelerated:

Figure 18-4: Shadow Financing in China

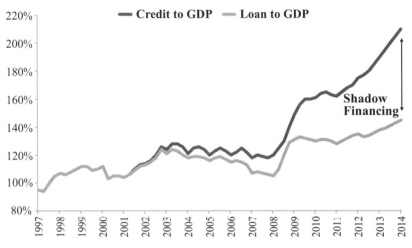

Source: Credit Suisse, The Brookings Institution

Since 2007, traditional bank lending in China declined as a percent of GDP and has barely grown since 2012. But since that time, shadow bank lending has skyrocketed, advancing to 60% of GDP in just two years.

Total bank and shadow bank lending is at 180% of GDP and rising rapidly. This is extremely high for an emerging country. In fact, it's higher than in most developed countries that have higher incomes and better credit.

I estimate China's total debt at a minimum of 295% of GDP and rising. You can see the breakdown in Figure 18-5.

This compares to Brazil, which has a debt-to-GDP ratio of 152%, India at 130% and Russia at 78%.

Emerging-country households, companies and financial institutions are not as credit worthy as developed countries, so any total debt ratios above 150% should be considered extremely dangerous.

China's numbers are off the charts for an emerging country and again shows how much more active China's government is in driving its economic growth through overbuilding. See for yourself:

Figure 18-5: China, Total Debt as % of GDP by Sector

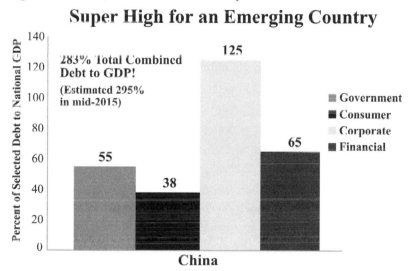

Source: "Debt and (Not Much) Deleveraging," McKinsey Global Institute, February 2015

The rise in shadow banking debt means that the Chinese government is losing control. It can regulate down payments and such, but if the lending is coming from this shadow banking system, the Chinese will continue to invest and speculate.

The local governments thrive on these endless building projects, as do their business cronies. And Chinese investors just love real estate; they have only minimal investments in stocks and bonds.

This has led to overbuilding in housing.

Figure 18-6 shows the number of housing units built in China since 2000 versus the number of new household formations.

Figure 18-6: Housing Units vs. Household Formation

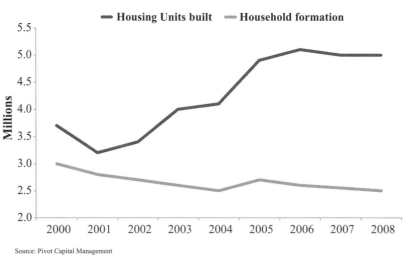

Building Houses for Nobody

Source: Pivot Capital Management

China has been overbuilding for more than a decade! Between 2005 and 2007, it basically built twice as many homes as it needed. That's about 2.2 million extra homes per year

The China Household Finance Survey published in 2013 showed 19 million housing starts in China versus average annual incremental demand of just 5.8 million in the first half of 2012. That's 3.3 times overbuilding.

It also showed that 53% of home purchases were for investments. In a country where home ownership is nearly 90% (the highest level in the world), who's left to fill the massive void of vacancies, particularly when most Chinese investors prefer not to rent their properties so they can keep them pristine and attractive for sale or use down the road? They're waiting for a big payoff that just isn't coming.

This next Figure, 18-7, shows the breakdown of China's world-leading home ownership level.

It's 92.6% in rural areas, where housing is much cheaper and likely self-built.

It's 85.4% in more expensive urban areas, and 89.7% overall.

This compares to 65% and falling in the U.S. and 60% in Japan.

Figure 18-7: Home Ownership Rates in China

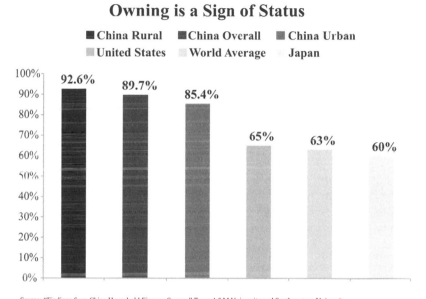

Source: "Findings from China Household Finance Survey," Texas A&M University and Southwestern University of Finance and Economics, Li Gan

This can only happen in a country with the highest valuations-to-income in the world because the Chinese save massively and are willing to live in very small spaces.

Home ownership is also an extremely important part of Chinese culture. In most cases, a man in China has no chance of getting a date or getting married if he doesn't own at least a condo or apartment.

There's Nowhere Else to Put Their Money

China's savings rates are beyond anything we could believe here in the U.S.

The average Chinese household saves 30% of its income. I know of very few U.S. families that can save that much!

China's rich save even more: 69% of income for the top 5% and 66.5% for the top 10%, who control 74.9% of the total savings in the country.

So the Chinese clearly have no problem making down payments and only 18% have mortgages at all. And given that banks pay nothing on deposits thanks to government policy, and the Chinese shun financial assets like stocks and bonds, there is a massive amount of money available for real estate purchases and speculation!

But these statistics would also suggest that the affluent Chinese own the vast majority of such real estate and Figure 18-8 bears that out.

The top 10% own 84.6% of household assets, which mostly consist of personal real estate. They also own 88.7% of non-financial assets, which include investment real estate and businesses.

Figure 18-8: China Household Assets of the Top 10% by Sector

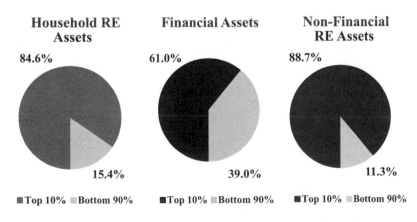

China's Top 10% Heavily Invested in Real Estate

Household RE Assets	Financial Assets	Non-Financial RE Assets
84.6%	61.0%	88.7%
15.4%	39.0%	11.3%
■Top 10% ▪Bottom 90%	■Top 10% ▪Bottom 90%	■Top 10% ▪Bottom 90%

Source: "Findings from China Household Finance Survey," Texas A&M University and Southwestern University of Finance and Economics, Li Gan

When China's real estate bubble bursts — and mark my words, it will — then it will be the top 10% that bears most of the losses. Their diligent savings will be wiped out.

And when the group that controls 60% of personal income stops spending and speculating in real estate… look out below!

If the top 10% stop speculating in real estate, slow their spending and leave the country, China will collapse like a house of cards! Its economy will reverse like nothing we've ever seen. It will not be a soft landing… it will be like an elephant falling out of the sky!

Although the affluent own 85% or so of this real estate bubble, poorer households also have the largest debt burdens from buying a little of this Chinese dream as well.

This next chart, Figure 18-9, shows the total loan-to-income ratio for the four different quartiles of the Chinese economy.

Figure 18-9: China, Household Loan to Income Ratios by Quartile

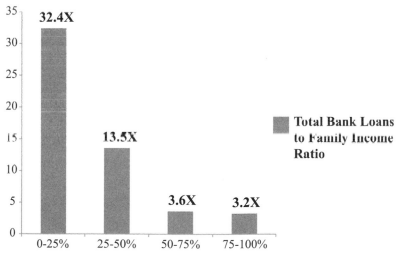

The Less Wealthy Chinese are at Even More Risk

Source: "Findings from China Household Finance Survey," Texas A&M University and Southwestern University of Finance and Economics, Li Gan

So if the economy collapses, the rich will lose massive amounts of wealth and assets, but the bottom half will be destitute!

The bottom 25% of income earners have loan-to-income ratios of 32.4 times. That is off the charts.

The third quartile (25% to 50%) is at 13.5 times. The second (50% to 75%) is at a more normal 3.6 times, and the top 25% is even better, at 3.2 times.

Most of these people don't even own their own land. Some own apartments in shoddy high-rises in the lower-tier cities. A few are renters in the cities. At least the ones still living on farms can support themselves at the most basic level... but the unskilled laborers in the cities have no hope.

The rural migrants can't afford a city apartment with its highest price-to-income levels in the world. They won't be able to have any basic services either... or even food, for that matter.

But that's not the worst of it. There's an even bigger problem brewing...

The Achilles Heel of the "China Miracle"

Today, 760 million people — 56% of the Chinese population — live in cities. Of those people, only 69% are registered urban residents. That leaves 247 million, or 31% of the urban population, as unregistered urban residents with no access to education, health care and any other social benefits.

They are basically "illegal migrants," and just like the "illegal immigrants" in the U.S., they will only stay as long as opportunities exist and an economic boom tolerates them.

Figure 18-10: China, Urban/Rural Population, Registered/Unregistered

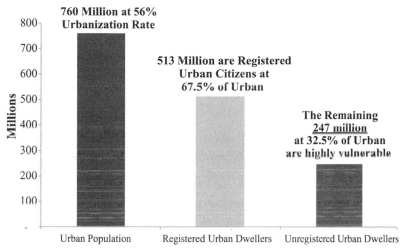

But what happens when the boom turns to bust?

Just as many of our illegal immigrants are returning to Mexico as fast as, if not faster than, new immigrants are entering, the Chinese illegal migrants are already starting to pick up sticks and head back to their family farms, if they haven't been paved over by crony developers.

Already, the outflow is underway...

The 800 Pound Elephant Leaving the Room

A major event has started that few have given the attention it deserves. China's huge migrant population fell for the first time in almost 30 years in 2015. Look at this next chart:

Figure 18-11: China's Working-Age Population and Migrant Workers

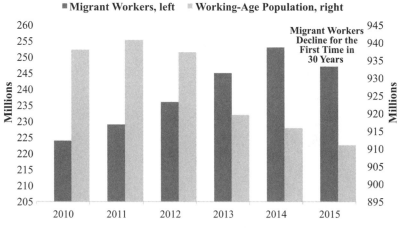

China's Urbana Migrant Workers
Start to Go Back Home

Source: China National Bureau of Statistics

The number of migrant workers dropped 5.68 million to 247 million in 2015. This follows growth rates falling two million a year since an annual peak of 12 million in 2010. So it's gone from 12 million-a-year growth to a *decline* of nearly six million in just five years...

And workforce growth (16 to 64-year olds) has been declining since 2011. It fell 4.87 million in 2015 alone and a total of 30 million since 2011 (it will decline much faster after 2025).

This brings us back to a crucial question: who is going to buy all of those empty condos or use all of the excess infrastructure and industrial capacity the Chinese government is so hell-bent on building when urban migration, the very engine of Chinese growth, has come to a halt and is even reversing?

Certainly not those migrant workers. They're moving back to the rice paddies and for obvious reasons: sky-high real estate, massive traffic and smog, slowing jobs and wages.

They're unregistered in the cities where they work, so they don't have access to education, health care or minor welfare benefits. They go back to their rural areas to visit parents (who are maybe taking care of the grandchildren due to lack of access to education and higher costs of living in the city). The contrast of cleaner air, safer food, natural beauty and higher wages in these rural areas causes some to simply decide not to go back to the hellish realm they worked in.

I have warned for many years that the greatest disaster in the world is these 247 million unregistered citizens trapped in cities when the overbuilding and work disappear. What are these people going to do? They can't *all* go back to their farms as many are paved over with empty condos!

There's One Morc Thing

China has accomplished its unprecedented over-building and urbanization by accumulating massive debt. Its total debt has grown 16.4 times since 2000 — from $2.1 trillion to $34.5 trillion estimated at the end of 2016.

The Red Dragon has been the greatest creator of money, with debt growing 4.8 times since 2009. That dwarfs all of the QE of the developed countries. It's on track to add a trillion dollars in 2016 alone, or 36% of GDP, bringing its debt-to-GDP ratio to near 300%.

As I said earlier, its total debt has grown 2.4 times GDP for 16 years (during the U.S. debt bubble our debt-to-GDP grew at 2.5 times but with far more credit quality and capacity in the private sectors). The greatest portion of this is attributed to corporations that are using government-backed loans to overbuild everything.

Corporate debt expanded from 72% to 125% of GDP just from 2007 to 2014. I expect much of that debt to go bad because it has largely gone into empty buildings and unprofitable state-owned enterprises with massive overcapacity.

Financial sector debt has grown from 24% to 65% in the same seven-year time period.

Take a look at this next chart. But I warn you, it's not for the faint of heart...

Figure 18-12: China's Debt by Sector as a Percent of GDP

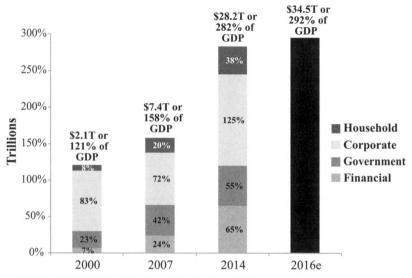

China's Debt Has Exploded 16.4 Times Since 2000

Source: "Debt and (Not Much) Deleveraging," McKinsey Global Institute, February 2015, Dent Research

How is this massive debt sustainable when so much of it went into creating empty capacity? And China has created government-backed debt and bonds for local building projects at the highest rate ever in the first quarter of 2016. Again, they are on pace to add another $4 trillion-plus this year!

This is absolutely insane and simply not sustainable.

China is careening headlong into a disaster of epic proportions... and the world seems to be cheering it on.

The country has created an insane infrastructure bubble.

It has the most overvalued real estate in the world, driven by the highest savings rates anywhere and the people's love of property ownership.

It also has the highest vacancy rates in cities, at 24% and rising.

What happens when tens or even hundreds of millions flee back to rural areas where they are registered and can survive on the land?

When China's real estate bubble bursts — and again, it will burst — wealth will evaporate faster than rain in the sun. And when its unprecedented real estate bubble bursts, the wealth of its citizens will evaporate as will their worldwide buying spree, just as occurred for the Japanese in the early 1990s forward. This will send a tsunami of real estate declines around the world.

There's no doubt in my mind that the Middle Kingdom is going to see the greatest debt crisis and bubble burst of any major country in modern history. It has NO chance of seeing a soft landing, but instead will fall over like an elephant.

It may be the last to fall thanks to such strong, top-down government control and lack of accountability, but it *WILL* fall.

Don't look to China as the model for capitalism. Instead, look to it as the prime example of why top-down government planning and endless stimulus only kills the golden goose of free-market capitalism, especially in an information revolution that makes bottom-up management and change much easier.

Steer clear.

The dragon is about to implode and it's going to take the rest of us down with it.

Before we move on to look at why and when the global debt and financial asset bubble will burst, and finally how to take advantage of the sales of a lifetime you'll shortly be handed, I do want to say one last thing about China.

While the Red Dragon's rapid urbanization has created an unimaginably ugly and dangerous monster of a bubble, it has taken many people out of poverty and raised the average standard of living from $2,000 per capita decades ago to $12,000 per capita (adjusted for purchasing power). Many people in China's cities today have incomes between $5,000 and $20,000.

My concern is that China is pushing this urbanization model at such a rapid rate that it will inevitably backfire. They are creating a massive underclass (247 million and now declining), while fostering a completely unaccountable upper class of party politicians and crony businessmen.

This is a disaster waiting to happen... and by the time China works off its incredible excesses at all levels, their demographic trends will become more like Japans from 2025 forward.

Farewell China, hello India!

CHAPTER 19

Why and When the Global Debt and Financial Asset Bubble Will Burst

THE MARKETS WERE SPOOKED downward into February 11, 2016 — losing more than 6% in less than two weeks mostly thanks to mounting global fears about banks.

The flagship German Deutsche Bank, with its ever-increasing non-performing loans, and Italian banks even worse, dominated the headlines.

Vying for attention was Japan's move to negative interest rates and the surprise pop in the yen, which just hurt their exporters and stock market more.

Seriously, when will these douchebags get it? If you keep doing desperate things, how can you have any credibility?

Off-the-charts stimulus has done *nothing* to revive Japan's coma economy, except in brief spurts. It's done little for our near-recessionary economy either! Things are getting out of control, as they inevitably do when you keep a "something for nothing" bubble going on pure stimulus.

Then Kyle Bass told CNBC viewers that China's bad-debt crisis is five times worse than the subprime loan crisis and will require the printing of $5 trillion to $10 trillion just to recapitalize the banks. This will result in a 15% to 30% devaluation of the yuan that would send shockwaves around the world. Commodity exporters (who are ailing) and global banks that lent money to Chinese companies are staring catastrophe in the eye.

Finally, someone talking some sense!

Only, then markets began to rally… when Mario Draghi, Japan, and other governments pledged more stimulus, and Janet Yellen says the Fed will at least look at negative interest rates — the markets are happy. Any crack addict gets happy when he's promised more crack!

That changes nothing! Central banks are losing control over their economies and we're seeing more evidence of this every day. They created a monster with their endless stimulus and free money. Now their monster is breaking free and will wreak havoc.

So, in this chapter, I'll give you details about the most distressed major global banks, the growing debt and banking crisis in Italy, and the dirty China bomb that's exploding… all to show you that, despite central bank arrogance and blindness, the greatest debt and financial asset bubble has begun to burst… and things are only going to get worse until this detox is over.

The Next Lehman Brothers

You know the reputation that Germany, Switzerland and Austria had for sound banking?

Well, they've turned that on its head.

Now they have the dishonor of leading the great global debt bubble as it bursts. Banking and investment banking in those countries have gone nuts. They've become speculators, not bankers or business builders.

Most people think that major U.S. banks, like JPMorgan at $51.9 trillion, have the highest exposure to the more than $550 trillion derivative market (that's not a typo!). They're wrong. That title goes to Deutsche Bank. At the time of writing, it had $54.7 trillion in total derivative exposure.

That's 20 times Germany's GDP, for crying out loud. This compares to $51.2 trillion at Citi, $43.6 trillion at Goldman Sachs and $27.8 trillion at Bank of America. And you thought German banks were more prudent. Ha!

Do you want to see a more responsible big bank in the U.S.? Wells Fargo only has $6.1 trillion derivatives exposure and that's why its stock valuations have been the highest, as I'll show you in a minute.

When global derivatives peaked at $700 trillion in 2012, they were 10 times global GDP! In response to this little detail, the slick gunslingers on Wall Street said: "Oh! That's nothing to worry about. Those derivatives are mostly insurance for lenders and bond buyers, courtesy of financial institution speculators — and the longs balance out the shorts." Oh, sorry, that was the Mad Hatter (Johnny Depp) in Alice in Wonderland who said that. Wait. No, it wasn't the Mad Hatter, but it sure sounds like something he'd say!

My response: what absolute B.S.! It's totally delusional.

The problem is that these highly leveraged financial securities are used as insurance but they have zero collateral behind them. So they're nothing like regulated insurance policies in the real world. When a speculator who has vowed to insure suddenly can't pay — because they're losing money in high-leveraged speculation — then what?

Then the total liability lands on the table and there's no balancing out... just like Lehman Brothers and AIG in 2008.

Credit default swaps were just another magic trick on Wall Street to create the appearance of greater risk management in an increasingly levered world. They bundled all types of questionable loans into "diversified packages" and insured them with B.S. credit default swaps. And rating agencies often looked the other way, even AAA rated this crap because they had to kiss the ass of their best customers on Wall Street.

If you haven't seen The Big Short movie yet, do yourself a favor and see it. Just remember when you're watching it: the reality was far, FAR worse than what the movie portrays.

All this make-believe financial chicanery went south in 2008, bringing the entire system to its knees... very nearly breaking it entirely. And now it's all starting to happen again. So much for learning from past mistakes!

In October 2015, Deutsche Bank posted its highest quarterly loss ever — $7 billion — from bad loans and investments, many of them highly leveraged, and there's much more to come when the global and European economy gets much worse ahead.

Of course, it doesn't stop there.

There's More Than One Bomb Exploding

Part of the recapitalization after the great recession from 2008 forward was to issue additional equity. But that's really expensive and dilutes shareholder stake… a double whammy after already losing more than 80% when the stock crashed. So the next best thing is to issue senior debt, but that also comes ahead of shareholders and hurts them and the other senior bondholders. That was a no go.

The easiest way to raise capital was to issue CoCo bonds, or a new second level of senior-level debt!

Ingenious.

Let's keep the bubble going!

102 billion euros (the equivalent of $113 billion) of these bonds have been issued since 2013.

I call them Coo-Coo bonds.

But listen to this one…

Deutsche Bank, for example, issues (present tense because it still did this at the time of writing) 6% high-yield bonds that are somewhat senior. But they're callable (if things improve they avert such high interest) and convertible into stock (if things go bad and the bank can't pay the interest).

Here's the clever part: not paying the interest isn't considered a default and they don't have to later pay back any interest payment they miss. They only pay interest if they have sufficient cash flow.

Is this what we have to do to get a decent yield in the zero interest rate economy? Far too many investors think so. Unfortunately, these bonds turned out to be much riskier than desperate investors thought. They, like everyone, are being forced to chase higher yields to meet retirement income, pension targets, and so on.

But banks don't care!

These bonds are structured totally in the bank's favor, not the investors'. When things go bad, the bank gets out of paying interest and the investors gets stuck holding a dud stock that will go down faster than the defaulting bonds.

These bonds have not defaulted yet, but their price has already gone down over 30% with yields spiking from 6% to 12% in anticipation just recently.

Here are two charts that tell the story of Deutsche Bank, the 2015 poster child for the new banking crisis…

The first shows Deutsche Bank's stock price:

Figure 19-1: Deutsche Bank Stock Price

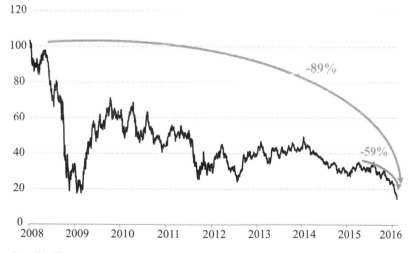

**Deutsche Bank Stock Crashes,
After Record Loan Failures**

Source: Yahoo! Finance

With that 2015 $7 billion loss — higher than any time in the great recession — and questions over the ability to pay their CoCo bonds' interest, Deutsche Bank's stock crashed.

As of February 11, 2016, it was down 89% from its early 2008 peak. It was down 59% from its 2015 high.

A major bank in Germany, Commerzbank, is down a whopping 97% since 2008 and 44% since 2015.

The second chart shows how yields on Deutsche Bank's CoCo Bonds have doubled since they were issued:

Figure 19-2: Deutsche Bank CoCo Bond Yields and 5-Year CDS Spread

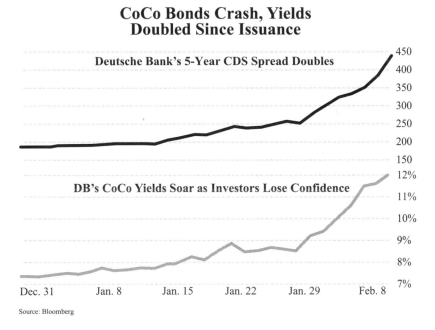

CoCo Bonds Crash, Yields Doubled Since Issuance

Source: Bloomberg

From January 1 to May 2016, the five-year CDS (credit default swap) spread in rates to insure (or look like insurance) its Coco bonds more than doubled from 1.87% to 4.38%. Most of that change happened after January 28.

The yields on those 6% bonds had risen moderately since 2013 up to 8% at the beginning of this year, but then suddenly spiked up to 12% into February 11.

Even everyday investors were fooled into buying these risky bonds. After all, the largest bank in Germany couldn't possibly go under, right? The German government would never allow it. Would they?

What a mess.

Deutsche Bank will sell off assets and employ other strategies to live as long as it can… and the German government will no doubt support the bank every way it can, but Deutsche Bank was dead as I was writing this book. It's just that no one had announced the funeral yet!

Since its crash, it's rumored that Deutsche Bank may buy back up to $3.34 billion in senior bonds above the CoCos. That would reduce their leverage and be a show of strength. Just a show. It will change nothing.

And Deutsche Bank has substantial exposure to the fracking industry in the U.S. and to Chinese companies. Both terrible, terrible places to be involved in right now!

The bank's CEO has strongly stated that the institution is totally sound. Yeah right! They all say that before the final curtain.

The truth is that such a move would deplete the very cash they need to pay those CoCo bonds and absorb increasing losses if the world economy gets worse   and it will get worse!

Allow me the liberty of tweaking this classic quote: the road to hell is paved with… greed and fraud.

Brothers in Arms

After Deutsche Bank, look at the exposure of the top 10 U.S. banks to this massive $550 trillion derivatives market in Figure 19-3. Total exposure to U.S. banks alone is $168 trillion!

Figure 19-3: Major Bank Derivative Holdings

The 10 U.S. Banks Most Exposed to Derivatives

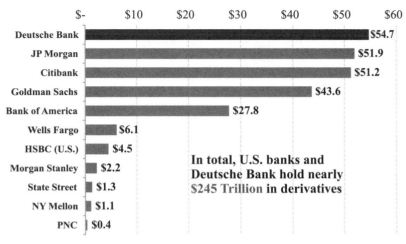

	$-	$10	$20	$30	$40	$50	$60
Deutsche Bank							$54.7
JP Morgan							$51.9
Citibank							$51.2
Goldman Sachs						$43.6	
Bank of America				$27.8			
Wells Fargo	$6.1						
HSBC (U.S.)	$4.5						
Morgan Stanley	$2.2						
State Street	$1.3						
NY Mellon	$1.1						
PNC	$0.4						

In total, U.S. banks and Deutsche Bank hold nearly $245 Trillion in derivatives

Source: Office of the Comptroller of the Currency, Quarterly Report on Bank Trading and Derivatives Activities

Clearly the problem doesn't stop with Deutsche Bank. They're not even the worst news.

Just look at how badly many western bank stocks have been hit. Figure 19-3 measures their current share value versus their book value or net worth at cost. Normally stocks trade well above book value (the higher the number the better), often many times more in a bubble like this one.

And here's more proof of the crisis unfolding:

Figure 19-4: Global Bank Stock Price to Book Value

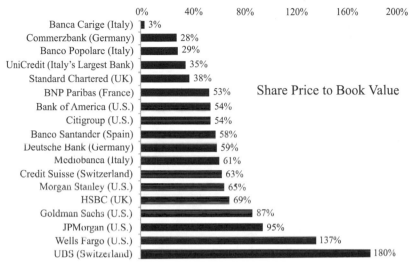

**Many Global Bank Stocks
Have Been Crushed Already**

Source: Bloomberg, Yahoo! Finance

Major banks normally trade at multiples of their book value, but now most are at fractions. This picture is ugly and it's only the beginning of the next, even greater financial crisis and deflationary deleveraging.

As you can see in Figure 19-4, Deutsche comes in at 59%. UBS in Switzerland is the prettiest ugly sister at this party at 180%, while Italy's Banca Carige is at a shocking 3% share value to book value. Clearly Europe is leading this banking crisis.

To get a better view of this, consider the stock prices since 2008 of four major banks in Europe and one in the U.S.

UniCredit, the largest bank in Italy, is the worst in this large-bank group. It's down 91% from its 2008 high and 58% from its 2015 high, as you can see in the next chart:

Figure 19-5: UniCredit Stock Price

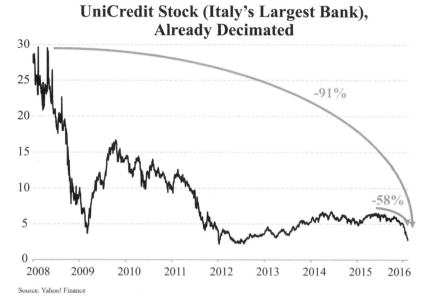

UniCredit Stock (Italy's Largest Bank),
Already Decimated

Source: Yahoo! Finance

Banco Santander of Spain has fallen 83% since 2008 and 57% since 2015.

Credit Suisse has seen a 79% and 58% plunge, respectively.

HSBC in the UK has fared the best, down only 66% since 2008 and 40% since 2015... but the UK has the highest global bank debt exposure, so don't take this as good news.

Even though U.S. banks have had a better recovery and easier and faster recapitalization, Citi has never really recovered from the massive crash in 2008. It's still down 88% from that top and 43% down since its recent high in 2015.

Clearly, the next banking crisis is rearing its ugly head. This time it's starting in Europe, where the next major sovereign default looks likely in Italy... the country considered too big to fail.

Already Bankrupt, Just Too Big to Fail

The other big news in the first quarter of 2016 was that the ECB and IMF finally reached an agreement to sell the worst loans from Italian banks to private investors… but with government guarantees.

Brilliant!

Another financial magic trick and cover-up. How many more rabbits can they pull out of this hat?

Why can't any government do the obvious (and best thing) and force banks to write off or restructure bad loans and have their stock and bondholders take the damn losses? It's just such short-sightedness on their parts and it's making the fallout as this global bubble bursts so much worse than it needed to be!

The response to the bubble burst in 2008 has been more and more free money and stimulus and more and more government guarantees. What government can guarantee everything if things go wrong?

Not a single one.

Bank deposits, mortgages, major corporations and banks, CoCo bonds… where does it end?

Many major government sovereign bonds will eventually come into question. It's inevitable. They have massively unfunded obligations like health care and retirement benefits they can never hope to pay on top of common debt ratios of 100% or higher.

I've been talking about the massive debt and overbuilding bubble in China for years and it finally seems to be bursting, as I explained in Chapter 17. It will be a major trigger for a global debt crisis and deleveraging — worse than 2008-2009. Another trigger is likely to come from Europe, especially from Italy.

Look at Figure 19-6. It shows non-performing loans in the worst demographic and competitive area in Europe: the southern region (with the exception of Ireland).

Figure 19-6: Italy's Bad Loan Problem

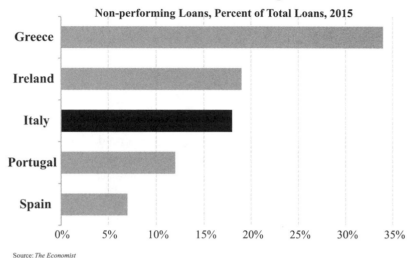

The Next Greece & Too Big to Bail Out

Non-performing Loans, Percent of Total Loans, 2015

No surprise here! Greece is first with 34% non-performing loans. That is beyond bankruptcy, even after many bail-outs.

Ireland is second at 19%.

But now look at Italy. It has grown from 8% in 2010 to 18%, currently. That's well ahead of Portugal and Spain.

When non-performing loans get to 10%, most banks are technically bankrupt because they typically only have around 10% in reserve (all that's required) and/or capital against loans.

On top of that, Italy's labor productivity has fallen from an index of 110 to 96. That's 13% down since 2000.

Its real GDP per capita has gone down 12% since 2004.

Its labor costs have risen modestly, instead of typically falling after a debt crisis and recession.

In short, it's not a good story here! Rising debt and falling income. Italy has been in recession five years out of the last eight and was back there again as I write this, despite Mario Draghi's QE bazooka and guarantees.

The country has the lowest college education levels of the major European nations, high taxes and reams of red tape, and an overwhelming underground economy that's stifling legitimate businesses and government tax revenues.

Many Italians migrate out to get better jobs. Of those who stay, nearly 70% work for firms with less than 50 employees.

Tax evasion is common because the government taxes wages more than it does spending.

Bribes are a necessity to get even the most mundane things done in its bureaucratic government.

Italy is clearly the next domino to fall in the Eurozone and it looks increasingly imminent. I see Italy becoming the next Greece by the end of 2016.

Remember Italy's leading bank, UniCredit, has crashed 91% since 2008 and 58% since 2015. Well, look at the worst leading bank failure there: Banca Carige. Its stock price has lost 99% since 2008 and 82% since 2015. Banco Popolare is down 92% since 2008 and 62% since 2015. Talk about blood in the streets.

Because Italy's government debt never enjoyed relief from bailouts, it keeps rising. It's currently 139% of GDP. It's the highest of the top four debt-to-GDP ratios in Europe and is only exceeded by Greece. Its private debt is not as extreme as many, so its total debt is 335% of GDP, but that's still high, especially given its recessionary bias in the last eight years and its falling productivity and GDP per capita levels I mentioned earlier.

The solution to these non-performing loans, which total $382 billion, is first to sell them to private investors with government guarantees. This began happening during Q1 2016. But the ECB is also considering allowing such bad loans to be pledged as collateral for loans to Italy… and then Italy simply doesn't pay the loans back, leaving the ECB holding the bag. If this happens, the citizens will be stuck with much of the loans in the end — yet another financial magic trick.

These are just more desperate short-term measures to deflect the debt crisis and to avoid having someone actually take the losses and restructure the debt. Keeping such deadly debt and zombie banks in the system weighs it down and makes a sustainable recovery impossible, something Japan has now proven for more than 26 years. Do you need more evidence than that?

The bottom line: Italy is way too big to fail. But the ECB, the euro and Eurozone simply cannot bail it out. So the Eurozone economy will continue to fail. That's the only scenario I see, especially with demographic trends so weak in the region for years and decades ahead. The ones most in trouble thanks to dismal demographic prospects ahead are Germany, Italy, Greece, Portugal and Austria — in that order. This is not going to end well.

Europe is already on the edge of deflation, much like Japan. Any slowdown and bank failures will create much deeper deflation, stock crashes and higher unemployment in short order. The region is likely to trigger the next larger financial crisis, not the U.S. who triggered the last one… unless China beats it to the punch. If Europe does start to crack apart by late this year, then China will follow and make the global crisis much worse.

As things get worse in Italy, Germany will likely advocate the same approach it did with Cyprus — a "bail-in." This is where larger deposits are converted to stock to cover the bad loans (like the CoCo bonds).

But who wants stock in a dying bank? Seriously!?

Non-performing loans in Cyprus in 2013 got as high as 51% before its bail-in. Today such non-performing loans are still 45.85%, or $30 billion. None were written off and only a minor 19% restructured.

That Cyprus bail-in took 47.5% of deposits — over $111,000 (100,000 euros) — largely hitting corrupt Russian oligarchs and larger small businesses.

Not too long ago I did an interview with Lydia Kyriakidou on Radio Paphos in Cyprus. She stated that most small businesses have never recovered from that debt crisis and bail-in. She knows from first-hand experience. She's a small business owner!

The Eurozone will never have a chance at recovery until it faces the music and restructures debt and that will be painful, period.

And the euro will have to restructure as well. One option would be to create two euro currencies. The first would include the stronger exporters and the second the weaker importers/debtors. That way the stronger currencies could cure the trade imbalances.

The bottom line is that the euro and Eurozone will not survive a debt crisis in Italy; not in its current form, with its current policies.

This will be the end of "endless" QE and guarantees of bad loans. These governments and countries just have to man-up, write down the damn debt and be done with it!

The bottom line is: European banks, which were slower to recapitalize in a much weaker economic recovery, are as likely to trigger the next global debt crisis as China. The frackers and energy companies will contribute as well, and remember: many large European banks are more exposed to that than most would assume.

Italy is where the banks and economy are weakest, so they're the next country to collapse. But it's too big to fail, so the Eurozone countries and the ECB will ultimately have to make investors and large depositors take the hit rather than their own citizens. The euro and Eurozone will change and restructure dramatically.

And all of this will set in motion the largest debt and financial asset bubble burst of them all: China. When the Red Dragon goes down and has to face its massive overcapacity and debt, we will fully see the next great depression and it will be ugly!

A note to readers in Australia and East Asia: Beware. You will feel this tsunami far more than we will in the U.S.

CHAPTER 20

Timing and the Finer Details

BEFORE WE MOVE ON to look at the opportunities ahead, let's get technical.

Figure 20-1 is the best chart for characterizing what is happening in the stock markets as this third and final bubble is peaking. I call it the Dow Megaphone pattern, and I've been monitoring it for years now.

It's possibly the most obvious pattern I've ever seen, yet no one is talking about it except the Australian Robert McHugh and thestreet.com.

There was a similar pattern for the S&P 500 when the Bob Hope generation was enjoying its peak spending phase (the tops were in 1965, 1968 and 1972). Each rally took the markets to new highs and each crash saw lower lows until the pattern ended with the nasty 1973/74 crash.

Well, in the Dow pattern today, it looks like we're finally peaking:

Figure 20-1: Dow Megaphone Pattern

Source: Yahoo! Finance

The Dow has made a slight "throw-over" above the top trend line between late 2014 and mid 2016. This is typical for the last "E" wave in the Elliott Wave Cycle.

This means the next crash should go to lower lows and be the worst, which, by my calculations, takes us to between 5,500 and 6,000 around late 2017 or so.

It's this pattern that has me convinced that 2016 and 2017 could be the worst years for the stock market has seen since 1930-1931, when investors endured the strongest crash of the great depression!

The three years it took the market collapse to play out back then saw an overall decline of 89%.

55% of that loss was endured during 1931. I see 2017 as being similar, with the second half of 2016 likely being the appetizer.

The length of the coming crash is likely to be somewhere between the 17 months it took the 2008/early 2009 crash to occur and the two years and seven months it took stocks to bottom during the tech wreck between early 2000 and late 2002.

So my best estimates are that the next and largest crash will bottom around December 2017. But if the markets correct and then hold up into late 2016, then the next crash will likely be longer and last into late 2019/early 2010.

Seeing the Signs

Each bubble has ended once the sharp bottom trend line is broken. The first sign that this final bubble was peaking came when stocks broke below the bottom trend line of the rally since early 2009 in August of 2015.

Figure 20-2 shows the break of the S&P 500 Channel:

Figure 20-2: S&P 500

S&P 500 Channel's Big Break in August 2015

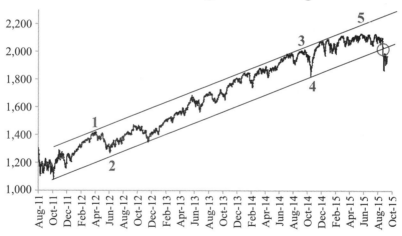

Source: Yahoo! Finance

Stocks were going up in a steep slope and within a narrow 10% range from late 2011 into 2015. But the momentum started to slow after late 2014 and stocks finally broke below the bottom trend line in the August 2015 mini-crash. That's when I told my newsletter subscribers that this great bubble was very likely over. And since we recently only got very slight new highs in the S&P 500 and Dow, with other U.S. and global indices failing to make new highs, I still believe this to be the case.

I call this a rounded top pattern, as I show in Figure 20-3:

Figure 20-3: S&P 500 Rounded Top

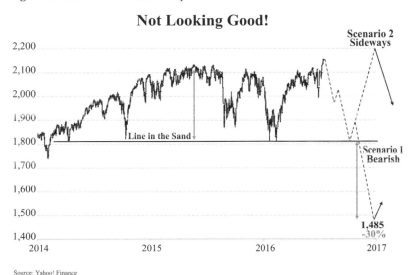

Source: Yahoo! Finance

As you can see, our stimulus-addicted market has been trying to do the same old thing it's done for the last seven years and rally to new highs under the assumption that central banks won't let the economy or the markets fail past a certain point (besides that, there's has been no other place for investors to go if they wanted any kind of decent growth).

But its efforts have been less fruitful of late. Stocks have gone nowhere since late 2014!

In this pattern, the first top was on May 18, 2015 at 2,134 on the S&P. The second top went only 1.9% higher to 2,176 on July 20, 2016. Stocks are very overbought and due for a substantial correction in the months ahead.

The S&P 500, since 2014, has formed a rounded top pattern, with many tests of the 1,810-1,820 level that have created major support in that area. Stocks have traded in a narrow range of around 325 points since 2014. So in the next crash, this will be the line in the sand. If the S&P 500 can break convincingly below 1,800, then this pattern projects another 325 points down to around 1,485 in a short period of time.

That would be just over 30% down from the July 2016 top and would be the final confirmation that this last and most extreme bubble is over and done! But recall that the next major target is around 5,500 in late 2017 and the ultimate target is 3,800 or a bit lower between early 2020 and late 2022.

Divergences Abound

Besides the two converging patterns I've just shown you, there are several contributing factors that convince me still further of the inevitable crash we'll see.

One is that smart money has begun running for the exits. This is a classic indicator that warns of trouble ahead. And it is visible through the divergence between large-cap and smaller-cap stocks.

When the dumb money piles in at the end, they buy household names like Apple or Coca-Cola. The smart money focuses more on smaller cap stocks as there is much more opportunity for finding undervalued stocks if you have the sophistication. That's why large cap stocks out-perform small cap stocks in the final stages of a long bull market.

Look at the next chart. It shows the typical stock (small cap) in the unweighted Value Line Geometric Index versus the S&P 500 large caps.

Figure 20-4: Small Cap Value Line Geometric Index vs. S&P 500

Everyday Stocks Underperforming: A Major Divergence

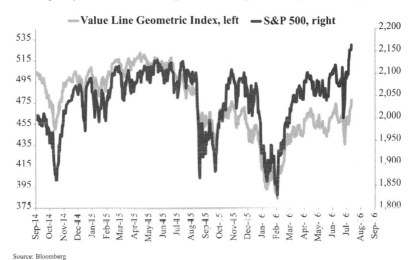

— Value Line Geometric Index, left   — S&P 500, right

Source: Bloomberg

Outlook as This Book Goes to Press

The markets are at a critical point in mid-July 2016. Despite the S&P 500 making very slight new highs, the Nasdaq is still 3% below its all-time high, the Russell 2000 is 8% below, and the Dow Transportation index is 13% below. Most major global markets are at least 10% to 20% from their 2015 highs (China is 41%).

As I pointed out in Figure 20-3, there are two likely scenarios, and the coming month should make those two scenarios more clear. U.S. stocks are very overbought as of mid-July and are due for a substantial correction. If that correction holds above the critical early 2014 support level of 1,810-1,820 on the S&P 500 during the typically weak period of September/early October, then the markets are likely to make one more run at new highs.

The more likely scenario would be that stocks break decisively below 1,800 on the S&P 500, then quickly collapse down to around 1,485 or so. Such a more decisive bearish move would likely occur by the end of 2016. That would make the S&P 500 down just over 30% and mark a clear end to the third great stock bubble since 1995.

I would see an even deeper crash into late 2017 in this scenario and the target would be around 5,500 on the Dow (a 70% crash from the top in July 2016). After a bounce into 2018, I would expect a final less severe crash that takes the Dow back to 3,800 or lower and the S&P 500 down to 430 or lower — an 80% crash.

If instead the markets do make one more run at new highs, then the crash scenario would be more brutal and most likely see a near three-year collapse down to my ultimate targets of 430 on the S&P 500 and 3,800 on the Dow (or lower). Such a bottom would most likely come in late 2019 or early 2020, when three out of my four key long-term cycles start to turn up again.

PART V

How to Get Rich
During the Aftershock

CHAPTER 21

Profiting from the Sale of a Lifetime: Investments

PROFITING FROM THE SALE of a lifetime we'll see ahead is as much about protecting yourself as it is about being ready to grab the opportunities that will present themselves.

So let's get the first part out of the way...

One of the things I hear most when talking with investors is this:

"I have a lot of dividend-paying stocks in non-cyclical industries that are globally diversified, so I should be OK in the downturn you're forecasting..."

Actually, no! You won't be.

The assumption behind this position is that many large multi-national companies are diversified, often in emerging countries that don't have downward pointing demographic trends. Many are in industries like food or toiletries, which aren't cyclical and are considered essential. And many pay dividends of typically 2% to 3%, bringing in some income to offset potential losses.

Here's the big problem with that view...

Between mid-2016 and late 2017, stocks are likely to see the biggest crash since late 1929 — certainly the biggest crash you'll ever see in your lifetime. Markets could lose as much as 65% to 75%. And nearly every stock will suffer, regardless of how diversified they are or whether they're in a cyclical industry or not as they did in the 1930s. Why? Because valuations or price-to-earnings (P/E) ratios decline across the board as the perception of risk escalates.

And any dividends they pay won't come close to offsetting the losses that will accrue during the first two years of the crash. Besides, during bad times, dividend-paying companies often cut their payouts to shareholders.

There's another big problem…

During the early stages of the crash, there are very few places to go if you want to put your money to work for you, unless you're prepared to short-sell stocks, and I don't recommend you do that unless you're following a proven system, like John Del Vecchio's *Forensic Investor*.

But there are places, so let's take a look at those now.

Rely on a Government Guarantee

High-quality, long-term government bonds (U.S. Treasurys) are a good place to start.

Figure 20-1 shows how they compared to stocks during the last economic winter season, including dividend and bond yields, which is called total returns.

Figure 21-1: Total Return on U.S. Stocks and Bonds

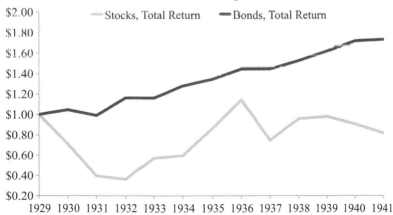

Bonds Did Much Better Than Stocks in the Great Depression

Source: JeremySiegel.com

(Note that this chart just takes average annual data and doesn't capture the exact peaks and troughs.)

During the Great Depression, bond yields and higher dividends on stocks increased the total returns on stocks, even though we saw the greatest crash in U.S. history. But, as you can see, stocks still got smashed. Sure, with adjustments for dividends, they got back to their highs in March of 1937, just seven and a half years after the peak in September 1929, but 12 years after that peak, stocks were still down 20%, even when adjusted for dividends.

(It's during those 12 years that investors saw the 20th century's sale of a lifetime, especially in late 1932 and early 1942!)

Clearly, holding stocks through an economic winter season like the one from 1929 into 1942, or even through the economic summer downturn of 1969 to 1982, just doesn't make sense.

On the other hand, total gains, with interest payments on high-quality, long-term government bonds, rose by 78% from 1929 to 1941!

Look to Triple-A Quality

The next hiding place is AAA Corporate Bonds.

Look at Figure 21-2. It shows how total returns on long-term government bonds and the highest-quality AAA corporate bonds compared during the last economic winter season.

Figure 21-2: Total Return on Long-Term U.S. Corporate and Government Bonds

Only High-Quality Bonds Gained
Throughout the Great Depression

━ U.S. Long-term Corporate   ━ U.S. Long-term Government

Source: Global Financial Data

Between mid-1931 and late 1931, the highest-quality, long-term government bonds spiked briefly from 3.15% to 4.3%. During that time, your government bonds would have *temporarily* gone down about 10% in value (which is not that bad), but your interest would have remained the same.

At the same time, AAA corporate bonds spiked from 4.4% to 5.45%, going down in value about 15% (and muni bonds jumped from 3.75% to 5.3%, going down more like 25%).

Then, after those minor setbacks into late 1931, all such bonds appreciated strongly as rates fell to the lowest levels of that era, into 1940 and 1941.

Bond values go up when interest rates fall (in this case from deflation in prices), and the longer the term of the bond, the more you gain.

For bondholders in the 1930s and early '40s, deflation became their friend, and the constant interest payments accumulated on top of that. The same will hold true during *this* economic winter season, once we move into a deflationary period from 2016 into 2022 or so.

Total returns, with interest, on government bonds were 78% from 1930 to 1941. Thanks to their higher yields, returns on AAA corporate bonds were even better, at 118% for that same period.

More than doubling your money in safer investments at a time when almost all other financial assets were down... now that's a good deal and a way to grow your cash value to buy real estate and stocks when they are at their lowest ebbs, as these bonds are very liquid when you need the cash.

Of course, this doesn't mean that just any old bond is a good place to hide. It is absolutely not. Nor are some of the more traditional "safe havens" you've no doubt heard of, like gold, silver and commodities. So here are some places, besides stocks and precious metals, to **avoid** during the next great crash...

Stay Away from Junk for Now

Where you *don't* want to go is into high-yield or junk bonds, at least not in the first major crash period into late 2017. The yields on such bonds skyrocket when the economy collapses, despite deflationary trends that follow, because of the sharply rising default risks, especially with riskier companies.

A quick look at BAA bond yields during the 1930s will illustrate my point neatly.

Figure 21-3: Corporate Baa Bond Yields

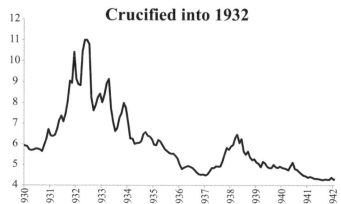

Source: Global Financial Data

(Note: These are not bond prices or total returns, just the annual yield.)

As you can see, yields spiked from 5.7% to 11% from mid-1930 into late 1932, when the economy was at its worst. Those bonds saw a sudden fall in value of near 45%. (Remember, yield up, value down.) Imagine how much lower-rated bonds fell!

Also, while they started down later than stocks, they didn't first bottom until stocks did in July of 1932. Rates ultimately fell to 4.2% by late 1941, due to deflation trends. That's because, when you consider the risk premium, junk bonds act more like the risk assets stocks, real estate and commodities.

Sales of a Lifetime Opportunity Alert

However, once the first major deflation crisis sets in, it can be very profitable to buy higher-risk or junk bonds, as deflation works in your favor and the worst companies default in the first few years and government stimulus programs kick in strongly again. Junk bonds would have been a great buy in late 1932 until 1941; but only then!

I expect that junk bonds could be a good buy around late 2017 and again in early 2020, depending on how this crisis unfolds.

Then there are utility stocks... Avoid them!

Demand May Be Compelling, But Don't Be Fooled

Many people think that they'll be OK in utility stocks like SCANA (South Carolina Electric and Gas) during the great crash ahead because such companies don't see demand go down that much, they pay high dividends, and they benefit from lower interest rates down the road, when we get deflation.

While this argument sounds compelling, don't be fooled.

Look at Figure 21-4. It shows the S&P Utilities from late 1929 into 1941:

Figure 21-4: S&P Utilities

Source: Global Financial Data

Utility stocks fell 89% into early 1935!

In fact, they crashed even before the broader stock market in early 1929, and lost 56% in a matter of months.

Sorry to anyone who hopes to hide in utility stocks! They're not the safe haven you think.

More than a decade ago I looked at a number of 1930s stock sectors to see if utilities, alcohol, casinos, movies, cigarettes… anything… did well during the bad times.

None did.

Not a single one.

The risk premiums on these stocks all went up and the stocks all tanked, losing anything from 50% to 90% or more.

Even the motion pictures sector suffered, falling dramatically. You'd think going to the movies would be a small expense that would hold up or maybe even rise during bad times. If I were suffering through an economic depression, I'd still want to spend a small amount on a movie ticket here and there. But clearly I would have been mostly alone in the theatre. That index dropped a whopping 97% when stocks bottomed in late 1932.

And telephone stocks also suffered. The index was down 76% at worst in late 1931. This brings me to the next "safe haven" to avoid...

Real Estate Won't Offer the Protection You're Hoping For

First let me say that, during the Great Depression, real estate didn't bubble up nearly as much as it did into 2006. There simply wasn't the same space for speculation. Not when the typical household had to put up 50% in down payments and only get a five-year mortgage with a big balloon payment due at the end. Fewer people could afford a home, never mind speculate.

Still, real estate prices dropped 26% into 1933. And just like the 2008 crisis, that really hurts when you have a big mortgage.

It wasn't until 1940 that prices got back to their 1925 peak.

Note that real estate tends to peak several years ahead of stocks as people buy their largest home about five years before their spending peaks.

By early 2006, real estate was central to the U.S. and global bubble, with more speculation and lending being done in real estate than in stocks. So it was no surprise that real estate fell 34% in just the first crash. That's massive for a sector that is less cyclical than stocks and is typically leveraged through mortgages.

During the next great crash, I expect real estate to fall sharply again, taking us down by at least 55% (maybe even 65%) total from the early 2006 top.

Even from the rebound in recent years, real estate would have to fall something like 40% or more from here. Ouch!

The biggest problem is that the richest people are now parking huge piles of money in the highest-priced, most desirable real estate areas like New York, San Francisco, London, Vancouver, Singapore and Sydney. They think the demand in those areas is so high, especially from the most affluent and foreign buyers, and supply so limited, that property in those cities just can't go down. *"They are unique and special places,"* or so the logic goes.

Well, if history means anything, they're wrong!

The greater the bubble, the greater the burst. And there is nowhere in the world where real estate is so unique that prices can only ever go up.

Foreign buyers are usually the first to vanish in bad times, and that's why it will be the most affluent households that see their wealth and incomes vaporized in this next crash.

Just look at home prices in Manhattan during the Great Depression as an example:

Figure 21-5: Manhattan Home Price Index

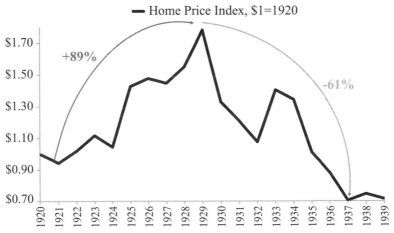

"Manhattan Home Prices Couldn't Crash," They Said...

— Home Price Index, $1=1920

Source: "Real Estate Prices During the Roaring Twenties and the Great Depression," Tom Nicholas and Anna Scherbina

After rising 89% in the boom from 1921 into 1929 (holding up four years longer than average home prices in the U.S.), Manhattan real estate prices collapsed 61% into 1937 (versus 26% for the average home). In 1939, they were still near their lows and didn't recover as fast as most home prices across the country.

New York home prices and rents didn't recover back to their 1929 highs until the late 1950s.

Since then, when home prices averaged $12 per square foot and rents cost $60 a month, prices have risen 100 times. Today, the average price per square foot is more than $1,400, while rents are up 64 times. To rent in New York nowadays costs upward of $3,850 a month.

And people think these prices can't fall! As they say in New York: "Get outta here."

I'll talk more about real estate in the next chapter.

For now, do yourself a favor: don't buy into the myth that you have no choice but to be invested in the stock markets. Those stable multinational, dividend paying stocks or utilities will do little to protect you. Or higher yield bonds.

When this whole bubble finally fails, be sure you're ready with...

✓ Cash, T-bills and high-quality CDs;

✓ High-quality, long-term government bonds (Treasurys); and

✓ AAA corporate bonds.

And be sure to **stay away** from...

✘ Utility stocks;

✘ Junk bonds;

✘ Stocks;

✘ Real estate; and

✘ Gold, silver and commodities.

The Trade of the Decade

Earlier I mentioned that you must stay away from junk bonds until it's time to snap them up after the crash. But I want to delve into bonds a little deeper, because it's in this sector that we find the trade of the decade.

All bonds have been in a bubble thanks to QE, which pushed the risk-free, 10-Year Treasury rate down to zero (adjusted for inflation).

That's about two percentage points lower than the market would have set them.

Said another way: 10-Year Treasurys have been just below 2% when they should be closer to 4%. That should end soon.

Take a look at this 10-Year Treasury Bond Channel in Figure 21-6:

Figure 21-6: T-Bond Channel

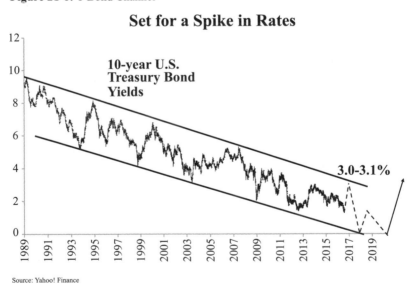

Set for a Spike in Rates

Source: Yahoo! Finance

As you can see, yields have declined steadily since 1989, largely because of the falling inflation trends (which I've been warning about since then). When such yields get near the bottom of this channel, they tend to rise. And when they near the top, they tend to fall. It's been a pretty consistent pattern.

Rates hit the bottom of this channel, at 2%, at the end of 2008.

Back then, we issued an urgent sell signal to our subscribers because rising yields mean falling bond prices. Good thing we did!

Then we saw another decline into late 2012, which finally bottomed at 1.38%.

Since then, they've been rising off and on and just hit a new all-time low at 1.36% in early July 2016. It's likely that the current rise will match what we saw after the Taper Tantrum of 2013, when rates moved off of 1.38% to reach 2.98%. So I think it's very possible that we'll see rates hit the top of this channel in the next several months, touching around 3.0% to 3.1%.

Why would this occur? The Fed and central banks have created this monster through a "something for nothing' highly leveraged trade from its zero short-term rate policies, making speculation and leverage cheap, and by continuing to buy their own sovereign bonds and push yields down and values up. Hedge funds and traders simply lever up and buy futures ahead of them. But in July of 2016 the smart money futures traders (commercials) are record short and the dumb money large specs are net long. That signals a major shift in rates upward over the next several months.

If this occurs, this move will both cause a stronger crash in stocks and real estate and will create the fixed-income trade of the decade I've been forecasting since late 2015!

And the next opportunity lies with the U.S. dollar.

Going from Strong to Stronger

I see the dollar rising strongly at least into mid-2017. Figure 21-7 shows my forecasts for the dollar index compared to a basket of our six major trading partners.

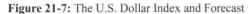

Sales of a Lifetime Opportunity Alert

Watch out for this in the early stages of the crisis. If rates head upward again temporarily into late 2016, back up the truck and load up on 30-Year Treasury bonds and AAA Corporate Bonds. The longer the duration of the bond, the greater the bang you get from deflation and falling risk-free interest rates.

Figure 21-7: The U.S. Dollar Index and Forecast

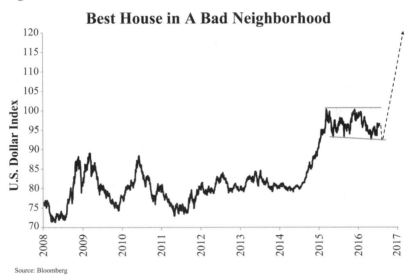

Best House in A Bad Neighborhood

Source: Bloomberg

I've marked the trading range we've been stuck in for a while. As you can see, I expect we'll break through this channel and move strongly upward, likely starting sometime in the second half of 2016.

As I have written about exhaustively, when debts and financial assets around the world deleverage, the dollar strengthens because the greenback is simply the dominant currency and we're the best house in a bad neighborhood, both after tapering in QE and with higher average GDP growth than Europe or Japan.

With more dollars destroyed, and so fewer doing the rounds, their value goes up.

At the time of writing, the greenback was up as high as 41% from the 2008 low. Besides the brief dip during the trade of the decade opportunity, I see nothing to indicate this will change in any way. If the dollar index breaks below the trading range between 92 and 100, then it should be an excellent buy as low as 86. If it holds 92, then it will be a good buy there.

Once we see 120, I will be neutral on the dollar because we'll have rebalanced with other currencies from the massive fall of the dollar between 1985 and early 2008 (which most people are unaware of).

Gold: $700 an Ounce Is Now In Sight

I've been forecasting since 2011 that gold would continue to melt down. It's been one of my forecasts that has possibly gotten the most attention and backlash, particularly from the gold bugs.

One analyst on *Seeking Alpha* is constantly berating me and arguing against my call that gold will melt down to $700 an ounce by mid-2017 or so… and maybe even go lower, reaching as low as $400 before the end of this commodity cycle in the early 2020s ($250 at worst). His comments are pretty insulting, but that's okay, because so far gold has done exactly what I've said it would.

And, as it stands, I'm on my way to winning my bets with Porter Stansberry (for $1) and Jeff Clark (for a Gold Eagle). I'm not going to go into too much detail here because, at the end of 2015, I released my book, *How to Survive (and Thrive) During the Great Gold Bust Ahead*. You can get this book at dentresources.com.

For now, suffice it to say Gold plunged out of a long trading channel in early 2013, falling to $1,180 an ounce from a high of $1,934.

Sale of a Lifetime Opportunity Alert

Bet on the dollar via the **PowerShares DB US Dollar Bullish ETF (NYSEArca: UUP)**.

Until we see the dollar go to 120 on the dollar index, it's open season!

Since September 2011, gold has seen a long decline that hit $1,050 right at the end of 2015.

Like I always say: "Things never go down in a straight line," so I have been forecasting gold to have a strong bear market bounce and it finally started in March 2016. I was expecting as high as $1,400 an ounce, but it now looks like $1,373 may have been it in early July. This is the last chance to sell as I see $700 as soon as mid-2017!

The impact of unprecedented QE wasn't to create inflation, as the gold bugs fretted it would, but to counter deflation and debt deleveraging.

In so doing, it only delayed the crisis.

Delayed... NOT prevented!

As we witness the global financial detox I described earlier, deflation will rear its ugly head again... and gold will fall. That's why I don't expect to see gold bottom until it hits $400 an ounce, likely between early 2020 and late 2022 — and next, the 30-Year Commodity Cycle peak is into 2038-2039... that's when I tell gold bugs we could see their $5,000 target... when they're dead!

Oil: $20 or Lower by Mid- to Late-2017

I've been saying for years that oil would see a major collapse, ultimately to as low as $10 to $20 a barrel. It's interesting that most people ignored this warning while haranguing me about my gold prediction.

Perhaps "oil ducks" aren't as common or vociferous as gold bugs.

Sale of a Lifetime Opportunity Alert

Investors have their last chance to sell gold now that gold got near my $1,400 target in early July 2016. You can also buy put options on gold or buy an inverse fund like DGZ with a first target of around $700 an ounce in gold by mid-2017 or a bit later.

Years ago, many told me such lows weren't possible. "OPEC and many oil exporters wouldn't allow it to happen," they said.

Yet oil prices hit $26 a barrel in February 2016.

And the world keeps pulling oil out of the ground and demand keeps slowing despite the rebound, as of writing, back to $50. That won't last because a more rapid fall in demand will be the next crisis, not the over-expansion of supply that caused the drop thus far.

I've heard many analysts and reporters say that lower oil prices would be a good thing for the U.S. economy. That may be true if the low prices were temporary... while still high enough to keep oil companies in business.

What has made low oil prices *bad* for us is the fracking industry and their junk bonds. The former has used the latter to finance their operations for years, at artificially low rates.

But frackers aren't low-cost oil producers like Saudi Arabia, Iraq or even Iran. While they became swing producers that added five million barrels of oil a day to global production, they did so using funny money. And so they created a glut of oil in a slowing world.

But frackers are now in a world of hurt... and the longer oil prices stay below $50 a barrel, the less they'll be able to afford to borrow new money at 12% plus interest compared to the 6% they got in the past (courtesy of the Fed's ZIRP policies).

Frackers are dying.

They'll default on their debts and when this $1 trillion industry goes belly up, it will rock this country to its very core. As the junk bond market collapses (it was already down 17% at the time of writing, with yields up as high as 12% in the energy sector), the situation will only become more ominous for the stock markets and the U.S. economy!

I now believe that oil is another of the major triggers for the next global financial crisis, just like subprime mortgages were in 2008.

The stock market reacts downward every time oil prices drop to new lows.

I have expected oil to bounce significantly sometime in 2016 as supply contracts, especially in the U.S., but it will eventually slump back down… and its downhill momentum could carry it to $18 to $20 for sure, and as low as $8 to $10 a barrel sometime between early 2020 and early 2023.

Sale of a Lifetime Opportunity Alert

Short oil, or frackers. Either will do.

Oil could lose another 80% from its $48 level (at the time of writing) by the end of this decade or early the next (which is only four short years away now!).

Follow the Baby Boomers

More broadly, there will be countless opportunities to take advantage of in areas that baby boomers will continue to drive as they age.

These include:

- Elective health care, like plastic surgery.

- Age-defying products, like vitamins, cosmetics and anti-wrinkle creams… anything that will help baby boomers to defy their aging for as long as possible.

- Cruises, because when you've done raising your family and working from nine to five, there's nothing more appealing that floating on the ocean for several days, where you can eat and drink yourself into a coma.

- Retirement/vacation (after the next real estate crash) and nursing/assisted living homes.

Really, the list is vast. But you have to wait until we see at least the next major stock crash, likely around late 2017.

It's difficult to pin down the exact details of the opportunities we'll see in these sectors. The extent of the crash will determine much of that. But keep your eyes firmly focused in those places. They'll become diamond mines, as will emerging markets even more, as I will cover ahead.

CHAPTER 22

Profiting from the Sale of a Lifetime: Business

AS I'VE SAID many times throughout this book, the current economic winter season will last until around late 2022, with the greatest danger periods for stock crashes and recessions/depressions into late 2017, from mid-2018 into early 2020, and finally between mid-2021 and late 2022.

In between, the economy should be more favorable for brief periods, with the next long-term boom starting by early 2023 or so.

The strategy for your business is similar to stocks…

Sale of a Lifetime Opportunity Alert

Sell your business or hunker down now and prepare for the sale of a lifetime on businesses in trouble or in bankruptcy, especially your competitors.

This is the best opportunity to build your long-term market share and profitability as major companies like General Motors and General Electric did in the 1930s depression.

Given that the economic winter season is about shifting market share to the most focused, dominant and efficient companies, your primary goal must be to gain market share at the expense of your competitors.

Also minimize your losses during challenging economic periods. That's when sales will fall and deflation will bring down your prices and margins drastically.

This is a once-in-a-lifetime, survival-of-the-fittest challenge from hell! The winners will gain dominance for decades to come, not just years.

In broader strokes, here are the nine most important principles for surviving and dominating in the years to come:

1. Cash and cash flow are critical to surviving the shakeout and having the resources to take advantage of unprecedented bargains in financial assets in the years ahead, especially around 2020.

The world will be on sale! When times get tough, the tough go shopping.

2. Identify segments that you can clearly dominate, or where you need to focus more narrowly, and sell off or shut down others. If you don't, the economy will do it for you, more painfully and less profitably.

Sell non-dominant product lines or businesses now to generate a cash hoard. This will give you ammunition to take advantage of the greatest sale in history on financial assets ahead. If you can't sell them, then cut them out to eliminate fixed costs or cash flow drains now and in the future when things get tougher.

3. Develop a clear definition of your customers and their needs to give your company direction, purpose, and focus. It's not what you think you do, but what your customers get from you that has meaning for them. It's not that you produce this product or service. It's about saving them time or money.

Do you add quality to their brand?

Do you allow them to focus more by taking on nonstrategic functions for them?

Do you allow them to adapt to changing market conditions with your flexibility?

Do everything possible to build customer loyalty in these times; it costs much more to acquire a new customer than to keep an existing one.

4. Be lean and mean, especially in danger periods like now and 2018–19. Cut fixed costs and overheads, and any variable costs, after allocating your fixed costs properly.

To allocate fixed costs, first ask what causes them. For your accounting department, transactions would likely cause its costs, so allocate costs to different products by that measure, not the normal allocation by dollar sales most accountants use.

Then define your direct or variable costs of producing and delivering an extra sale and subtract that from your sales revenues. That gives you your contribution margin.

Products with higher contribution margin are more profitable with growth and will increase your cash flow more in the downturn.

After cutting your fixed costs to the bone and curbing your worst products, know your break-even level to cover your fixed costs. It's below that where your company will get into trouble and start to fail. You have to do everything to not get there.

5. Defer major capital expenditures — plants, warehouses, stores, major computer systems, real estate or office purchases — until the next major crash and economic downturn, when you can acquire such assets at much lower costs from competitors that are in trouble.

In this next financial crisis, banks will have more failing loans and will be looking to offload those assets to companies like you at 20 cents–plus on the dollar... if you have cash and cash flow.

6. Focus on short-term investments that increase high contribution margin sales or cut short-term costs. This could mean investing in software applications that help you lower your marketing or production costs. It could mean direct marketing expenditures that allow you to get on Google's top listings in your keyword category and then only pay per click — and you know you can make cash flow gains on those clicks.

Again, increasing cash and cash flow is critical to surviving and having the financial power to acquire assets at bargain prices ahead.

7. Sell non-strategic real estate and lease instead, as there are likely to be losses in the property market and then little or no gains above inflation for years and even decades ahead.

In other words, only own real estate if it's critical to your defined customer end results, your image, customer service, delivery, or other systems.

Selling real estate at a profit while things are still good can add a lot to your treasure chest for buying more valuable and strategic assets in the worst years of the downturn ahead.

Remember, real estate can become stunningly illiquid, stunningly fast.

8. Identify in advance the competitors that you know are the weakest and the desired assets (customers, employees, business assets, real estate, product lines, and technological systems) that you want to acquire from them or out of bankruptcy if they fail or get in trouble.

Estimate the cash you would need to do that.

Be ready to move quickly and decisively when the crisis happens.

9. Look at your employees and identify who is weak and questionable. Fire them now, not only to cut costs, but to have the courtesy to give them a better chance of getting another job before the economy fails.

Hire only employees who have a proven track record of creating results and are oriented toward a customer end-results focus. Reward them if they create results in the downturn ahead, even if your company's overall profits go down.

CHAPTER 23

Profiting from the Sale of a Lifetime: Real Estate

REAL ESTATE MARKETS throughout much of the developed world have rebounded since 2012. While this has marked a significant turnaround from the collapse between 2007 and 2011, it has also led the market into a false sense of security.

This rebound was primarily induced by zero interest rates and mortgages that are at least two percentage points lower than markets would set. That obviously makes a big difference in affordability of real estate... a "free lunch" courtesy of the Fed.

Only it's Sushi, and it's going to go bad!

Those who believe the next few years will be a time of growth for real estate are in for an unpleasant surprise. My research shows a crushing downturn is just around the next corner. This chapter, therefore, serves as a warning of what lies ahead.

Remember, to be able to take advantage of the sales of a lifetime you're about to witness, you must protect yourself first by preserving the value of your assets and creating as much cash and cash flow as possible.

In the last property crash, U.S. residential real estate tumbled by 34% and commercial real estate collapsed by 43%.

Yet, during the worst year of the Great Depression — 1933 — home prices only fell 26% on average because speculation wasn't easy back then with 50% down payments and five-year balloon mortgages.

Make no mistake about it: the fragile U.S. real estate market is now ripe for an even bigger fall.

It's not just the U.S., though. We're on the verge of a global real estate bubble burst. Its devastation will be felt around the globe, from London to Paris, Shanghai, Mumbai, Sydney and Vancouver, to name but a few.

I will show you how the inevitable bubble burst ahead is likely to play out in both residential and commercial real estate.

I strongly advise you to use this chapter to gauge your risks and prepare for the inevitable. Because, unlike the stock market, the risks in real estate differ substantially in different cities and countries.

Where the Risks Are Greatest in the U.S.

The real estate bubble in the U.S. between 2000 and 2006 was not quite as extreme as Japan's 1986 to 1991 bubble. During those six years, Japan's housing prices increased a whopping 160%, compared with 127% in the U.S. If our retracement echoes the Japanese experience, we should see a 49% fall from late-2014 price levels.

Figure 23-1: S&P/Case-Shiller 10-City Home Price Index

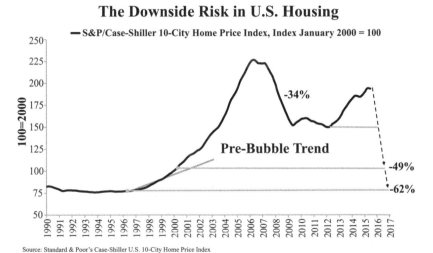

The Downside Risk in U.S. Housing

— S&P/Case-Shiller 10-City Home Price Index, Index January 2000 = 100

Source: Standard & Poor's Case-Shiller U.S. 10-City Home Price Index

(Note that even though the chart projects the lows into 2017, the ultimate bottom is more likely to come in the early 2020s.)

Given that real estate prices vary greatly from region to region, I always say that the best way to gauge your downside risk is to look up the value of your property in January 2000.

This isn't a perfect indicator, but it's the best I have found in a market that varies in time and degrees much more than the stock markets.

When the bubble bursts, this is the point to which your property is likely to fall — or perhaps even 10% to 20% lower.

You can see in Figure 23-1 that the key support levels for the residential real estate market took hold in January 2000, when the bubble really took off, thanks to the transfer of speculation into real estate after the collapse of the tech bubble.

As a rule, bubbles always retreat from their peaks to where they began, or even a bit lower, as I explained right at the beginning of this book.

This is what forms the likely range of downside exposure over the following years, when net demand stops sliding — at least temporarily — and the next global boom begins.

To just erase the bubble that started in January 2000, home prices would have to fall 56% from their top in early 2006. That's 49% from the recent highs in early 2016.

If home prices fall back to their previous lows of 1996, that would mean a 67% decline from the top and 59% from recent highs. The 59% decline would be more in line with the fall in Japanese home prices at 60%. And commercial real estate will fall even more, just like it did last time around.

All of this means that you have to prepare yourself for what's coming, because your residential and commercial real estate, along with your investment portfolio, is likely destined for deeper declines than we saw during the great recession and its aftermath.

And not only will the next downturn be much deeper, it will stretch across the globe. I expect all major real estate markets around the world to crash as the popcorn popper accelerates.

In the U.S., the greatest bubbles occurred primarily on both coasts. Between the Rockies and the Appalachian Mountains, the real estate bubbles were less extreme and, in some cases, minimal.

Cities like Dallas, Houston, St. Louis and Kansas City bubbled mildly into 2006.

Smaller central cities, like Omaha, Nebraska, bubbled less.

The exceptions are now North Dakota, Dallas and Houston, thanks to the U.S. fracking industry, and Austin, the new hipster city in Texas and Denver, the new Pot Capital.

The table below shows the downside risk from where the bubble started in individual cities, often between 1997 and 2002.

The third column shows the worst-case scenario — if prices fall back to the next lower support level, which was typically 1996 for the overall market. I look at the more specific next lower support levels for each city.

Figure 23-2: How Bad Can This Get

City	Downside Risk to Bubble Origin	Downside Risk to Next Lower Support Levels	City	Downside Risk to Bubble Origin	Downside Risk to Next Lower Support Levels
San Francisco	-56%	-70%	Dallas	-41%	-47%
Boston	-55%	-66%	Seattle	-40%	-61%
Denver	-54%	-72%	Charlotte	-36%	-46%
New York City	-50%	-60%	Atlanta	-34%	-45%
Minneapolis	-50%	-43%	Tampa	-33%	-51%
Los Angeles	-47%	-69%	Chicago	-31%	-47%
Miami	-45%	-62%	Detroit	-27%	-44%
Washington, D.C.	-45%	-58%	Phoenix	-27%	-59%
San Diego	-43%	-67%	Las Vegas	-20%	-44%
Portland	-42%	-52%	Cleveland	-17%	-38%

With this, you can gauge your likely downside risk of a price tumble to the levels of where the bubble started or a bit lower.

Only at the first point can you feel better about investing in real estate again — and at the lower level you can feel really good — but don't expect a robust rebound.

I would advise that you own for utility or rent for the sake of cash flow in the future, rather than for appreciation.

San Francisco was perhaps the greatest bubble outside of downtown Manhattan. Its natural downside risk would be 56%, the highest in this chart. But worst case, it could be as much as 70%... ouch!

Boston is next at -55% and -66% worst case.

Then, surprisingly, Denver at -54% and -72% worst case. Maybe the pot business will offset that somewhat.

Then comes New York at -50% and -60%, and Manhattan will be much worse with its $5,000-plus prices per square feet and condos that have sold for as high as $100 million plus, with a new pent house set to come on to the market for $250 million! We could see 80%-plus downside on the high end, which already started cracking in late 2015 and early 2016.

Other high-risk areas are L.A. and Miami, especially South Beach and downtown Miami.

Then there's D.C., with high downside risks but higher employment in a downturn thanks to higher government spending during such periods.

Then you have medium-risk cities — San Diego, Portland, Dallas, Seattle — with 40% to 60% downsides at worst.

The lower-risk cities, while still substantial, are: Charlotte, Atlanta, Tampa and Chicago with more like 30% downside risks and 40% to 50% at worst.

And finally, the lowest-risk cities are Detroit, Phoenix, Las Vegas and Cleveland. They have been already beaten down and are slower to recover. In those places there's more like 20% risks and higher in the worst case.

The Fall of the Super Cities

Signs of trouble in the commercial real estate sector are already evident globally. For example, the richest family in China was feverishly dumping its commercial real estate holdings throughout 2015. But this family is not alone.

One of the clearest recent trends in developed countries is the veritable cornucopia of foreign money being invested by the super-wealthy in the world's most attractive large cities, especially cities where foreigners can get their kids a good English-speaking education.

These cities include London, New York, Toronto, Miami, Los Angeles, San Diego, San Francisco, Vancouver, Singapore, Sydney, Melbourne, Brisbane, Auckland and Dubai.

I show the downside risk of these cities in Figure 23-3:

Figure 23-3:

Key Global Bubbles and Bursts		
City	Downside Risk to Bubble Origin	Downside Risk to Next Lower Support Levels
Rio de Janeiro	-56%	-69%
Mumbai	-47%	-83%
Dubai	-47%	-67%
Sydney	-47%	-65%
London	-45%	-76%
Shanghai	-44%	-86%
Toronto	-42%	-56%
Brisbane	-39%	-69%
Vancouver	-36%	-64%
Singapore	-33%	-50%

These cities are the bubbliest in residential real estate as well.

Most people think that the super-rich will always buy in these desirable areas, but history proves otherwise. Because these cities are prone to the biggest bubbles, they also have the greatest downside.

The ultra-rich have always represented the smart money. When the bubble starts to burst, a chunk of this group will be the first to get out — but for many, it will be too late.

This is exactly why I predict that these super cities around the world will crash the hardest. And many of the ultra-affluent, who have been driving these real estate bubbles, will see their wealth evaporate — just as the Japanese did when their bubble peaked in 1991. Wealthy Japanese used their instant riches from the country's real estate bubble to buy overseas. But when Japan's bubble burst (ultimately 60% in residential and 80% in commercial) their wealth vanished and they became sellers, both overseas and at home.

Shanghai faces losses of 81% to 86%. Yet cities like Shenzhen (an industrial city outside of Hong Kong) and Beijing are even pricier and could fall even more.

London comes next at 62% to 72%, then Rio at 60% to 72%.

Even the cities with lower downside risk, in Australia and Singapore, range from 37% to 67%.

This is how bubbles work. The same speculators and trends that inflate bubbles, end up collapsing them. I see the highest risks of falls as high as 70%-plus in these super cities.

Real Estate Bubbles Globally

Real estate bubbles are generally even more extreme in the major cities around the world than they are in the U.S. Indeed, there are many global cities that have yet to peak.

I will start with my favorite city in the world...

Sydney: The trends here are very similar to trends in other major bubble cities, like Melbourne, Brisbane, Vancouver and Toronto. After the U.S. subprime crisis and the real estate collapse between 2006 and 2012, prices in Sydney have continued to climb.

Australia has the most favorable demographic trends in the developed world, largely thanks to the volume and quality of its immigration over many decades. It is one of the very few developed countries to have a millennial generation substantially larger than its baby boom (along with Israel, Sweden, Norway, Switzerland, Singapore and New Zealand).

At the same time, demographics and strong exports have kept Australia's economy more buoyant.

It also continues to benefit from strong immigration from Asia, especially the affluent from China. It's China's second foreign real estate market after the U.S. The Chinese are the strongest factor that continue to drive Sydney's high real estate prices ever skyward. The same phenomenon has been occurring in Melbourne, Brisbane, Vancouver, L.A., San Francisco and Toronto.

Real estate prices in Sydney began to accelerate around mid-1998, and then saw a mild correction after early 2003 into 2005. After that, Sydney's prices surged 64%.

To reset back from current levels, prices would have to fall 37%.

When Sydney sees a demographic decline from 2025 forward, its property prices could fall back 59% to its early 2000 levels.

The downside risks over the next several years are similar for Melbourne, where real estate could lose up to 46%.

Brisbane has a 38% downside risk.

Look at Sydney's history of prices in Figure 23-4:

Figure 23-4: Sydney Real Estate

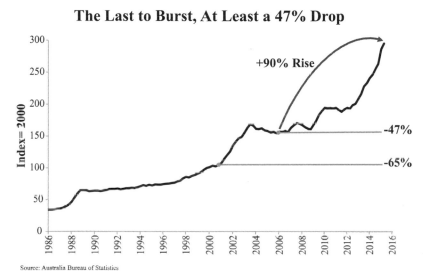

The Last to Burst, At Least a 47% Drop

Source: Australia Bureau of Statistics

Vancouver: Real estate prices in this Canadian metropolis would have to fall 30% just to erase the bubble from mid-2009, and 63% for prices to decline back to early 2000 price levels.

In Canada, the real estate downside is now worse than the U.S. because prices have continued to rise.

Take a look:

Figure 23-5: Vancouver Real Estate

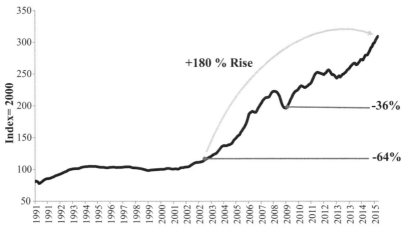

Source: Teranet, National Bank of Canada

Toronto: Given Canada's weakening demographic trends and high export levels, it will feel the global downturn more than the U.S.

By that token, real estate prices in Toronto would have to see a 36% decline to erase the bubble from mid-2009, and a 60% fall for prices to reach the levels of early 2000.

Figure 23-6: Toronto Real Estate

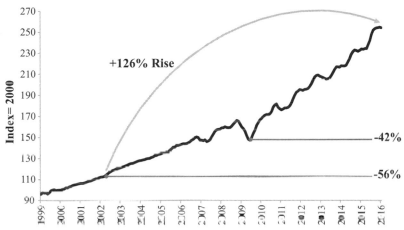

Source: Teranet, National Bank of Canada

London: The UK capital is the most overvalued English-speaking city in the world. It's bubble — 65% since mid-2009 — would suggest a decline of at least 39% and potentially as much as 64% to return to early 2000 levels.

London is a major global financial center. Given that this coming financial crisis will hit cities with major financial centers the hardest, I expect London to trend toward the worst-case scenario.

Paris and Rome are even more expensive.

Figure 23-7: London Real Estate

One of the Largest Bubbles in the Developed World

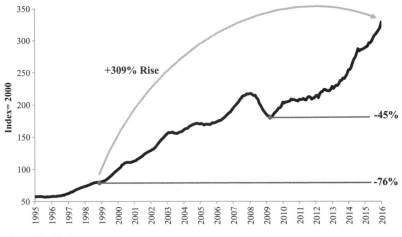

Source: UK Land Registry

Real Estate Bubbles in the Emerging World

Lastly, real estate bubbles in the emerging world have been the most extreme since 2000.

I have focused a lot in the past on Shanghai and the unprecedented China bubble, which I think will be the greatest bubble to burst. I also think it will have the greatest domino effect on global real estate markets, because the rich Chinese, like the affluent Japanese in the late 1980s, have been the greatest bidders in the top cities of the world.

As for the rest of the developing world, I'm going to use Mumbai as an example, because it's similar to Shanghai and the major Chinese cities in its extreme appreciation.

Mumbai: Real estate in this Indian metropolis has been on a tear since late 2000 — with 500% appreciation. This is similar to Shanghai's 587% price surge since 2000.

I show Mumbai's massive rise in Figure 23-8:

Figure 23-8: Mumbai Real Estate

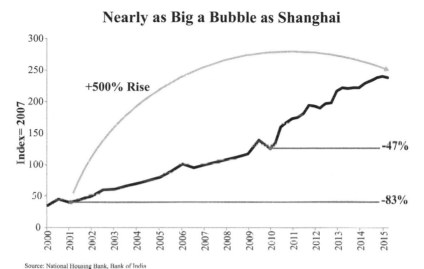

Nearly as Big a Bubble as Shanghai

Source: National Housing Bank, Bank of India

A large part of this acceleration took place at the beginning of 2010, with an 83% increase in the last five years alone.

Mumbai has two key support points.

If it falls back to the bubble from early 2010, that would mean a 46% decline.

If it falls back to early 2006 levels, prices would fall 59%.

A decline to early 2000 levels would see a massive 79% drop, similar to Shanghai.

Expensive Real Estate and Outrageous Rents

To wrap up this chapter, I'll show you the overvaluations of real estate in key cities and the very different rental affordability.

Let's start with this next table:

Figure 23-9: U.S. Home Price Valuation Levels in Major Cities

The Most Expensive Cities For Home Buying

City	Sales Price/Income Ratio	Median Sale Price	Median Household Income
San Francisco	11.4	$ 1,100,000	$ 96,900
New York	11.0	$ 1,200,000	$ 109,000
L.A.	10.4	$ 653,000	$ 63,000
San Jose	7.1	$ 750,000	$ 106,300
San Diego	6.7	$ 490,000	$ 73,000
Seattle	5.6	$ 500,000	$ 89,600
U.S.	5.3	$ 283,775	$ 53,657
Miami	5.0	$ 250,000	$ 49,900
D.C.	4.7	$ 510,000	$ 109,400
Denver	3.8	$ 300,000	$ 79,900
Atlanta	3.4	$ 240,000	$ 70,700
Dallas	3.3	$ 235,000	$ 70,500
Chicago	3.1	$ 240,000	$ 77,700
Phoenix	2.9	$ 185,000	$ 64,000

Source: Housing and Urban Development, Trulia, Zumper

Note the much higher-than-average incomes in Washington D.C., New York, San Jose and San Francisco, and the very low incomes in Miami and L.A.

The extremes in valuations are surprising, ranging from over 10 times income in San Francisco, New York and L.A. to under 3.5 times income in Phoenix, Chicago, Dallas and Atlanta. This makes a big difference to where you own.

And this last Figure shows you how insane rents are:

Figure 23-10: U.S. Median Rental Price Valuations in Major Cities

The Rent's Too Damn High!

City	Median Rental Price of 2 Bedroom Apartment as a Percent of City Median Income
Miami	61%
San Francisco	57%
New York	42%
Chicago	41%
Los Angeles	37%
Boston	33%
San Diego	32%
San Jose	32%
Washington, D.C.	31%
Seattle	31%
Atlanta	27%
Dallas	26%
Denver	26%
Phoenix	18%

Source: Housing and Urban Development, Trulia, Zumper

The most extreme rent as a share of income is in Miami because residents there have the lowest median income of any major city.

San Francisco is next at 57% thanks to its super high prices.

The most affordable city for renting and for buying is Phoenix. That's after it was one of the bubbliest cities in the first bubble and crashed nearly 50%.

Boston and Washington D.C. are surprisingly affordable for renting, despite high prices. You can thank higher incomes in the area for that.

Again, my advice is:

• Sell all non-strategic real estate for your business and personal use now.

- Your business is better to lease than own for the next several years.

- Keep your primary home, but only if you plan to stay in it for the long term. If you plan to downsize or move in the next few years, sell now!

- Certainly sell vacation homes that are not dear to your heart, or that you don't use more than several weeks a year.

CHAPTER 24

Profiting from the Sale of a Lifetime: Emerging Markets

I WOULD BE REMISS if I didn't also discuss the opportunities that you'll find in emerging markets after this next great crash.

It's no secret that I'm no fan of mainstream economists. Most of them are highly intelligent, but misguided. Even Adam Smith, the much-celebrated 18th century Scottish moral philosopher and the father of modern economics, didn't quite get it right. His theory that rational self-interest and competition behave like an "invisible hand," guiding the free market and society toward innovation and economic growth, was a stroke of genius. It was a revolutionary idea, and while it may have set in stone capitalism's intellectual foundations, it fell short of capturing the big picture.

The real story is that there is more than one invisible hand. The first is demographics and it has shaped the rise and fall of empires and societies since the dawn of time. That's why it's one of my key indicators.

The other great "invisible hand" is urbanization, which I talked about in great detail in Chapter 17.

Together, these two "invisible hands" are guiding one developing country right to the forefront, making it my number one pick post-crash.

I'm talking about India.

While the rest of the developed and emerging world will struggle to recover from the carnage, so giving us that sale opportunity of a lifetime, India — before any other emerging nation — will be ripe for long-term investment likely after the next crash bottoms, long before the final bottom around late 2022.

The Fire in India's Belly

The developed world has already urbanized. Seventy to 80%-plus of their populations already live in or near cities. Only 20% to 30% remain in rural areas. As such, the rate of urbanization has slowed to practically zero in these countries, the United States and Western Europe included. Future growth in these nations will be based solely on demographic and productivity advances.

Take Great Britain, for instance. Thanks to a wave of new technology — the spinning Jenny, the steam engine, the water frame and the foot-powered trip hammer — Britain enjoyed the world's first industrial revolution and was thus the first country to urbanize rapidly.

And its wealth and dominance grew accordingly. In 1700, only 12% of Britain's population was urban. By 1870, that number had grown to 43%. By 1939, it was 80% urbanized. Since then, the UK's growth prospects have been moderate, at best. And they'll continue to slow as we move forward.

Urbanization in the U.S. followed a similar path. We were only 20% urbanized in 1860, just before the Civil War. But by 1919, we had 50% of our population in urban areas. By 1960, 70% lived in or near cities and that number topped 80% in 2000. And just like the UK, since then we've struggled to keep our growth rate at 2% or 3% a year.

The emerging frontier is a different story. Most developing countries didn't begin their urbanization movements until recently. China's urbanization didn't really take off until the early 1980s. Yet it has urbanized at the fastest rate in modern history, which is why everyone mistakenly believes China is an unstoppable force. China is still just 56% urbanized.

India's urbanization started even later, in the early 1990s, and is picking up the pace rapidly. Right now, it's about 33% urbanized.

By comparison, Kenya is just 26% urbanized while 86% of Brazil's population lives in urban areas, which is one of the many reasons Brazil is not near the top of my watch list for future investments.

Here's a chart showing the different levels of urbanization across 12 countries:

Figure 24-1: Urbanization Rates in Major Countries

Who are the Most and Least Urbanized Countries?

Country	Current Rate of Urbanization
Brazil	86%
United Kingdom	83%
United States	82%
Mexico	79%
Germany	75%
Malaysia	75%
Russia	74%
South Africa	65%
China	56%
Philippines	44%
India	33%
Kenya	26%

Source: United Nations Population Division

This move from rural to urban areas, and the speed at which it takes place, results in at least a doubling, and more like a tripling, of income without higher education or particular skills. A rural rice farmer can become a taxi driver overnight! And with money, that rice-farmer-turned-cab-driver buys more food and consumer goods. He plays his part in driving the economy upward.

Right now, China's GDP per capita is three times India's. Yet, India is doing remarkably well, considering it is much less urbanized and has made far less infrastructure investment.

That spells extraordinary potential for India, particularly as it seems more capable of moving into higher-end commodity or industrial sectors that see greater GDP-per-capita growth for every percentage growth in urbanization.

Added to this is the fact that China is considering investing in India's infrastructure. That alone is like a gift from heaven. And if India can attract massive foreign investment — which is highly likely when China falls — its status as the next big thing is certain.

The following chart neatly compares the rate and slope of urbanization between the three largest BRICs — Brazil, India and China. As you can see, they've all progressed toward the higher-end of GDP per capita versus urbanization. Many countries like the Philippines or Kenya have progressed, but on a much more gradual slope and at a much slower pace.

Figure 24-2: Urbanization Rate vs. GDP per Capita (PPP) in China, India and Brazil

Source: United Nations World Urbanization Prospects, The Conference Board, Dent Research

I like this chart because it shows another important factor of urbanization. It tells me that most emerging countries experience a straight-line progression of growth in GDP per capita as they urbanize.

The biggest exceptions have been Japan, Taiwan, Singapore and South Korea. They were able to leapfrog into higher value-added industries and achieve GDP per capita similar to that of developed countries. They've progressed on an exponential or S-Curve instead of in a linear way.

Japan and South Korea progressed from emerging to developed country status in as little as three decades. Malaysia is the only other "Asian Tiger" to finally reach developed country status at $26,000 GDP per capita and 75% urbanization.

But I see no other emerging countries poised to make that leap to $20,000-plus GDP per capita levels of the developed world ($40,000 is more typical).

As a result of the differing rates of urbanization, emerging countries have widely varying GDP per capita ranges. Average income per urbanite in poorer places like the Philippines or Kenya sits between $2,000 and $5,000. In the middle zone, like Indonesia, it's $7,000 to $11,000. And for the higher-end places like China and India, it's about $13,000 to $17,000 (I've adjusted these figures for lower costs of living in those countries).

In short, India's urbanization trends are on track to take the country towards what China has been able to achieve.

And India has the added bonus of no overblown, government-fueled infrastructure bubble. In fact, India has greatly underinvested and with the trend towards increasing investment already under way, it has the potential to urbanize more rapidly than ever before.

India Trumps China on Demographic Trends as Well

Besides its strong urbanization trends, India is also backed by good, solid demographics. Workforce growth is a strong indicator of demographic trends in emerging countries, and here too, India trumps China…

Figure 24-3: Workforce Growth and Projections in China, India and Brazil

Here Comes India

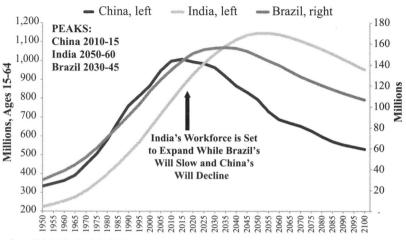

Source: United Nations Population Division

Clearly, China's workforce growth is already peaking and will see modest declines into 2025. After that, its workforce will shrink more rapidly for decades.

But look at India's workforce growth. It won't plateau until between 2050 and 2060! That means that apart from the being the first emerging nation to recover from the next crash, it has at least five decades of urbanization ahead as it drives toward the 80% threshold. And about four and a half decades of demographic growth to which it can look forward.

Talk about two powerful invisible hands pushing India up!

But it gets better. Coupled with the power of its population size, its citizens have a strong creative and innovative spirit. I've been to India three times since 2006, and while I stayed in luxury hotels I still witnessed first-hand the grime, the poverty, and the cows walking in the streets. Many roads where impassible because they were so riddled with potholes. Yet the population innovates... they overcome.

And things look even better now with the country's first ever growth- and capitalistic-oriented leader — Narendra Modi.

When I talk to major business people in India, and present my demographic and urbanization argument for why their country has such potential, they always say: "But you don't understand our bureaucratic and socialistic government." Now, under Modi's leadership, that has a chance to change!

A while back I saw an interview on CNN with Fareed Zakaria and Modi. Fareed asked whether Modi thought China has an advantage because it isn't a democracy and so can push growth faster from the top down. Modi argued that India's greatest strength was that it is a longstanding democracy in the emerging world and that would empower it toward more solid and sustainable growth.

I agree. But India needs to continue to step up its investments in infrastructure that have begun in recent years. It needs to attract much more foreign direct investment from countries like China, the U.S. and in Europe.

As that happens, it will create huge opportunity for us. We'll witness an economy that's likely to grow rapidly into at least 2055, and more likely up to 2065 to 2070, driven by the two invisible hands of demographics and urbanization.

The Cycles That Point to India

Besides urbanization and demographics, there's one other key cycle I watch that forecasts India's rise to dominance: commodities. I discussed my hierarchy of cycles for developed worlds in Chapters 9, 10 and 11. For developing countries, I have a slightly different hierarchy of cycles. These are:

1) Urbanization Rates and the slope of GDP Per Capita growth.

2) The 30-Year Commodity Cycle.

290 The Sale of a Lifetime

3) Demographics, but workforce growth rather than the Spending Wave.

4) The Geopolitical Cycle.

5) The Boom/Bust Cycle.

The commodity cycle is a key difference in the hierarchy I use when analyzing developed and emerging countries, because the emerging world relies far more on commodities.

Commodities as a percentage of total exports for Brazil are 63%!

Saudi Arabia exports 89%!

Any decline in prices or demand severely impacts those countries as these industries are a major part of their stock markets.

But those countries that have lower exposure to commodity prices and exports are less affected. Such places include Mexico, Thailand, Indonesia, Cambodia, Vietnam, Myanmar, Turkey… and India.

India's total commodity exports are just 35% of its exports, giving me yet another reason to call the country the next big thing, even before the next commodity boom from around 2023 to 2039.

All of this explains why I see India as the next big thing after the global crash ahead… and why you should have it on your radar as prime hunting ground for sales opportunities of a lifetime!

I also see Southeast Asia as next in line for rising urbanization and higher productivity and work ethic than most emerging countries. Thailand's demographics are maturing, so the best countries would be Vietnam, Cambodia, Myanmar and Indonesia, in that rough order.

A FINAL WORD

THERE YOU HAVE IT. everything you need to know about the reset of 2016 to 2022… what the triggers are that have set the global collapse in motion… how bad things will get… and most importantly, what opportunities you'll find ahead.

These are once-in-a-lifetime opportunities.

They only become available after major resets.

Men like those I told you about in Chapter 13 — Benjamin Franklin, Mayer Amschel Rothschild, John D. Rockefeller (and even the mafia) — made fortunes that have spanned generations by being ready and willing to take advantage of those opportunities.

Now, it's your chance.

As I began by saying, after 35 years spent studying cycles, I can tell you that they all have the same characteristics.

They all have hierarchies.

They all have seasons.

And they all bubble up in the economic fall season and end in a terrible winter burst.

We're in the midst of that economic winter season… a time when we clear the decks with a devastating crash and debilitating deflation.

Central banks have, for the first time in history, printed massive amounts of money to stave off the inevitable financial crisis and reset. Now such futile and irresponsible efforts are increasingly failing, as common sense would dictate.

The economy and markets shed the excesses created during the preceding economic fall bubble boom season and clear the decks for new blossoming in innovation and an economic spring boom.

After the Roaring '20s came the Great Depression.

After the booming or Roaring 2000s came the great recession.

After the blustering bull market of 2009 to 2015 will come a shakeout more painful than anything we've seen before.

Winter follows fall, without fail.

It was my purpose with this book to prepare — and so protect — you from the carnage ahead and allow you to not only survive, but prosper.

We are on the cusp of witnessing the biggest explosion of opportunities in generations. This is the stuff that makes millionaires and billionaires. With the help of this book, you may very well be the next Rockefeller or Vanderbilt.

I hope I have been successful in imparting the urgency of making radical changes in your investment, business and living decisions, rather than just incremental. That's what it takes to create "extreme wealth" in a once-in-a-lifetime reset like this one ahead.

More importantly, I hope *you'll* be successful.

Strap in. We're in for one hell of a ride.

Good luck and thank you for reading.

APPENDIX

Cycles Discussed in This Book

I'VE MENTIONED DOZENS of cycles throughout this book. Some I discussed in detail. Some I mentioned only in passing. Some of my favorites I didn't even mention at all. Here's a list of those you'll find in this book, with a brief explanation. Use this as a quick reference guide.

The Human Sexual Response Cycle: Researchers Masters and Johnson found that men generally rise steadily during arousal into the peak of the orgasm. Thereafter, they "cool down" rapidly. Women, on the other hand, often have three peaks in their orgasms before the speedy reset to normal. Bubbles almost always follow one of these two cycles.

8-13-Year Boom/Bust Cycle (AKA Sunspot Cycle): When sunspot activity peaks or bottoms, there is an accompanying market upset, typically within a few months to a year.

30-Year Commodity Cycle: This cycle is particularly significant for emerging markets, which rely heavily on commodity imports and exports.

34-36-Year Geopolitical Cycle: For 17 to 18 years, this cycle is positive. During that time, very little goes wrong in the world. However, when the cycle turns negative, political tensions spike, civil unrest becomes rampant, and generally risk and fear are high.

39-Year Generational Spending Wave: Every generation has predictable spending habits that see people spending more as they raise children, and then save more and spend less as they head into retirement.

45-Year Innovation Cycle: During the positive arm of this cycle, clusters of breakthrough technologies are adopted en masse and saturate the market. In so doing they help us take leaps forward in productivity and efficiency. During the neutral arm of this cycle, those technologies are tweaked, but no longer have any significant impact on how we conduct business or live.

Past 50-60-Year Kondratieff Wave: Developed by Nikolai Kondratieff, this cycle follows the alternative intervals of high growth and low growth in the economy.

80-Year 4-Season New Economic Cycle: This involves two booms and two busts as the economy moves through economic seasons during which inflation heats up or cools down, like the annual climate cycles.

165-Year East/West Cycle: Power shifts from East to West every 165 years, on average.

250-Year Revolution Cycle: This sees massive changes in societies and economies, business and politics. The changes are so significant, life, business and investments are literally no longer what they once were.

500-Year Mega Innovation Cycle (AKA Inflation/Deflation Cycle): Inflation rises and peaks every 500 years.

5,000-Year Civilization Cycle: This is the development of towns into cities into megacities.

100,000-Year Glaciation Cycle: Represents the predictable heating and cooling of earth around a hierarchy of three predictable cycles.

One Billion-Year Climate Cycle: The overarching cycle that has determined life on earth since the beginning of time.

Acknowledgements

My thanks go to Shannon Sands, Publisher of Dent Research; Teresa van den Barselaar for editing this book, my monthly newsletter *Boom & Bust* and my alternate-monthly newsletter *The Leading Edge*; Jennifer Junggust for proofreading this book; Jennifer Somerville for getting this book pulled together; David Okenquist for research (both for this book and all my other outlets); Megan Johnson for marketing; Stephanie Gerardot for publicity; Chris Cimorelli, editor of *Economy & Markets*; and my partners at Dent Research, Rodney Johnson and Harry Cornelius.